Chuck D. Pierce
& Robert Heidler

A TIME TO
PROSPER

Finding and Entering
God's Realm of Blessings

Regal

For more information and
special offers from Regal Books, email us at
subscribe@regalbooks.com

Published by Regal
From Gospel Light
Ventura, California, U.S.A.
www.regalbooks.com
Printed in the U.S.A.

Library of Congress Cataloging-in-Publication Data
Pierce, Chuck D., 1953-
A time to prosper : finding and entering God's realm of blessings /
Chuck D. Pierce and Robert Heidler.
pages cm
Includes bibliographical references and index.
ISBN 978-0-8307-6533-1 (trade paper : alk. paper)
1. Wealth—Biblical teaching. 2. Wealth—Religious aspects—Christianity.
3. Christian life. I. Heidler, Robert D., 1948- II. Title.
BS680.W38P54 2013
241'.68—dc23
2013002607

Rights for publishing this book outside the U.S.A. or in non-English languages are
administered by Gospel Light Worldwide, an international not-for-profit ministry.
For additional information, please visit www.glww.org, email info@glww.org, or write to
Gospel Light Worldwide, 1957 Eastman Avenue, Ventura, CA 93003, U.S.A.

To order copies of this book and other Regal products in bulk quantities,
please contact us at 1-800-446-7735.

CONTENTS

1

GOD'S PROMISE OF PROSPERITY

CHUCK D. PIERCE

"A time to prosper!" What an interesting, wonderful phrase, thought, interjection and decree. In a world where there is chaos and poverty, to hear these words brings excitement mixed with skepticism. As you read this book, we want to turn your skepticism into faith and your excitement into a manifestation of reality in your life! God intends for us to live peacefully. His goal is for us to cultivate and multiply in the place He assigns us. He means for us to be efficient in what we do, maximizing our allotted time and space. His ultimate goal for us is to live in harmony with Him and with those who enter our lives and spheres of influence.

Faith works in time and space! Prosperity is proportionately related to faith! *A Time to Prosper* will help you understand your time, your space and the dimension of faith that is linked to multiplication. In the midst of your time and space, faith must not only rise but also grow to deal with all the tests that attempt to stop your progress and your prosperity.

So many of us have been sorely tested in the areas of finances, particularly in regard to provisions and supply. The atmospheres in the heavens and earth, however, continue to change rapidly. This is a season of "looking beyond." We can use the Word of God to do war in the area of finances; and in the following pages, you will learn how some key laws and your testimony can lead to a future of financial peace. God's will is that you extend the testimony from your testings of the last season into the next season. Your testings are major components of your testimony, but the seeds and sacrifice sown during your testings will cause the growth of a greater faith at an appropriate time in your future! These types of testings produce testimonies that have a multiplying, combustible power and create triumph and prosperity.

This is a time to go deeper into the things of God. You will search for answers to a matter and find that you understand more deeply what you have been seeking to understand. You will find the missing link, the lost puzzle piece, of the vision you are carrying in your heart. You will gain understanding of the circumstances of the past season that left you perplexed, which will produce a new hope and strength in you. You *can* prosper in every situation, and every circumstance *can* work for good on your behalf!

Pray Big and Expect Changes

Most people do not see prosperity in their lives because they do not expect to prosper! "Expect." Look at that word for a moment. Say the word aloud. Feel the weight and power of the word as "expect" leaves your tongue and passes into the atmosphere around you.

God created us with a built-in barometer of expectation. That expectation barometer should register at least 9.8 on a scale of 1 to 10, with 10 being the highest expectation (the .2 is a factor that causes us to rise up and war for the final increase). But how does this work?

What we expect from life is often a direct result of our desires, whether they are Holy Spirit-prompted or not. We expect many things as humans, and many of us are not satisfied until our expectations are met. "Expectation" is defined as "a strong belief that something will happen or be the case in the future."[1] Not surprisingly, "desire" is defined in much the same way: "a strong feeling of wanting to have something or wishing for something to happen."[2]

Expectation is linked with the concept of the future and the emotional ability to embrace what should happen. Therefore, without healthy emotions, our expectations suffer. This, in turn, produces what is described by a phrase that couples an emotional spiritual state with an accounting term: "hope deferred." Hope is the expectation of faith—what we were trusting would manifest in a touchable form—and "defer" means to put off.

Some of you might have deferred your ability to prosper because your hope of the future has been wounded. If you're one of these people, here is a good prayer to pray:

> *I expect You, God, to meet me at every corner. I expect Your presence to overtake me when I least expect You to help me. I expect and desire the best that You have for me. I expect You to open my eyes to that which I have not been able to see or attain. I MEAN TO PRAY BIG! I know that You delight in me and long to make my desires the same as Your best for me. Restore me and redeem the wasted time linked with past failings.*

Break Out of Your Shell!
Remove Waste and Poverty!

This is a time to break out of the shell of your last identity, whether good or bad. God is doing a new thing with His people and creating a new model of Kingdom authority in the earth. You are part of this! It is time to break the spirit of poverty from your life Poverty thinking is contrary to faith, and without faith you cannot please God. You please God when you have a mind to prosper. Thinking prosperity is the same as grasping the promise. You must break out of the shell of insecurity that convinces you that you cannot succeed. Joshua 1:8 says, "Study this Book of Instruction continually. Meditate on it day and night so you will be sure to obey everything in it. Only then will you prosper and succeed in all you do" (*NLT*).

When you look at the stages of a chick hatching from an egg, you find a timed process that leads to victory and breakthrough. The egg has three main parts: yolk, albumen (egg white) and shell. The yolk is where the chick forms. The albumen, along with the shell, protects the chick. The shell also changes coloration, depending on its surrounding environment. The chick can hatch by either natural or artificial incubation. The natural process just leaves everything to the hen, from laying the egg to kicking the chick from the nest. Here is the process:

1. The chick swallows the liquid in which it has been "swimming" and stores the water it acquires in its body tissues.

2. The yolk sac, with the unused remains of the yolk, is pulled into the chick's body (along with portions of the allantois). In this way, the chick is provided with a food

store on which it can depend during its first few days of
life outside the egg.

3. Changes occur that enable the chick to breathe air. During most of its development, the chick obtains oxygen
   from the gases diffusing into its blood via the thin mem-
   brane of the allantois. But when it hatches, the chick, cut
   off from this supply, must use its lungs. To make the
   transition easier, the chick begins to breathe while it is
   still enclosed in its shell. As a result of evaporation, an
   air space forms at the blunt end of the egg. Just before
   hatching, the chick, with the beak claw, pierces the mem-
   brane and breathes in the air from this space.

4. For a while the chick derives oxygen from both the air
   inside the egg and from the blood pumped from the allantois; but by the time the chick hatches, its lungs are
   fully operational.

5. The shell enclosing it is weakened by the removal of minerals. This is a neat arrangement, because these very same
   minerals are required to make the chick's skeleton hard
   and able to function when the bird finally emerges.[3]

There are a couple of items to note about the development of a
chick. Within the shell, the heart forms first. This ties in with the
formation of the allantois, a thin sac that forms as an outgrowth of
the chick's stomach. This will eventually surround the embryo and
press against the inner walls of the shell. As the chick grows, waste
products are produced. These products would poison the chick if
they were not removed.

Although we will discuss the concept of desire later in this
book, let me say now that some of our desires can become toxic to
God's desire for us and prevent us from succeeding in His perfect
will here in the earth realm. Once the desires of our hearts form,
we must allow all of our personal waste to be removed so that we
develop God's heart. Once we have our desires aligned with God's
desires for us here in the earth realm, we properly form His will
and vision.

I believe that this is what happens to us. We form heart issues within our present shell, but then we receive the call to break forth into the prosperity that God has destined for us. I have always said that any person can reform a habit, be delivered and be ready to begin a new cycle in 28 days. That is similar with the chick that is ready to break out of its confining eggshell. After 28 days, the time comes to break out! The forming process is complete, and the pecking to break out begins.

In Luke 13:34-35, Jesus states, "O Jerusalem, Jerusalem, the one who kills the prophets and stones those who are sent to her! How often I wanted to gather your children together, as a hen gathers her brood under her wings, but you were not willing! See! Your house is left to you desolate." Not only does the Lord want us to be gathered under His wings and achieve proper form, but He also wants us to listen carefully to His divine instructions so that we prosper. He prefers that we take our form in such a way that desolation remains far from the destiny He has intended for us. May our hearts rise up with a desire to prosper!

I sense that many of you reading this are saying, "Now is the time!" I liken you to a chick that has been forming, and I declare that you will peck your way out of your last cycle of poverty and enter into a new world of limitless possibilities. I declare that the time has come for the old shell of insecurity, failure, unbelief, doubt, double-mindedness, disappointment, disinterest and disillusionment to break from you.

The Lord has given you a way to absorb the wastes from your hurts, pains and losses of the past season of trials and tests. Find your small window of reviving and start breaking out. May you not despise small beginnings and begin to strive to break into the "air" of the new. May you let go of your last cycle of formation, and may you come out into a broad and enlarged place. May you not fear the near space ahead of you but be ready to prosper in new ways. May you enter a new timeframe of development, authority and multiplication.

I declare that the last season of prosperity and glory will be minimal compared to what you are about to experience. I declare that the seed you have sown upon the water will bring many treasures back to you. I decree that this is a time for you to prosper! Psalm

66:10-12 says, "For you, O God, have tested us; you have tried us as silver is tried. You brought us into the net; you laid a crushing burden on our backs; you let men ride over our heads; we went through fire and through water; yet you have brought us out to a place of abundance" (*ESV*).

Claim the Prosperity Knit Within You

When God created humans, He meant for us to cultivate, prosper and multiply in the Garden of Eden that He planted for us. He meant for the Garden to increase in glory and wealth. His desire was for us to secure all that was within the boundaries of the Garden and to multiply each seed, herb and animal therein.

He knit within humans the DNA of earth. Within that DNA, there are codes of prosperity and stewardship. Psalm 139:13-16 says,

> For you formed my inward parts; you knitted me together in my mother's womb. I praise you, for I am fearfully and wonderfully made. Wonderful are your works; my soul knows it very well. My frame was not hidden from you, when I was being made in secret, intricately woven in the depths of the earth. Your eyes saw my unformed substance; in your book were written, every one of them, the days that were formed for me, when as yet there was none of them (*ESV*).

God wove you together and formed you like the chick so that when you break out, you have a purpose to accomplish. He made you to be one with His heart of multiplication and prosperity. He made an atmosphere conducive for the DNA of humans and the DNA of the earth to bring forth the ultimate will of heaven. This allows the reflection of heaven to be seen in earth.

Of course, you know our story of failure. We listened to a voice that caused us to misuse a resource of the Garden for our own benefit. This caused our stewardship role of the Garden to be dismissed. But God! He did not leave us but activated a plan for us to regain our dominion and authority. Like a brooding hen, He sat on us until we were ready to embrace His time of visitation and break out into a new season of prosperity.

Align Yourself with God's Plan of Prosperity

In *Time to Defeat the Devil,* I wrote the following:

To prosper means "to advance or gain in anything good or desirable." To prosper means you have successful progress in any enterprise, business, or undertaking. To prosper means that you obtain your desire. Success from a Hebrew perspective means that there is already *help on your road* so you will accomplish your destined goal.

God's plan from the beginning was for us to prosper. So many people have problems with the concept of prosperity. In the Western world, *prosperity* and *making money* seem to be synonymous. God's prosperity was part of the garden plan! He planted a garden, put man in the garden, and told man to watch and cultivate the garden. His goal was that the glory and prosperity of the garden would increase and cover the whole earth. That is still His plan of fullness. To this day, the only thing that wars with this plan is the serpent or adversary. Jesus came to overthrow the power of the wrong communion that occurred between man, woman, and the serpent in the garden. Jesus' work on the cross was a full work of redemption. Father's sacrifice of His Son defeated the serpent's voice. Jesus' resurrection broke the serpent's headship. However, mankind must enter in to this full victory on a daily basis. We each still have a garden or portion that we have been given to prosper in.

One of the most incredible truths revealed by God to mankind was the covenant that He made to Abraham. Abram, who became Abraham, became His offspring. Many years later, God, through His own son, *Yeshua,* then offered all mankind the ability to enter this inheritance. Those who would be grafted in to the power of this inheritance that was created from God and Abraham's union would have access to all the blessings of the agreement that was made between the two. Through the family of Abraham, God had an incredible plan to bless mankind.

Abraham, the father of Israel (his grandson Jacob's new name), was the firstborn prototype of prosperity. Israel was first denoted in Exodus 4:22 when God said, "Israel is My son, My firstborn" [NKJV]. The Lord then brought all of Israel out of Egypt by armies. Even in Egypt, the people prospered for a season. Though they fell into slavery, when He brought them out by armies, a great plunder of Egypt came with His covenant people. This plunder would be used to form what was necessary for God's people to worship in the future.

Deuteronomy 8:18 says, "And you shall remember the LORD your God, for it is He who gives you power to get wealth, that He may establish His covenant which He swore to your fathers, as it is this day" [NKJV]. That means that Adonai will give you the power to get wealth today, just like He did then. In the *New Living Translation* we find a little different aspect of this verse: "Remember the LORD your God. He is the one who gives you power *to be successful*, in order to fulfill the covenant he confirmed to your ancestors with an oath" (emphasis added). Success means that on your road God has already made available what you need to accomplish His purpose for your life.

The covenant that God made with Abraham was beyond any that had been seen or formed in the earth realm. This covenant was not limited to the confines of time or space. There are times when God limits generational flow of blessings and curses for ten generations. However, this was not so with Abraham. Abraham's blessings were open-ended to all who would bless Abraham and his offspring as a nation. In today's world, many want God's blessings, but they do not want to be grafted into the covenant plan of God through Abraham.

God's intent was to bless all nations. However, the only thing that can secure blessings for a nation is for that nation to stay in right relationship to the Abrahamic covenant. Nations and people do not have to be related to Abraham to experience the promise of prosperity. Through the Lord Jesus Christ they can be rightly related and claim Abraham as their father and watch the fullness of their destined blessings unfold (see Rom. 4:11–12; Gal. 3:29).[4]

Another important fact in this paradigm of understanding the prosperity linked with Abraham was that he was declared to be righteous before he was circumcised. Unswerving faith had been a demonstration of Abraham's life for many years. Like most of us, he had belief.

However, there came a moment when Abraham submitted himself fully to God. This became the moment when God committed to Abraham's future. God said (and I paraphrase): "Use a blood sacrifice. Worship your way into this new place. By your worship, I will commit to you. Even when other nations attempt to overtake you, I will come to your aid. Yes, if you sin, you will have consequence, but I will never forsake you" (see Gen. 15). This dialogue occurred when Abram was 75. He was given covenant status without being a Jew. This covenant alignment was a forerunner of how Jesus would graft the Gentiles into the Jewish nation. Salvation and covenant would come to all humankind without works. We are saved by grace through faith, not of works, lest any person should boast (see Eph. 2:8-9).

Recognize How Prosperity Works

Prosperity occurs when we enter into the fullness of God's plan for our lives. Just as He promised Abraham, God begins to bring us to our land. When we submit to His plan of prosperity for our lives, He cleanses us from all idolatry and unfaithful ways. This submission causes hearts of stone to be replaced with hearts of flesh (tender hearts to hear God). He places His Spirit within us.

God then opens doors that are linked to abundance—not just worldly abundance, but abundance of revelation to understand who God our Creator is through His Son as well as who we are. He blesses the works of our hands. He fills us with revelation. He gives us boundaries and says, "Take dominion! Prosper on every front. Be like Nehemiah." In his day, Nehemiah saw Jerusalem in ruins and began to rebuild walls, restore gates, hang doors and ready the place for a new move of worship. We have to submit ourselves as Nehemiah did.

Are the Jewish people more prosperous than others? Well, I think some could argue that they are, since per capita they are one of the wealthiest people groups in the world. They constitute around 2 percent of the population of the world, yet they rank in the top percentile of those holding wealth worldwide.

Are the Jews smarter than everyone in the world? They do possess a high level of intelligence, but just having a high intelligence quotient does not make a person prosperous. Then what makes a person prosper? Here are five keys that we will investigate as we move deeper into the discussion of prosperity, success and the operation of multiplying resources:

1. Understanding the world in light of who you were meant to be

2. Understanding the power of firstfruits, or giving the first and best to the One who gave His best to you

3. Being positioned in God's perfect time in your life cycle

4. Receiving the favor of the One who created you

5. Being shrewder than the world system around you

With these five keys in hand, you will be able to prosper and succeed in your place, sphere and time.

Take Hold of God's Promise of Prosperity

In *Restoring Your Shield of Faith*, Robert Heidler and I discuss the promises that God keeps:

> We [always] need to know what God has promised. Too many Christians don't know God's promises. Some have been told it is God's will for us to live in poverty. If we believe that lack of provision is what God wants, then we will never have faith to overcome a financial setback. In fact, we will probably become irresponsible, which will make the problem worse rather than improve it.
>
> We need to know God's will. Where do we find God's will? It is revealed in the Bible. To bolster our trust in God for our finances, we can read passages that describe God's will for us to prosper.

Psalm 23:1 is one of those verses. It reads, "The LORD is my shepherd; I shall not want." This verse is very clear. God says His standard is that we be short of nothing that we need.

Everybody loves to recite Psalm 23. We sing about it, talk about it, utter it at funerals and put it on wall plaques. Psalm 23 makes us feel good when we read it, but there is not one Christian in a hundred who believes this promise is true—by "believe" I mean applying it in our life and expecting it to happen.

A lot of Christians claim to believe the Bible but make silly comments such as "I don't believe in that prosperity stuff." What happened to Psalm 23? God's Word says the Lord is our shepherd and we will have no lack.

Let's look at two other passages:

Psalm 34:9 (*NIV*) promises us, "Those who fear him lack nothing."

Psalm 84:11 (*NIV*) expands upon the promise: "The LORD God is a sun and shield . . . no good thing does he withhold from those whose walk is blameless." God wants us to know that He is our sun (our provider) and our shield (our protector). Because He is our sun and shield, He will not withhold any good thing from us.

That's the promise of God's Word. If we walk with God and adhere to His standard, then His will for our lives is that we lack no good thing. Having enough is supposed to be the norm, not the miraculous exception.[5]

We need to activate the truth and Spirit of His Word in our lives and manifest the reality of God in the earth. This book is meant to help you break the mentality of poverty and need. The Word declares, "You know the grace of our Lord Jesus Christ, that though he was rich, yet for your sakes he became poor, so that you through his poverty might become rich" (2 Cor. 8:9, *NIV*).

Steward Your Portion

We each have a portion that we have been allotted by God. Our destiny has boundaries meant for multiplication, increase and fullness.

Each of our lots should reflect God's fullness, since He allowed us to be stewards of a portion of His wonderful creation. If we would always draw near to God, we could resist any foe threatening our portions and gain wisdom to dismantle the enemy's schemes to distort our property lines and our prosperity for generations to come. Satan's temptations are meant to keep us from multiplying and increasing in the portion that each of us has been allotted.

The goal of the book you now hold is to help you achieve the goal summed up in this verse: "Beloved, I pray that you may prosper in all things and be in health, just as your soul prospers." (3 John 2) This book will help you plant your feet and become stable so that you can prosper. This book will also help you understand the keys to taking hold of all that God intends for you so that you may truly prosper in all things. God longs for you to prosper and succeed in life. He longs for you to accomplish all that He has destined for you to accomplish. And He longs to lead you down the road to possessing your inheritance.

In *Possessing Your Inheritance*, Rebecca Wagner Sytsema and I share:

> One of the most beautiful stories about possessing inheritance comes from 2 Chronicles 20. In the context of this passage, a federation of enemy nations was coming against the tribe of Judah to overtake it. In days past, God had prevented Israel from invading these nations, because God always knows what wars can be won (see v. 7). He knew that as these enemy nations came together, their multiplied strength would overpower Judah.
>
> Perhaps you can relate to this story, feeling as though many enemies are coming against you. It may seem that when you have defeated one, another rises. You may have seen many things in your life fall into rubble. But take heart! God is with you and He has a plan for overthrowing your enemies.
>
> Such was the case in 2 Chronicles 20. Judah's king at the time was Jehoshaphat, who was a godly man. Through prayer and fasting, Jehoshaphat sought the Lord for a strategy to defeat the enemies standing in the way of Judah's God-given inheritance (see v. 3). God is always faithful to those who cry out to Him. When Jehoshaphat cried

out, God answered through a prophet who gave the following detailed instructions for victory:

1. They had to let go of fear. It was not their battle; it was God's (see v. 15).

2. They had to position themselves to meet the enemy head-on (see v. 17).

3. They were to stand still and see the salvation of God (see v. 17).

4. They had to believe by faith that God would defeat their enemies.

5. They had to believe the word of the prophets over their lives and inheritance (see v. 20).

As they followed God's plan, Jehoshaphat led them into worship and instructed the people to posture themselves in faith. Faith is that pause between knowing what God's plan is and seeing it actually take place. Faith sees the ruins. Faith sees what has been torn down. Faith sees what has never been completed. But faith can look at a situation and see what God sees—the thing already rebuilt or completed.

So as [the people] mingled their worship with faith, and obeyed God, the enemies who were set against them were utterly destroyed, and total victory was theirs (see v. 24). In fact, they saw their enemies turned against each other and every one was killed. Not one had escaped (see v. 23). . . .

Jehoshaphat sought God and was successful in what he was to accomplish. God also longs for us to succeed—every one of us. He did not create us to be sad, defeated failures. Although that does not mean we will never *experience* failure, it does mean we are not created to *be* failures. Ponder, for a moment, the beautiful words of Psalm 139:17-18:

How precious also are Your thoughts to me, O God! How great is the sum of them! If I should count them, they would be more in number than the sand; when I awake, I am still with You.

Chuck D. Pierce and Robert Heidler

God's loving and precious thoughts were not only for David, who wrote this psalm, but they are also for each and every one of us. Part of God's redemptive plan for our lives is to see that we gain whatever we need, whenever we need it, in order to accomplish His purposes for us. Those purposes include our success.

Success is defined as "turning out well or attaining a goal." It means to flourish, to prosper or to thrive. Such is God's will for our lives. Psalm 1:3 says the godly person "shall be like a tree planted by the rivers of water, that brings forth its fruit in its season, whose leaf also shall not wither; and whatever he does shall prosper." There is a portion, both spiritual and physical, that God has set aside for each of His children. As we learn what our portion is, and God moves us toward it, we become successful in our walk with Him.

Such was the case with Peter. When Jesus first laid eyes on Peter, He saw far more than a local fisherman. He saw a man with a high purpose in the kingdom of God. "Then Andrew brought Simon to meet Jesus. Looking intently at Simon, Jesus said, 'You are Simon, the son of John—but you will be called Cephas [which means Peter]'" (John 1:42, *NLT*).

The name Peter means rock. Though Peter had his ups and downs while a disciple, and even denied Christ at the Crucifixion, the Lord still said to Peter, "And I also say to you that you are Peter, and on this rock I will build My church, and the gates of Hades shall not prevail against it" (Matt. 16:18). And so it was that Peter became a great apostle, spreading the gospel and eventually giving his life for the cause of Christ.

Even though Peter was nothing particularly special at the time of their meeting, Jesus saw in him a great destiny. I suppose that Jesus knew a bumpy road would lie ahead for the young disciple. Even so, He set a course to lead and guide Peter through to the place where he would become a highly successful citizen of the kingdom of God, upon whom the Lord said He would build His Church.

Today, the Holy Spirit sees us just as Jesus saw Peter—reaching our fullest Kingdom potential. No matter where we are in life, or how insignificant we may feel, the Holy Spirit can see ahead to the day when we are successfully fulfilling the destiny for which we have been created. Just as Jesus called Peter by his new name long before its meaning became clear, so the Holy Spirit calls out to us in this hour—as children of destiny and success, even though we may seem far from it.

Specifically, the Lord longs for us to succeed: by moving our lives forward; . . . by causing us to prevail over the enemy of our souls; . . . by causing us to act wisely and strategically; by promoting us to new levels at the right season; and by helping us to achieve our destined purpose when we cry out to Him along our paths.

In essence, as God's children, He longs for us to succeed even as He succeeds![6]

Five Keys to Success

In *Possessing Your Inheritance*, Rebecca Sytsema and I note that achieving the success and prosperity that God has for us is not automatic just because we are His children. We have to cooperate and participate in God's plan to help us move toward all He has for us. The following are five keys that can help us along the way:

1. Put God First

"No one can serve two masters; for either he will hate the one and love the other, or else he will be loyal to the one and despise the other. You cannot serve God and mammon. Therefore I say to you, do not worry about your life, what you will eat or what you will drink; nor about your body, what you will put on. Is not life more than food and the body more than clothing? For after all these things the Gentiles seek. For your heavenly Father knows that you need all these things. *But seek first the kingdom of God and His righteousness, and all these things shall be added to you.* Therefore do not worry about tomorrow, for tomorrow will worry about its own things" (Matt. 6:24-25,32-34, emphasis added).

As this passage so clearly states, we cannot serve both God and the love of wealth (at the same time). God is not merely a means to our financial security. People with that attitude will never reach their full potential until their hearts have been changed. God is not our servant. Instead, we are His servants. The apostle Paul, one of God's greatest success stories, wrote, "I know how to be abased, and I know how to abound. Everywhere and in all things I have learned both to be full and to be hungry, both to abound and to suffer need. I can do all things through Christ who strengthens me" (Phil. 4:12-13).

We may experience times of hunger in our lives, but if we are following God and seeking Him first, those times can be considered as a few pages in the book of our ultimate success. God knows what we need. The promise in Matthew 6 is that if we seek Him first, He will see to it that what we need, when we need it, will be there for us.

2. Follow Covenant Agreement

Every one of us who has experienced the saving grace of God has entered into a covenant agreement with Him. Many analogies are used throughout Scripture to define the relationship: He is our Father; we are His children. He is our Shepherd; we are the sheep of His pasture. He is the Head; we are the Body. He is the Master; we are the servants.

Each of these analogies paints a simple picture. [When we are touching and agreeing with our Maker, Jehovah, He will] provide for our needs . . . promote us to the next level . . . teach and guide us . . . help us move forward and prevail. . . . [When we submit to our Holy God, He makes sure] that we have a portion and an inheritance. But, it is up to us to obey His commandments at every turn in order to see all His provision come to fruition. If we break the covenant through disobedience, rebellion, unbelief, sluggishness, forgetting God or hidden sin, we bring peril to our own success.

3. Seek Strategy from God to Reach Your Goal

The concept of reaching toward a goal is both wise and biblical. In Philippians 3, Paul writes, "No, dear brothers and sisters, I am still not all I should be, but I am focusing all my energies on this one thing: Forgetting the past and looking forward to what lies ahead, I strain to reach the end of the race and receive the prize for which God, through Christ Jesus, is calling us up to heaven" (vv. 13-14,

NLT). Here Paul reveals that the success God has for us is not just for this earthly life, but will continue in heaven.

Reaching toward our goal of godly success seems to have a dual purpose. First, we are reaching toward our God-given potential to accomplish His plan for us while here on earth. Second, we are laying up a prize in heaven that is eternal. What a complete picture of success! God has a strategy for each of us to reach our goal. By seeking Him, we will gain pieces of the strategy along the way. As we are obedient to follow that strategy, we will one day stand before Him with confidence, knowing we reached the end of the race with success.

4. Live in Christ

"For I live in eager expectation and hope that I will never do anything that causes me shame, but that I will always be bold for Christ, as I have been in the past, and that my life will always honor Christ, whether I live or I die. For to me, living is for Christ, and dying is even better" (Phil. 1:20-21, *NLT*). Here again Paul brings success into an eternal perspective. To live for Christ and to honor Him in all that we do will bring us ultimate success and prosperity, whether we live or die. Many honorable saints throughout the history of the Church have shed their blood as martyrs for Christ Jesus. These are great success stories in the Kingdom.[7]

5. Give Your Way into Freedom!

Success is as simple as knowing that when we allow Christ to lead us, we will always prosper in our souls, and we will be blessed in all areas of life, both now and eternally. Each one of us has a God-given destiny of success. That is a part of the inheritance we have as children of God. But what does having an inheritance in God really mean? Let's take a look.

Give Your Way into Freedom

Although we will be discussing giving throughout this book, I want to point out a few items about it here. As I wrote in *Redeeming the Time*:

Giving is a way of life for Pam and me. As a matter of fact, most people think I am motivated by prophecy because I am a prophet. However, what motivates me is giving. God has shown me the power of seedtime and harvest. The issue of giving is probably one of the most controversial topics in the body of Christ. Giving does not mean bringing a check or dollar to the church. Rather, giving is built around a covenant relationship that is linked around an altar of worship. Giving occurs when we recognize that our King is righteous and legitimate. We bless the Lord so that He will take His stand righteously on our behalf. Giving occurs when we worship. Giving occurs when we respond to authority with generosity and blessing. Giving occurs when we realize the lesser is blessed by the greater—that God is the greater King and we should want to give all to Him. Giving occurs when we do not hold back what we have been entrusted with by the Lord.

Here are some things to remember about giving:

- God gave! He sent the expression of Himself through His Son as man. His Son gave His life for our freedom (John 3:16).

- We should give because we recognize that our *King is righteous* and legitimate. When you give, only He can rise up over you in certain dimensions and serve as your judge. Only He can make you righteous.

- We give when we worship. Worship is an expression of faith in someone greater than ourselves. Our being gives of its life back to its Creator when we worship.

- We give when we respond to authority with generosity and blessing. I love to give to those who cause my destiny to move forward.

- We give when we realize the lesser is blessed by the greater.

- We give when we do not hold back what we have been entrusted with and that over which we have stewardship.[8]

Here are a few additional items to consider about giving:

- When we give our first and best portion, He blesses all the rest that remains! This is the firstfruits principle!

- Sow seed and you will reap a harvest. This will be a time that we bring forth seed after our own kind (see Gen. 1:13). On the third day the Lord created seed time and harvest principles. However, remember that after this, the ground fell into a curse. Cain offered the fruit of the ground; Able offered the best. The redemptive power of the Lord Jesus Christ broke the curse. This is a season that our fruit will be seen. We must be purified, because what we sow we will reap. Then our best will be seen. We must ask the Lord to draw His best from us. The enemy is going to resist your gift coming forth. And now is the time for you to be released into a new anointing. Resist the enemy and he will flee.

- Honor the Lord with your firstfruits. Proverbs 3:10-11 states, "Honor the Lord with your possessions, and with the firstfruits of all your increase; so your barns will be filled with plenty, and your vats will overflow with new wine." Firstfruits-giving is a way of life for Pam and me, since when you understand firstfruits giving, you will prosper. (We will discuss more about firstfruits giving in a later chapter.)

The rest of this book is aimed at helping you break into God's timing for prosperity. Once you understand the cycles (of life and the calendar) and the various laws (of recovery, use and multiplication) that are in operation, you can position yourself to receive the fulfillment of God's promise of prosperity. We want you to learn how to first seek God and His Kingdom so all things will be added to you.

Notes

1. *Oxford Dictionaries,* 2013, http://oxforddictionaries.com/us/definition/american_eng lish/expectation, s.v. "expectation."
2. *Oxford Dictionaries,* 2013, http://oxforddictionaries.com/definition/english/desire, s.v. "desire."
3. Robert J. Mangile, "The Egg Hatching Process," *American Pigeon Journal,* August 1992, p. 31.
4. Chuck D. Pierce, *Time to Defeat the Devil: Strategies to Win the Spiritual War* (Lake Mary, FL: Charisma Media, 2011), pp. 15-17.
5. Chuck D. Pierce and Robert Heidler, *Restoring Your Shield of Faith: Reach a New Dimension of Faith for Daily Victory* (Ventura, CA: Regal Books, 2004), pp. 20-22.
6. Chuck D. Pierce and Rebecca Wagner Sytsema, *Possessing Your Inheritance: Take Hold of God's Destiny for Your Life* (Ventura, CA: Regal Books, 1999), pp. 38-41.
7. Keys #1-4 taken from Pierce and Sytsema, *Possessing Your Inheritance,* pp. 41-44.
8. Chuck D. Pierce, *Redeeming the Time: Get Your Life Back on Track with the God of Second Opportunities* (Lake Mary, FL: Charisma Media, 2009), pp. 195-196.

2

THE DOMINO EFFECT

CHUCK D. PIERCE

When I was growing up, one of the things I enjoyed doing was taking box after box of dominos and lining them up. I would barely touch the first and then watch the first touch the second, the second impact the third, and so on until the 500 tiles were all completely lying on each other. The sound! The motion! The effect of one tile causing the whole 500 to move into a new order was thrilling!

The domino effect is a chain reaction that occurs when a small change causes a similar change nearby, which then causes another similar change, and so on in linear sequence. The term is best known as a mechanical effect and is used as an analogy to a falling row of dominoes. It typically refers to a linked sequence of events where the time between successive events is relatively small. It can be used literally (an observed series of actual collisions) or metaphorically (causal linkages within systems such as global finance or politics).

If we are willing to change our minds and submit to God's way for our lives, new joy will arise and create an incredible domino effect in our lives that will, in the end, produce prosperity. To change your mind should make you think of the word "repent." Repentance comes from experiencing the goodness of God. Because of God's faithful, forbearing love, He passes over the sins and wrong ways of thinking that humankind harbors to demonstrate at the present time His righteousness, which is love, peace and joy through the Holy Spirit (see Rom. 2:4; 3:25-26).

This domino effect of repentance will eventually produce a mindset that causes us to walk in God's perfect timing, pressing toward His plan of abundance for our lives. Third John 2-4 says, "Beloved, I pray that you may prosper in all things and be in health, just as your soul prospers. For I rejoiced greatly when brethren came and testified of the truth that is in you, just as you walk in truth. I have no greater joy than to hear that my children walk in truth."

Prosperity is the result of a quality of life that is produced by being aligned with God's Word and will. The meaning of the Greek word translated as "prosperity" means "there is help on the road." Prosperity is not a fleeting moment where things all align and we have what we want. Prosperity is an ongoing experience that is produced by thinking the way God thinks. This produces wholeness in our lives and makes things complete around us. Repentance leads to joy, which results in prosperity.

Joy Is the Push that Sets Things Moving

I think many people overlook their call to success or miss their moment to succeed. After that they walk in defeat. This can produce grief, which results in having less strength in the future. Don't forget that God can redeem lost time, waste, mistakes and just plain old ignorance and stubbornness when we ask Him for help. A new influx of joy can break us out of the shell that is surrounding us and cause strength to arise that we can bring forth into our future. New joy revives our expectations in God, the One who can cause us to prosper and increase.

Earlier today, I was reading Jacqueline Varnedoe's new book *Becoming Joy Carriers*.[1] This book really spoke to me. Nothing is needed more in today's chaotic world than a good dose of joy! Not only do we need to be filled with joy, but we also need to carry joy!

Joy can be difficult to define. Joy is not necessarily a positive attitude or pleasant emotion. Joy is both an emotion and a fruit, and it is linked with delight. Many levels of joy are described in the Bible, including gladness, contentment and cheerfulness. The joy that the people of God should have is pure. This joy rises above circumstances and focuses on the character of God who originates and emanates His emotion through us when we experience His will.

The joy experienced by righteous children of God is produced by the Spirit of God, who is working all things together for our good. This joy causes us to see our future. This is what makes joy different from happiness and causes us to rise above sorrow and loss. We go through so many adverse, trying times as we walk through this world that we need something to help remind us that "the joy of the LORD is [our] strength" (Neh. 8:10). If the enemy can remove your joy, he can remove your strength. Strength is the ability to withstand our next attack. Therefore, maintaining strength is key to our Spirit-filled life.

When the second of our twins died, we had an outdoor memorial service for him. During that service, Pam stood up and sang a beautiful song out over the field where they were interred. It was an incredible moment. One week after the death of the second baby, a friend called and said she had a real problem with the fact that God had allowed their deaths. She was also having a problem with how Pam was dealing with this trauma—with seemingly unshakable faith. One of the most impacting things I have ever heard anyone speak came from my wife's mouth on that day. Pam told our friend, "If there's one thing I've learned in my life, it's that the quicker I submit to the hand of God, the quicker I can resist the devil. I have chosen to submit to God's hand in this circumstance. And in submitting to the hand of God, He will give me the ability to overcome the enemy so that the double portion that has been robbed will be returned."

The Lord was speaking through my wife. Those words went deeply into my spirit, and I have carried them since that time. Even when we don't understand what has happened in our lives, in the midst of our loss and resulting grief, we need to learn to submit quickly to God's greater plans for our lives. When we submit, we stand under. The concept of submitting is the act of allowing the wings of His goodness and grace to spread over us and shelter us from the accusatory thoughts of the enemy, the fray of the world and the condemnation of our own mistakes. If we always submit our lives to God, we can resist the roadblocks we encounter in our destined paths. Truly, when we submit, we learn that loss has great benefit. We should allow God to work our situations for good and respond to His love, no matter how difficult our circumstances may be. Loss can turn into joy!

Although we could have been devastated by what happened to us, Pam and I both were able to recognize that even in the midst of the trauma of the loss of two children, God was working out a higher-level promise of restoration on our behalf. Loss can produce a great acknowledgement of God within us, if we submit to His hand.

Chuck D. Pierce and Robert Heidler

When we submit to an all-knowing God who loves us and knows the best for us, we move from devastation to prosperity. The incredibly hard things that we go through will truly become some sort of blessing in the hand of the Lord and will produce a greater prophetic fulfillment in our lives. Yes, a sad, bad, unbearable time can become a joy-filled moment, when we place that moment in the hand of God and give Him thanks for the moment. Time then takes a turn. The harsh memory of pain from the loss of expected joy can now be redeemed. The situation can become a transforming work of grace that can be seen in us for a lifetime.

There is a certain level of joy that we would never come to know if we did not experience loss. The deeper the sorrow, the more capacity for joy we seem to have. After experiencing loss, nothing seems the same. The Bible is full of references about mourning turned to joy:

> For His anger is but for a moment, His favor is for life; weeping may endure for a night, but joy comes in the morning. You have turned for me my mourning into dancing; You have put off my sackcloth and clothed me with gladness (Ps. 30:5,11).

> As the days on which the Jews had rest from their enemies, as the month which was turned from sorrow to joy for them, and from mourning to a holiday; that they should make them days of feasting and joy, of sending presents to one another and gifts to the poor (Esther 9:22).

> For I will turn their mourning to joy, will comfort them, and make them rejoice rather than sorrow (Jer. 31:13).

> To console those who mourn in Zion, to give them beauty for ashes, the oil of joy for mourning, the garment of praise for the spirit of heaviness (Isa. 61:3).

John 16:16-23 is a beautiful passage in which Jesus prophesies His own death and resurrection. Verses 20-22 speak directly of the sorrow and joy that the disciples were about to experience:

Most assuredly, I say to you that you will weep and lament, but the world will rejoice; and you will be sorrowful, but your sorrow will be turned into joy. A woman, when she is in labor, has sorrow because her hour has come; but as soon as she has given birth to the child, she no longer remembers the anguish, for joy that a human being has been born into the world. Therefore you now have sorrow; but I will see you again and your heart will rejoice, and your joy no one will take from you.

Grief has entered into the supply line of many people. This in turn has produced sorrow. Sorrow and joy are firmly linked, perhaps because the deeper we experience sorrow, the more capacity we have for joy.

In this season, so many people have lost their savings, seen businesses fail, and floundered in their attempts to survive the world economic situations. These situations should spur us on to gain a new appetite to prosper. The hungrier we are, the more satisfying a good meal is to us. God knows this. Although we may only see the sorrow and tears of the night, He has planned a bright and beautiful morning full of joy. Pam and I are so aware of this principle that we chose to put John 16:22 on the headstone of our twin sons, knowing that one day our sorrow would turn to a joy that no one could take from us.

One reason God may have for bringing joy after a season of sorrow is to bring a new wind of strength to our spirits. Grieving robs us of strength. There is a weakness that comes from carrying an emotional and spiritual load during difficult circumstances. But God knows that joy brings a new vitality and strength, "for the joy of the LORD is your strength" (Neh. 8:10). Joy produces the kind of strength we need to move into our next season.

Like the disciples at the crucifixion of Jesus, we may go through intense and even confusing losses. But, like the disciples at Jesus' resurrection, great joy awaits us, a joy that no one will be able to take away.

"Restore to me the joy of Your salvation, and uphold me by Your generous Spirit" (Ps. 51:12). Our enemy longs to rob us of our joy and get us out of the salvation process. That does not mean that he can steal our salvation by robbing our joy, but he can steer us away from the forgiveness, healing, prosperity and restoration that are by-products of our salvation. His strategy, many times, is the same one he used on King David: He causes us to sin. Nothing will rob us of the joy of the Lord in our lives as effectively as sin.

But these are days in which God is longing to restore joy to His people through deeper levels of repentance. In repairing the breaches that sin has caused, God is able to restore joy. Proverbs 17:22 says, "A merry heart does good, like medicine." Joy works like a medicine that brings healing to our bones. That is why Scripture says that the joy of the Lord is our strength; joy brings with it the power to heal and maintain the health God has for us.

Even though David sinned and lost his joy, we see from Psalm 51 that he was able to ask the Lord to restore that joy to him. Through the blood of Christ, we are positioned with even greater favor than King David had to ask the Lord to forgive our transgressions and restore the joy of our salvation.

Expect God to Bring Change and Renewal in Your Life

When we walk in defeat, we are blinded to our future and the provision that the Lord has for us. God has ways to redeem what has been lost and to open our eyes to our future. This is an amazing testimony of God's ability to keep those things that we have committed to Him. Janice Swinney, one of the pastors and administrators here at Glory of Zion International, recently had one of those incredible God interventions, one that will encourage you to look again and see what the Lord has for you:

> My father has been gone for 11 years, and I have had little contact with his wife since his death. On March 8 of this year, I received word of my stepmother's death. She and my father were married for 24 years and were both blessings to their children and their grandchildren.
>
> In preparation of their passing, my father and stepmother had established a living trust with my older brother as the grantor trustee. The estate was a combination of assets

that my father (and mother) had accumulated through-out their lifetimes, as well as property that my stepmother had inherited from her parents. Over the last 20 years, there has been much prayer go up regarding this particular inheritance, partially due to some unresolved issues of this blended family.

Upon her death, I called my spiritual authorities, Chuck and Keith Pierce, discussed the change that had occurred in my life, and asked for prayer. Both Chuck and Keith spoke into the situation. So many times when the Lord hears our prayers, He starts working, but we must "look" to see Him in our midst.

On March 10 while I was sitting at my desk at GO, at 2:50 PM, the Lord spoke to me and said, "Go now and get some cash to pay Joshua Awbrey back for your lunch." Immediately, I left the office and drove to the Racetrack Gas Station near the church. I used the ATM to get $50 cash (two $20 bills and one $10 bill). I then went inside, purchased a Diet Coke, and handed the cashier the $10 bill. He gave me change of $9 and some coins.

I returned to the office, and as I was counting out the $8 to pay Josh, I saw that one of the dollar bills had hand-writing in ink on the front of it. I looked again and became completely speechless! My father's name—last and first—and the number "768" were written on one of the dollar bills. At first, I was speechless and overcome with amaze-ment and awe. This was so supernatural. Only God could have orchestrated this moment!

I was so excited! I then reached for my phone to call Keith Pierce and give him the testimony of the sign. I was only giving the high points! Then I said, "Oh, Keith there is also a number written here—it is 768. What does that mean?" He answered with, "I'll call you back." In less than five minutes he called back and told me the Lord had said to look at the seventh book (Judges) in the sixth chapter and the eighth verse. That verse says, "That the LORD sent a prophet unto the children of Israel, which said unto them, Thus saith the LORD God of Israel, I brought you up from Egypt, and brought you forth out of the house of bondage" (*KJV*). Verse 9 goes on to say, "And I delivered you out of the hand of the Egyptians, and out of the hand of all that oppressed you, and gave you their land" (*KJV*).

As I was praising and thanking the Lord for this supernatural sign of the assurance of my inheritance I heard the Lord laugh. He said, "It is My pleasure to give you the Kingdom. Just believe. Do not allow a cap to come over your faith by trying to imagine how I will do a thing. JUST BELIEVE THAT I AM!"

While pondering the path of this, I realized how incredible the timing of each step was. Being at the right place—in this case the exact cashier at the racetrack, at the right time—moving with the voice of the Lord was as supernatural to seeing the sign as the sign itself. This situation gave me a great deal of respect for those Israelites at that first Passover who stayed under the blood covering until the Sign of deliverance came.[2]

Look again! God is there! He will give you the signposts of how change and renewal can come into your life in a moment. In an instant, everything changes. God comes down and reveals Himself, and you see into a realm that you could not see into before. Signs point you along your path of faith! He guides you into a new season. This is a perfect time for you to war your way into the provisional inheritance of your future!

Jehovah Plus

Several of the people at Glory of Zion International are wine connoisseurs. Recently, we were discussing how the anointing is like the grapes in a cluster. Just as you need more than one grape to begin to make wine, so too more than one spiritual dimension or gift is necessary to accomplish all of God's purpose. Brian Kooiman, my personal assistant of many years, sent me his observations after a recent service:

> One of the prophetic words from yesterday's service was that in the cluster we would begin to identify the individual grapes. I felt the Lord tell me to study grapes to see what we could hear spiritually from the different types of grapes. Lori and I actually have forty flashcards for different varietals. The first grape I studied was *Cabernet Sauvignon*. Key points were: "This well-known grape is actually a hybrid offspring of Cabernet Franc and Sauvignon Blanc (a red grape and a white grape . . . producing a very rich red grape). This grape is frequently blended with other grapes. The purpose is to add depth and discipline to blends, creating wines of great character. This grape produces a wine that improves beautifully with age.
>
> In this cluster season, I am hearing the Spirit of God say, "Allow the hybrid to be welcomed. Not only the purebreds or the supposed purebreds can bring their gift to the table in days ahead. The blending of gifts results in added depth, discipline, and great character. Some grapes/gifts specifically help things endure and cause movements to be sustained with excellence."[3]

This illustrates the same principle as when God began to "add to" His character, or further reveal different aspects of His character, to those to whom He had already displayed His nature. When you "add to" God as the eternal, self-existent One, the God of Revelation, the God of moral and spiritual attributes (righteousness, holiness, love), the Lord of Redemption and the Lord of Israel, something historical happens. Our understanding of God is enhanced and a progressive revelation of what we already have understood is produced (see 1 Cor. 10:11). So think of how God had already revealed Himself, and then notice how the Lord was expanding the Israelites' understanding of who He would be to those in covenant with Him:

- *Jireh—The Lord Will Provide.* "I have provision for you to see." God revealed this at Moriah (see Gen. 22:1-19), at what would become the threshing floors purchased by David (see 3 Chron. 3:1) to display His future plans.

- *Rophe—Healer.* God's revelation of this aspect of His character is described in the book of redemption, Exodus. At Marah, God showed that He heals life's wounds and sweetens life's bitter experiences (see Exod. 15:22-27).

- *Nissi—Banner.* God came down at Rephidim during the battle with Amalek. God revealed that He would do miracles and wage war in a hostile world on behalf of His covenant people (see Exod. 17:8-16).

- *M'Kaddesh—Holy.* "I will show you the holy way to walk." God began a new experience of setting His people apart (see Lev. 20:7-8).

- *Shalom—Peace.* "I will atone, bring harmony, and produce wholeness." God revealed who He was to Gideon. He later said, "You should have entered into rest, but . . ." (see Judg. 6:11-24; Isa. 30:15).

- *Tsidkenu—Righteousness.* To Jeremiah, God showed Himself as a righteous Branch and King who would appear in the future (see Jer. 23:5-6). In doing this, He let His people know that His promise would never fail. The people might fail in their stewardship of the promise, but God would not fail. Eventually, He would bring the people back into right standing in the land He had given them.

- *Rohi—The Lord Is My Shepherd.* God showed His people the need to follow Him. "I will feed and lead My flock to pasture." David's life and his journeys became a prototype of God doing this in the lives of those who had covenant with Him (see Ps. 23).

- *Shammah—Jehovah Is There.* "At your lowest ebb, I will be there." Even as the Israelites were in exile, God revealed that they would be restored (see Ezek. 48:35).

There is a place and time, a moment of change, where God Himself comes down and shows each one of us that whatever we need and whenever we have a need, *in Him we are fulfilled*—He has all. Therefore, once we learn God's method of "adding to," we can begin to "add to" our identity and our level of abundance.

Our Desire Should Be to Expect Blessings

As I said in the first chapter, we must expect to prosper! Expectation is linked with the function of desire. In later chapters, I will be explaining our human nature and how we are made in God's image—spirit, soul and body. But for now, let me explain one of the soul's functions that affects the spirit of a person: desire.

Desire was the part of the soul that was affected most when Eve ate the forbidden fruit. Genesis 3:16 says, "To the woman [God] said: 'I will greatly multiply your sorrow and your conception; in pain you shall bring forth children; your desire shall be for your husband, and he shall rule over you.'" Woman's soul was shifted at that moment. In Hebrew, the word translated as "desire" means that there is a stretching out after something that you wish for, a longing for something that is deep and driving your emotions.

Even though in the seed of woman was the overcoming ability to dethrone the serpent and take dominion over his voice, the seed would have to learn to submit the desire of the soul to God. This is a war situation, because desire is one of the functions of the emotion of humankind. James says it this way:

> What is causing the quarrels and fights among you? Isn't it because there is a whole army of evil desires within you? You want what you don't have, so you kill to get it. You long for what others have, and can't afford it, so you start a fight to take it away from them. And yet the reason you don't have what you want is that you don't ask God for it. And even when you do ask you don't get it because your whole aim is wrong—you want only what will give you pleasure (Jas. 4:1-3, *TLB*).

Jesus dealt with the same issue as He taught those who followed Him. Mark 9:35 says, "And He sat down, called the twelve, and said to them, 'If anyone desires to be first, he shall be last of all and servant of all.'" He shared that each disciple would have to determine where his impulses were, and each would have to learn to regard others as greater than himself. Jesus showed each disciple that his intentions would have to realign with God's purposes.

Desire means much more than merely long for, ask for or demand. Our prayer life is developed through desire, and the whole of our personalities is wrapped up and dependent upon our desires being in submission. Misplaced desires can easily become covetousness. Also, a skewed desire can lead to envy and jealousy. When the whole soul submits to a desire that is sinful, our lives shift and we miss the mark of God's targeted plans for us. Then the soul falls to lust (see Num. 11:4,6). This creates an iniquitous pattern that affects all of society. Desire can be stimulated by the will to get rich (see 1 Tim. 6:9). The love of money is the root of all kinds of evil. Another manifestation of wrong or misplaced desire occurs in illicit sexual acts (see Matt. 5:28).

The desires of the flesh and of the thoughts of humankind can lead to destruction, not prosperity. When we gratify our flesh and satisfy our illegal desires, we open ourselves to many evils. Galatians 5:19-21 admonishes us by revealing: "Now the works of the flesh are manifest, which are these; adultery, fornication, uncleanness, lasciviousness, idolatry, witchcraft, hatred, variance, emulations, wrath, strife, seditions, heresies, envyings, murders, drunkenness, revellings, and such like: of the which I tell you before, as I have also told you in time past, that they which do such things shall not inherit the kingdom of God" (KJV). These all work against the principles and laws of prosperity (which we will discuss in the last chapter of this book).

The apostle Peter shared it this way:

Therefore, since Christ suffered for us in the flesh, arm yourselves also with the same mind, for he who has suffered in the flesh has ceased from sin, that he no longer should live the rest of his time in the flesh for the lusts of men, but for the will of God. For we have spent enough of our past lifetime in doing the will of the Gentiles—when we walked in lewdness, lusts, drunkenness, revelries, drinking parties, and abominable idolatries. In regard to these, they think it strange that you do not run with them in the same flood of dissipation, speaking evil of you. They will give an account to Him who is ready to judge the living and the dead (1 Pet. 4:1-5).

He went on to add:

The Lord knoweth how to deliver the godly out of temptations, and to reserve the unjust unto the day of judgment to be punished: But chiefly them that walk after the flesh in the lust of uncleanness, and despise government. Presumptuous are they, selfwilled, they are not afraid to speak evil of dignities. . . . Having eyes full of adultery, and that cannot cease from sin; beguiling unstable souls: an heart they have exercised with covetous practices; cursed children: Which have forsaken the right way, and are gone astray, following the way of Balaam the son of Bosor, who loved the wages of unrighteousness; But was rebuked for his iniquity: the dumb ass speaking with man's voice forbad the madness of the prophet. These are wells without water, clouds that are carried with a tempest; to whom the mist of darkness is reserved for ever. For when they speak great swelling words of vanity, they allure through the lusts of the flesh, through much wantonness, those that were clean escaped from them who live in error. While they promise them liberty, they themselves are the servants of corruption: for of whom a man is overcome, of the same is he brought in bondage. For if after they have escaped the pollutions of the world through the knowledge of the Lord and Saviour Jesus Christ, they are again entangled therein, and overcome, the latter end is worse with them than the beginning. For it had been better for them not to have known the way of righteousness, than, after they have known it, to turn from the holy commandment delivered unto them (2 Pet. 2:9-21, *KJV*).

If desire is not submitted to the power of the Spirit of God, we go "haywire," as they used to say in East Texas when I was growing up. Haywire was used to keep the entire bale of grass together after haying. However, if that wire came loose, then the whole bundle would go every way imaginable. Desire is the function of the emotion that causes us to look forward. Desire is also linked with the deep longing of an individual that can cause us to expect God to move on our behalf. Unless desire is in check and submitted to God, our whole destiny can go in many directions and will never fully manifest during our lives.

Expectation Is Not the Same as Desire

Desire and expectation are closely related. Basically, expectation is that which is looked for to come at a future time. The word means "anticipation of something happening; a confident belief or strong hope that a particular event will happen; a notion of something; a mental image of something expected, often compared to its reality; expected standard: a standard of conduct or performance expected by or of somebody."[4] One of the three Greek words translated in the New Testament as "expect" is *prosdokao,* which means "to look forward." You know something is going to happen or probably will occur, so you allow your emotions to be released in a way that has you watching for a manifestation. What you are looking forward to seeing manifest may not be all good, and you may watch in hope or dread (see Luke 3:15; Acts 3:5). Prophets can tell the future to forewarn individuals of what is coming in days ahead, but no matter how or what they prophesy, they should create a faith element of what will be seen.

Another Greek word translated as "expect" is *ekdechomai* (see Heb. 10:13), which means to wait because you are assured that you will realize what you are waiting on, much as the husbandman waits for the processes of nature (see Jas. 5:7) and the patriarchs for the divine promise (see Heb. 11). *Apokaradokia*, or earnest expectation, describes the stretching forth of the head toward an object that is anticipated (see Rom. 8:19; Phil. 1:20). We are now in a time to stretch out as far as we can stretch and expect God to stretch His hand to meet us.

Aligning Our Expectations

One time I was preparing to speak on expectations, and I asked my daughter to help me communicate this concept to the people I was planning to address. She wrote and then spoke the following:

> As human beings, we are at odds constantly with our fleshly desires, our godly desires, and our limited understanding of destiny and time. We live in a world that blares the message of *following whims*, *doing what you feel*, and *creating your destiny*, without ever mentioning the Father's plan. It is very easy to get out of God's timing in our quest to get what we hope for and to miss destiny moments along the way.
>
> When I was younger, I had pretty strong opinions about what I was supposed to have, be, and become. Okay, I'm just going to say it: I was stubborn. I thought I knew myself so well that I didn't need anyone else's input. Little did I know, God knew my heart better than anyone, including me. At the beginning of life, when things are just getting going, it is so easy to get caught up in our own expectations, never looking to our Father to see if that, in fact, is His amazing plan. It came out in many ways as I walked through childhood and adolescence, but one particular story comes to mind when looking back.
>
> One Christmas, like most kids, I had a very specific list of wishes. I spouted it off to anyone who dared ask me what I wanted for Christmas, and was very clear that these were the things I should be given. I wanted a doll, an Easy Bake

Oven, and more clothes for my doll "Green Baby." Now, there was nothing wrong with my wants. They were normal expectations for a little girl. My brother, Daniel, who is three years older, also had a list of things he'd had his eye on. He wanted a Nintendo, a small TV to play it on, and an iguana. Looking at our two lists, his was the more extravagant and odd of the choices (I mean, really, an IGUANA). So Christmas arrived, and I was filled with high expectations that my desires would be fulfilled.

In my family, we open gifts on Christmas Eve, in a whole frenzy of laughter and eggnog. The day came, and our gifts were handed out. I was given a set of diamond studs, a coat and watch, and a beautiful jewelry box. Meanwhile, Daniel received a TV, a Nintendo, and an iguana. He got an IGUANA! You can probably picture my response. I threw down my watch and shoved aside the ornate jewelry box that would someday hold many prized possessions and trinkets of sentimental value, and stormed through the house. I was blazing mad, not to mention completely determined to spoil Christmas for everyone.

For months, when I looked at Daniel's iguana or played on his Nintendo, I would get mad all over again. And why not? I had been so clear. There was no reason I shouldn't have gotten what I wanted, my list was so reasonable and useful, and normal. My parents tried to explain the gifts. Dad even went so far as to get me more jewelry to store in my jewelry box, but his act of love wasn't enough. "But, honey, these are things you can cherish," Dad said.

"I don't want to cherish them," I pouted. I couldn't see then the outcome of those gifts, or comprehend the reason I had gotten them. I had no foresight and concept of the future. All I could see was a dashed expectation and a hope deferred.

Oftentimes, when our expectation is not met, we are too stubborn and blind to see the gift God has presented us instead. Years later, while getting ready to leave my home in Texas for a strange new one in Colorado, I remember packing up that very well-used jewelry box, hardly remembering the time as a child when I didn't appreciate it. Fortunately for us, God has His expectations in line when it comes to His children.

One of my favorite movies as a kid was Disney's *The Little Mermaid*. In the story, Ariel is the beloved daughter of King Triton. She is headstrong and gifted, but she has a very peculiar desire for a mermaid—to be human. "To be part of their world," as the song goes, is her greatest desire. She knows this is not something that her father agrees with, therefore Ariel thinks he would not understand, let alone care about the desire of her heart.

Through a series of events, Ariel falls in love with a human prince. Now, meanwhile, there is a sorceress named Ursula who wants to destroy King Triton at any cost. She had once been a member of his court but had been banished many years before. (Sound like a familiar villain?) She turns Ariel into a human at the cost of Ariel's voice and the promise that Ursula will own her soul if Ariel is unable to live up to her side of the bargain. However, Ursula never intended for Ariel to live up to her side of the deal.

In the end, Ursula is destroyed, but Ariel remains a mermaid, believing her hope of being with the prince is lost forever. Her father, who loves her and knows that she is not meant to stay where she is, transforms her easily. Ariel discovers that her father was always able and willing to give her the desires of her heart, if she would have just waited.

We can be so like unstable teenage mermaids sometimes. Often, we try to circumvent the Lord in the quest toward our destiny. We want to make it happen and, sometimes, we want to make it happen at any cost. Thankfully God is ever faithful to teach His children good, though at times difficult, lessons.

In the business of our desires, the perilous area for us humans is timing and choices. We think we know what we want and we *expect* that there is a clear path to obtaining that desire. Often we don't see choices and how they will affect our path, and we rarely see God's heart for us. All we know is that something in us *wants*, and we have to go for it. We have hungry eyes that lock onto our goals like a homing beacon. This kind of single-mindedness is great when applied to the things of the spirit or the plans of the Father, but it's not so good when applied to what the ego wants.[5]

Our Expectations of Others Are Related to What We Do Ourselves

I want my kids to prosper. One of my greatest heart's desires is to see *all* people prosper. No matter who the people are, if God has brought them in my path, I start declaring prosperity over them.

I have six children and have always worked with people (my trade was in the human resource field), and I realize that expectation of others is an issue that one must master in life. How we expect others to perform can be a blessing or a snare. Many times we expect others to do what we do. Actually, this falls in the category of "an eye for an eye." If we are not careful with expectations, we become disappointed, judgmental and/or critical. We must learn to look at someone's potential and encourage that person to succeed in the best that God has for his or her life.

Many children have been ruined because their parents had such high expectations of them that they could not reach. However, there is a fine line for parents to walk. We must motivate our children to reach for the best without overly refining them or being overly disappointed when they regress or shrink from success.

There is also a fine line to walk with the people with whom we work. Our expectations of others are keys to how achievement is experienced. If a fellow worker wants to succeed, it will be easier for us to accomplish the overall goal of a corporate project. However, if a fellow worker has no self-destined expectation, the attitude of the whole group will be affected, as will their ability to reach the intended goal.

As a general rule, people want to achieve. Most of the time, people who are motivated to achieve will work hard regardless of how everyone around them works. People who have little motivation will work harder if they think their comrades will not work hard. In other words, they will have a desire to pick up the slack if they feel they will be held accountable for the tasks at hand. In addition, if a person knows someone is watching, he or she will tend to work harder than he or she would otherwise.

Personal motivation or expectation of others relates to how we loaf or achieve:

> Four researchers set up a study of "social loafing," using college students who were invited based on being in the top or bottom 25 percent of their classes in "achievement motivation," defined as, "the tendency of an individual to work toward the achievement of personal goals or standards." They were paired off, told they were in a study on e-mail communication, then separated by screens and not allowed to talk. They were asked to come up with as many ideas as they could for use of a particular item, but unknown to them, the messages they supposedly exchanged with their partners were fake. Some people were led to believe their partners would try hard on the study, and others the opposite. Also, although the researchers could count how many ideas every individual came up with, some students believed only the total amount of ideas produced by both people could be counted. (In other words, if any of those people tended to be a social loafer, they would think they could get away with it.)
>
> The results identified only one combination of factors in which people loafed: People with low personal motivation who thought their partners were going to work hard and that their own output could not be counted did not work very hard.[6]

Teachers' Expectations Affect Student Performance

I have worked with many gifted individuals. Also, I have had many disciples who I was responsible to mentor. I had to learn quickly with gifted and talented children not to give them the answers, but to develop within them the ability to problem solve and creatively produce. Most of these have succeeded in life. Here are some observations from key educators concerning their students:

> The expectations teachers have for their students and the assumptions they make about the potential have a tangible effect on student achievement. Research "clearly establishes that teacher expectations do play a significant role in determining how well and how much students learn."[7]
>
> Students tend to internalize the beliefs teachers have about their ability. Generally, they "rise or fall to the level of expectation of their teachers. . . . When teachers believe in students, students believe in themselves. When those you respect think you can, YOU think you can."[8]
>
> Conversely, when students are viewed as lacking in ability or motivation and are not expected to make significant progress, they tend to adopt this perception of themselves. Regrettably, some students, particularly those from certain social, economic, or ethnic groups, discover that their teachers consider them, "incapable of handling demanding work."[9] Teachers' expectations for students—whether high or low—can become a self-fulfilling prophecy. That is, students tend to give to teachers as much or as little as teachers expect of them.
>
> A characteristic shared by most highly effective teachers is their adherence to uniformly high expectations. They "refuse to alter their attitudes or expectations for their students—regardless of the students' race or ethnicity, life experiences and interests, and family wealth or stability."[10]

Now, the Spirit of God, our great teacher, knows how we are knit together. He knows why the Father made us and what He made us to accomplish. He knows how to activate gifts within us so that we prosper. His manifestation in us is meant for us to profit! First Corinthians 12:7 says, "But the manifestation of the Spirit is given to each one for the profit of all"!

Learn How to See Your Blessing

I mentioned earlier that in 2 Chronicles 20:20, God tells us that if we honor the prophets, we will succeed. When Robert Heidler taught about blessing recently, he shared that 12 years ago, his family was in a desperate financial situation. He and his wife both had surgery the same year, and their medical bills overwhelmed them with debt. Debt piled upon debt! The interest charges on their credit cards were exorbitant, and they saw no hope of escape. They had lost their expectation of God.

Robert came to me and told me that the only way he knew to try to deal with the debt was by increasing the amount he paid each month. Yet when he paid just the minimum payments on all the credit cards, he was often left with less than $20. There was no way for him to increase his payments, and he and his wife felt trapped. Robert tells the story this way:

> Linda and I went to Chuck and asked for prophetic counsel. We wanted to see if the Holy Spirit had a path that would lead us out of that prison of debt. Chuck's word to us was very simple, but very difficult. He said, "You need to sell your house and pay your debts." That was a hard word! We had lived in our house for 16 years. We had raised our kids in that house. It was hard to think about selling it to pay our debts. But we saw no other way, so we decided to follow Chuck's prophetic counsel. (It's important to see that this was a prophetic word for us; it might not be God's plan for you. But God does have a plan for you!)
>
> It took us a full year to get our house ready to sell. But during that year, something incredible happened. As we worked to prepare our house for sale, the property values in our neighborhood skyrocketed, and the interest rates fell. At the end of the year, we sold our house, paid off all our debts, and had enough money to build a much nicer house than we had before. So God's plan to get us out of credit card debt was to give us a wonderful new house. God had a way, but it was not a way we could have ever figured out

with our human minds. It could only be seen as the Holy Spirit was released to shine His light on our situation. We had lost our expectation in God working until we heard the word from heaven and entered into heaven's blessing by letting go of what we had and receiving something greater.

God wants to break off whatever curse you are under so that you can experience His blessing. Robert and Linda's curse was debt linked with infirmity. They chose to be blessed. God has a path to blessing for you too, just as He did for Robert and Linda. God wants you to see His path to your blessing. God's Holy Spirit is your menorah. He is there to reveal His wisdom and plan. Let Him shine His light on your path. Walk in the light of the Spirit—and see the path to your blessing!

One key to seeing God's path of blessing is to look beyond where you are so that you can see into the place that the Lord has already prepared for you. When you have vision, you do not go backward; you expect the Lord to perform His word on your behalf. Let the shout of the Lord rise up, and may you shout, "My blessings are on the way!"

See Your Future and Go Beyond

The author of Hebrews says the following about seeing beyond our present situation:

> Therefore, as the Holy Spirit says: "Today, if you will hear His voice, do not harden your hearts. But instead warn (admonish, urge, and encourage) one another every day, as long as it is called Today, that none of you may be hardened [into settled rebellion] by the deceitfulness of sin [by the fraudulence, the stratagem, the trickery which the delusive glamor of his sin may play on him]. For we have become fellows with Christ (the Messiah) and share in all He has for us, if only we hold our first newborn confidence and original assured expectation [in virtue of which we are believers] firm

and unshaken to the end. Then while it is [still] called Today, if you would hear His voice and when you hear it, do
not harden your hearts as in the rebellion [in the desert,
when the people provoked and irritated and embittered
God against them]" (Heb. 3:7-8,13-15, *AMP*).

Seeing then that the promise remains over [from past times]
for some to enter that rest, and that those who formerly
were given the good news about it and the opportunity,
failed to appropriate it and did not enter because of disobedience, Again He sets a definite day, [a new] Today, [and
gives another opportunity of securing that rest] saying
through David after so long a time in the words already
quoted, Today, if you would hear His voice and when you
hear it, do not harden your hearts (Heb. 4:6-7, *AMP*).

My wife seems to have the keys to being free. She keeps her life
simple, and she remains focused. Pam's favorite Scripture is Ephesians 5:8-16:

For you were once darkness, but now you are light in the
Lord. Walk as children of light (for the fruit of the Spirit is
in all goodness, righteousness, and truth), finding out what
is acceptable to the Lord. And have no fellowship with the
unfruitful works of darkness, but rather expose them. For
it is shameful even to speak of those things which are done
by them in secret. But all things that are exposed are made
manifest by the light, for whatever makes manifest is light.
Therefore He says: "Awake, you who sleep, arise from the
dead, and Christ will give you light." See then that you walk
circumspectly, not as fools but as wise, redeeming the time,
because the days are evil.

This is a life principle in which she has walked for as long as she
has known Scripture and been aware that there was a God in heaven
who was there for her.

When I wrote *Redeeming the Times*, I asked her to write the foreword. Here is what she shared:

> Time . . . We waste it, manage it, even kill it, but when it's gone, we can never get it back. Or can we? In this book by my husband, Chuck Pierce, the concept of redeeming time is explored through the eyes of a man who understands and appreciates the value of time and the need that all of us experience: the need to buy back time, correct our mistakes, and wipe clean our spiritual slates.
>
> Chuck and I both experienced childhoods stained with alcoholism and its accompanying effects. Like the children of many alcoholics, we felt cheated out of normal, functional family life and would have welcomed the opportunity to go back in time and get another chance with one or both of our parents. And yet, we both recognize that who we are today is largely due to the circumstances of our childhoods. Fortunately, we don't have access to a literal, physical time machine, so we aren't free to go back and tamper with the challenges that shaped us. We do, however, have access to the redemptive power of the eternal One who makes all things work together for our good and His purposes.
>
> The concepts and principles set forth in this book center around the mystery and wonder of time as God defines and ordains them. In spite of how we humans squander the time we are given or try to manipulate the clock to fit into our plans, God is ultimately the One in control. Because of this, we can enter into a new dimension of faith where time is concerned. With a new understanding of time and God's redemptive plan for each one of us—whether past, present, or future—we can embark on a whole new adventure where time is concerned.
>
> Regardless of your circumstances right now, you can face the future with hope knowing that the God of your past and present is ordering your steps.[11]

Chuck D. Pierce and Robert Heidler

You must break into God's cycles of blessings, see new doorways, and go beyond your present. Open your heart and your mind to the reality of God's presence in every cycle of your life, and prepare to shift into new calls and new victories.

Satan's Plan Is to Divert Us from God's Path

As I said earlier, prosperity could be defined as "help on the road." Unfortunately, on that road (the path that God has for us), there are also many things the enemy uses to try to divert us and blind us from moving into the promises of God. Anytime we are blinded by a force, we lose the power of prosperity. In *How to Minister Freedom*, I wrote:

> Even though God plans for us to be whole and successful, we have an enemy that has a plan contrary to our Maker's. This enemy, Satan, and all of his hordes of demonic spirits, would love to see us fragmented instead of whole. Satan delights in setting us on a wrong path so that we cannot accomplish God's kingdom purposes for our lives and advance His kingdom in the earth. Satan's purpose is to interrupt God's plan for us to have successful lives. At any one of the stages of our lives, the enemy would love to block us from moving any further in God and His purposes. If he can do this, the destiny that God has for each of us cannot be completed. In his attempt to keep us from reaching our destiny, Satan uses the following 10 ways to sidetrack us, divert us or fragment us:
>
> 1. *Cares of the world*—We divert our eyes and desires to the world around us instead of keeping our eyes upon the One who made us.
>
> 2. *Anxiety*—Anxiety is friction within our inner person that keeps us from walking in peace, or wholeness.
>
> 3. *Weights on our spirit*—These weights are burdens that we bear in the flesh.

4. *Unforgiveness*—Unforgiveness is holding resentment toward an individual who has wronged us.

5. *Poisoned spirit*—We allow the hurts that we encounter in life to cause a root of bitterness to arise within our spirit and eventually defile our whole body.

6. *Grief*—Grief is a function of loss that can be embedded in our emotions. Grief has a time frame. If we go past that time frame, the enemy produces hope deferred within us. We then lose our expectation in God and others.

7. *Unstable emotions*—Instability is the lack of being able to stand. Our emotions eventually rule us, and life becomes a roller coaster.

8. *Accusations*—The accuser of the brethren loves to reproach us and remind us of everything that we have done wrong.

9. *Condemnation*—Condemnation is the opposite of conviction. Whereas conviction leads us to grace, condemnation says that there is no way out for any wrongdoing we've done.

10. *Sin and iniquitous patterns*—Sin's author is Satan. Unconfessed sin can lead us to a pattern of iniquity. Iniquity diverts us from the path of life.

Each of these issues can fragment the way we think and cause our spirit to lose the power that God has made available to us. God has made us spiritual, soul and body; and He ordained us to be whole. If Satan can trap us with any of the above issues, . . . our mind becomes divided (our way of thinking becomes unsure), and we lose the power of the Holy Spirit flowing through our spirit.

When we minister deliverance to others, we need to understand how the enemy attacks us in each of these areas. We need to remember that deliverance is not just setting people free of demonic forces; it is also bringing people into a place of renewal so the life processes of God begin to flow through them and they begin to operate in life, and not death. In order to do that, we need to minister deliverance to the whole person.[12]

Let Go and Prosper!

I think the greatest war we face is over the idea of increase. We were meant to increase, not just to maintain. We are being transitioned and repositioned in the new season. Now is the time for us to break past destructive ways of working and old, cyclical poverty mentalities. We must move out of our up-and-down ways, which are creating emotional instability. We must break the power of rule by and in the flesh, we must get to know the Holy Spirit, and we must yield to God's ways. We must embrace the war of the season ahead and leave the old wars of last season behind!

A good way to understand this is to liken it to the time when the Cold War was ending between the United States and the Soviet Union. One type of war was ending and another was beginning. Similarly, we are letting go of last season's building plans and pressing in to find the new prototypes that heaven will release so that we can build the church life of the future. Once this is completed, we will unlock the Kingdom that is within us, the floodgates will open, and God's glory will fill the earth.

We are called to prosper! I do not mean just with material blessing, but also in our call and every other aspect of our lives. In the next chapter, we will seek to better understand God's timing and covenant agreement with humankind that allow us to prosper.

Notes

1. Jacqueline Varnedoe, *Becoming Joy Carriers* (Thomasville, GA: Calling to Excellence, Inc., 2012).
2. Janice Swinney, personal communication, March 20, 2010.
3. Brian Kooiman, personal communication, April 27, 2010.
4. *Encarta World English Dictionary* (North American Edition), 2009, http://www.bing.com/Dictionary/Search?q=define+expectation, s.v. "expectation."
5. Personal communication, December 11, 2009.

6. J. Hart, et al., "Achievement Motivation, Expected Coworker Performance, and Collective Task Motivation: Working Hard or Hardly Working?" *Journal of Applied Social Psychology*, 2004, vol. 34, no. 5. http://www.suddenteams.com/teamres/indiv_loafing.htm (accessed April 2010).

7. Jerry Bamburg, "Raising Expectations to Improve Student Learning," *ERIC Digest* 378 290 (1994), quoted in Linda Lumsden, "Expectations of Students," *ERIC Digest,* 409 609 (July 1997), quoted in *KidSource OnLine,* 2009. http://www.kidsource.com/kidsource/content4/student.expectations.html (accessed April 2010).

8. James Raffini "Winners Without Losers: Structures and Strategies for Increasing Student Motivation to Learn," *ERIC Digest* 362 952 (1993), quoted in Linda Lumsden, "Expectations of Students," *ERIC Digest,* 409 609 (July 1997), quoted in *KidSource OnLine,* 2009. http://www.kidsource.com/kidsource/content4/student.expectations.html (accessed April 2010).

9. Peggy Gonder, "Caught in the Middle: How to Unleash the Potential of Average Students," *ERIC Digest* 358 554 (1991), quoted in Linda Lumsden, "Expectations of Students," *ERIC Digest,* 409 609 (July 1997), quoted in *KidSource OnLine,* 2009. http://www.kidsource.com/kidsource/content4/student.expectations.html (accessed April 2010).

10. Barbara J. Omotani and Les Omotani, "Expect the Best: How Your Teachers Can Help All Children Learn," "The Executive Educator," EJ 519 766 (March 1996), quoted in Linda Lumsden, "Expectations of Students," *ERIC Digest,* 409 609 (July 1997), quoted in *KidSource OnLine,* 2009. http://www.kidsource.com/kidsource/content4/student.expectations.html (accessed April 2010).

11. Pam Pierce, foreword to *Redeeming the Time: Get Your Life Back on Track with the God of Second Opportunities,* by Chuck D. Pierce (Lake Mary, FL: Charisma House, 2009).

12. Chuck D. Pierce, "How Satan Diverts Us from the Path of God," in *How to Minister Freedom: Helping Others Break the Bonds of Sexual Brokenness, Emotional Woundedness, Demonic Oppression and Occult Bondage,* ed. Doris M. Wagner (Ventura, CA: Regal Books, 2005), pp. 40-42.

3

The War for Prosperity

Chuck D. Pierce

In chapter 1, I briefly discussed our relationship as blood-bought believers with the covenant of Abraham. Abraham became the father of the Jewish nation, and there is much progressive revelation of Scripture related to Abraham's seed and all of those who are grafted to this seed. Only those who share in the faith of Abraham can share in the eternal blessing of this covenant and all the available prosperity that is linked to it. Through Messiah's seed, all nations and people can prosper if they operate under the power of this blessing. As individuals come to faith in Yeshua, the ancient promise given to Abraham is being fulfilled, and a door for incredible blessings opens to each believing individual.

Cross Over and Prosper!

Abraham was confronted and visited by the Lord on several occasions. On one of those occasions, God spoke to him the incredible promise that would change the course of history. That promise included land, children and riches. Embedded in the promise was an inherent power that would be shared with anyone who aligned with it. God said only to Abram, "I will bless those who bless you and curse those who curse you!" (see Gen. 12:3).

According to Genesis 14, Abraham was called and created the Jewish race from this covenant. Later, he was sent to recover his nephew Lot, who had gotten caught up in the war of the land where the Hebrews coexisted with other tribes and kingdoms. Kings rose against other kings, and in the midst of the uprising, a portion of Abraham's family was captured. Now Lot, who had lots of problems, was still family. The Bible says that Abraham had to go from Beersheba all the way to Dan to recover this portion of his family.

Not only did he recover Lot, but he also gained the spoils and booty linked with war. He was not afraid to cross over and war for the best that God had promised.

This was a defining moment for the Hebrew! The word "Hebrew" comes from the word *abar*. *Abar* means "to cross over." Abram, the Hebrew, was the one who crossed the river. Through covenant with a holy God, Abraham—and all of those linked with him—would be a crossing-over people. The act of Abram crossing the river Euphrates was a dynamic moment that defined his identity in God's eyes and thus his name. Abram was the first Hebrew and always by faith crossed over any barrier that would prevent him from seeing the fullness of the promise that had been spoken to him. By continually crossing over, he became known as the father of nations.

Just as crossing over became a defining characteristic of Abram, crossing over should be a defining characteristic of everyone aligned with this covenant. But for you to be fully grafted into this covenant, you must be willing to cross over. If crossing over is not functioning within you, something has not been activated in you. If you need help in this area, your prayer should be, "God, come intervene in my life, and I will move to the other side."

You are part of a people who cross over! Unlike Abram, who crossed over by himself the first time, you can collectively cross over with other believers into a new place. That is the whole tribe concept. We can all go across! We just have to find our time and our positions, and we have to be able to see God's presence moving so that we all move in order over to the other side.

Just like Abram, certain acts that you do name you spiritually. Specific acts of faith that you perform create the godly identity of your bloodline. You are then grafted into the covenant that identifies you as unwilling to stop, rest and be denied the riches of the promise.

Likewise, acts of iniquity done by you or those who have gone before you create an imprint of iniquity in your bloodline. For instance, if your family has robbing God in their bloodline, that identity is passed from generation to generation. Thankfully, every one of these iniquities can be overturned by the redemptive power of God. There are defining godly characteristics locked up in our bloodlines that God is ready to unlock. There are characteristics linked with prosperity that God wants to bring forth in each of us that will make His Body look and perform in the way He intended from the beginning of time. So, ask the Lord to show you anything in your life that you have never let Him draw out of you.

To see the life of Abram unfold was one thing, but then to see the blessings stored in one generation manifest 12 ways 4 generations later is an amazing dynamic. Abraham's covenant blessing was passed to Isaac, then to Jacob, and then to the 12 tribes. By the fourth generation, all the dynamics of the curses and blessings were manifest. What had prospered in one generation had continued to prosper, but what had been infiltrated by the enemy's plan and the flesh and mind of humankind to work against prosperity was also in operation. Each tribe had specific strengths as well as weaknesses.

Again, as Paul says in 1 Corinthians 12:7, "But the manifestation of the Spirit is given to each one for the profit of all"! Where one tribe was strong another might be weak, but when they moved and acted as one covenant entity, they were a mighty force with which to be reckoned. This is the way the Body of Christ today needs to be functioning and moving. If we would submit to the Holy Spirit and allow Him to move in us and use us, the whole profits! Through the Holy Spirit, we profit!

Prosperity in Circumcision— the Sign of Covenant

For Abraham, the sign and submission of circumcision came when he was age 99. *El Shaddai*, "The Sufficient God," called Abram to perfection. In the account in Genesis 17, the Lord is basically saying, "Weaken your organ of propensity [the way of prosperity through flesh] and then watch Me multiply you. I am a miracle-working, sufficient God. Take My sign of covenant, cut away, be perfect, and then conceive in holiness. I will change your name from Father of One People or Father of One Land (Abram) and make you Father of Many Nations (or Multitudes)." Abram's identity was being shifted to prove that his prosperity and propensity in the future were not to be dependent upon himself. The prosperity from our own flesh does not last. However, when we stop and recognize God's sufficiency, He acts to secure our inheritance!

We must demonstrate our faith by works, but our relationship with God cannot be merited through works. Abraham would multiply by "cutting" a covenant relationship with a holy God. All of those who align with Abraham will have the same ability to prosper and multiply if they trust in and rely upon the God who aligns with them.

Understanding Holiness

Holiness is one of the foundational principles in the Word of God. Holiness means not common to the world's blueprint. You can flow in the Spirit without having to have your hair or clothes look a certain way. Holiness allows you to be free to wear your hair any way you wish as long as it enhances God's character and reflection through you.

Holiness does not mean you have to follow a long, legalistic set of rules of what not to do. Holiness is about showing honor, so it does require a need to honor your body so it doesn't become defiled. Holiness also means you honor God by putting Him first in every area of your life. If you understand holiness, then you will better understand what we will discuss about firstfruits, which is the outward action of putting God first and giving God the first in every area.

How Prosperity Works

When you enter into the fullness of God's plan for your life, God begins to bring you to your land, just as He promised to do for Abraham. When you submit to His plan of prosperity for your life, He cleanses you from all idolatry and unfaithful ways. This submission causes a heart of stone to be replaced with a heart of flesh (a tender heart to hear God). He places His Spirit within you. He then opens doors that are linked to abundance—not just worldly abundance, but abundance of revelation to understand who God your Creator is through His Son as well as who you are. He blesses the works of your hands. He fills you with revelation. He gives you a boundary and says, "Take dominion! Prosper on every front. Be like Nehemiah."

(In his day, Nehemiah saw Jerusalem in ruins and began to rebuild walls, restore gates, hang doors, and ready the place for a new move of worship.)

You Are a Hebrew

Through Christ, you are grafted into the inheritance of Abraham, so you are a Hebrew. The Bible is written from a Hebraic perspective. As a Hebrew, you have access to God's calendar. You can understand the time to cross over into the new. As we've discussed, Abram, the Hebrew—the one who crossed over—was the key to our becoming who we are destined to be. I always say that we are a crossing-over people. When we move by faith, we cross over from one place in our lives to another. We go from blessing to blessing. Because God's plan was to graft us into the blessings of Abraham, we must use the covenant revelation that was released biblically to help us tell time.

The Lord built His revelation to people around three feast seasons: (1) Passover, a celebration of our deliverance and redemption; (2) Pentecost, a celebration of God's provision; and (3) Tabernacles, a celebration of our fullness in God. Jesus fulfilled all the feasts, but now we and the nations must enter into the blessings of these feasts. The time for that is now, because now we can access and see into a new dimension of God's plan in the earth. (Discussions later in the book will help you understand these feasts, as well as the power of firstfruits—the celebration of *Rosh Chodesh*.)

A Fresh Anointing Is Being Released as We Cross Over

Once you have submitted your life to the Father through the Son, the Spirit will always enable you to face each transition, each crossing over, into a new dimension of promises and blessings. So keep going forth. You are anointed!

The *mashach,* or anointing, lives in you. This anointing is linked with the Messiah. One way to think of it is to picture oil smeared all over you. Another way to see the anointing is to think fullness.

Imagine growing full from the inside out. As the fullness continues to expand, any yoke binding you breaks. Your whole atmosphere changes. Trauma and unforgiveness leave your body. You begin to worship in a new and fresh way, and you begin to interact with the angelic hosts. A new wave of the Holy Spirit overtakes you. You find creative ways to give. You have faith to declare that your seed will multiply and your resources will multiply. You recognize spiritual forces around you that are blocking your flow of life.

See Your Provision!

Abraham was a rich man. He was most likely the richest person in all of his part of the world at the time. He had gone through a process with God. This process had included leaving his home and business in Ur of the Chaldeans, settling in Haran, reforming his supply line and watching God work on his behalf. As stated earlier, the promise of God included material goods, land and blessings to all of those who would connect with and bless Abraham. When Abraham moved to Canaan, he was moving to a new boundary. By doing so, he could receive the best that God had for his life.

Much warfare followed Abraham's choice to follow God, and the warfare started within his family. For instance, he had to separate from Lot, his nephew. Lot always seemed to choose money over morality. So Lot chose a wonderful portion of land, and Abraham took what remained. Wealth and lust for more always bring out the worst in people. There was quarreling and strife in the family, but Abraham submitted to God, allowed Lot to choose first and trusted God to give him his portion. After Lot's departure, God repeated His promise to Abraham: "to you I will give . . ." (see Gen. 13:14-17). Abraham would possess land and would have children, and the inhabitants of Canaan would even honor him as a ruler.

Lot happily settled in Sodom and became a victim in a war involving the major kings in the region. When that happened, Abraham did not shirk his family responsibility. He mobilized his disciples and went into battle and rescued Lot. He also retrieved and returned all the property that had been looted. But he remained humble in the midst of this great victory.

In this process, Abraham entered into a new level of communion with the king of Salem, Melchizedek. He was a priest of God, the Most High. Melchizedek released a new type of blessing on Abraham: "Blessed be Abram of God Most High, Possessor of heaven and earth; and blessed be God Most High, who has delivered your enemies into your hand" (Gen. 14:19-20).

A blessing always indicates that God is the source of all good. The word "blessing" is translated from the same word that means "a spring." So God is like a never-ending spring that provides a constant flow of life to His children. When we bless God, we acknowledge His majesty. Abraham gave a portion of what he had to Melchizedek. From that time forward, God found ways to "cut" covenant with Abraham and ensure a godly covenant with His people in the earth.

This covenant included children. The understanding of this blessing was a difficult concept for Abraham, since he and Sarah were barren and seemed unable to produce a child. However, Abraham and God began to communicate; God gave forth revelation, and Abraham began to develop faith for the future. Abraham knew that having a child or developing an inheritor for his promise was a key component to having a future. Reading through Scripture, the longing in Abraham and Sarah to build a future is clear. God had created a world for them to have dominion in, but their future had to be secured through the covenant that was in their bloodline. So they were tested.

Tests Produce Prosperity

The tests we go through are not meant to destroy us but to create an overcoming spirit within us. There are many challenges that you will go through in life, but because of the good that results from the tests, you have reason to do so. Psalm 66 says, "Shout! Your tests have created an enlargement and fulfillment!" (paraphrased).

Abraham and Sarah attempted to create an inheritance through Sarah's slave, Hagar. However, contention, confusion, competition and discontent came from their attempt to work out this promise.

Separation needed to occur again. Sarah finally said, "Cast out this bondwoman and her son; for the son of this bondwoman shall not be heir with my son, namely with Isaac" (Gen. 21:10). Abraham had to give up one son to embrace another.

Ten Major Tests Abraham Faced

Abraham actually had 10 major tests—all of which produced prosperity in his life:

1. Exile from a portion of his family and from his homeland
2. Hunger and famine in Canaan
3. Corruption in Egypt, resulting in Sarah's abduction
4. Separation from Lot and engagement in warfare to retrieve Lot
5. Union with Hagar, after assuming that Sarah would never give birth
6. Commandment of circumcision
7. Giving of Sarah to Abimelech to protect himself
8. Casting away of Hagar while she was pregnant
9. Giving up his son Ishmael
10. Giving up his promised son, Isaac, binding him on the altar, and trusting God with the future that he thought he had attained (the greatest test)

As you can see from this list, Abraham was not through being tested when he had to choose whether to give up Ishmael. His next test came over his promised son, Isaac. The same God who revealed Himself to Abraham, manifested the promise to him, and made covenant with him was now telling him to give up that promise. The tenth test was the faith release that produced the testimony and infused prosperity into the generations that followed. Through all of Abraham's tests—even though he did not do everything correctly—he submitted his heart to God and was eventually exalted. In the last test, he displayed his complete trust in the God whom he had followed for many years from Ur of the Chaldeans into Canaan, down to Egypt, amidst the Philistines and then to Mount Moriah.

Abraham's Greatest Test

When the Lord requested the final test of Abraham, his response was immediate: "Here I am!" Abraham was almost 140, and Isaac was around 37. In no way could Abraham have forced Isaac to submit to this new test. This giving of Isaac was different than the giving of Ishmael. Abraham had to trust God with his entire future. The giving of Isaac meant that there were no other sons to give away. The inheritance that he had trusted to receive—the promises, the future—all had to be lain on the altar.

From studying Genesis 22, we find that Abraham and Isaac went to worship together in complete harmony. There was a moment on this journey, however, when Isaac realized that this test was not only Abraham's, but also his. He realized he was the offering. He asked, "Where is the lamb for the sacrifice?" (see Gen. 22:7).

Abraham, by faith, replied, "God Himself will seek out and provide the lamb. God's plan of provision is great, and we will watch to see this manifest! But if there is no lamb, then you, my son, will be the offering" (see Gen. 22:8-9).

Rejoicing to Obey, Though Not Happy in the Process

Elohim had appeared and commanded Abraham to offer up a sacrifice—his only son. Wow . . . what faith! With every test, our faith level must rise, just as it did with Abraham. With every test, we must find out what to say. Abraham made a major faith statement: "I and the lad will go and worship and come back" (see Gen. 22:5). Abraham did not know how, but he did know the God that he had been following now for almost 10 decades. *How* is never the issue, but knowing the *who* of our faith is the significant key to our future.

There is a joy in fulfilling God's will. However, feeling follows faith. Like Abraham, sometimes we can be saddened that our choice creates a shift that causes our future to hang in the balance. Binding Isaac on the altar represented total submission. Two generations laid their lives on the line to accomplish the will of God. Abraham lifted his eyes, and there he could see a new provision. This level of faith and interaction revealed what had been hidden from him but now was in full sight. Vision for the future was opened. The prophetic word (to add to what God had spoken before) was released again. God spoke again and included future generations in the next promise.

God has proved that in our testings, the provision for our futures is always waiting—and not only provision, but revelation as well. Revelation releases vision. Abraham named the place "Hashem Will See," or as we know it, *Jehovah Jireh*, "God the One Who Causes You to See Your Provision." This created an event, a precedent, a prototype. From this time forward, all of Abraham's descendants—natural or grafted into the promise—would be able to see their futures and find their provision.

See Your Provision

Jireh is a seeing word. In this season, this becomes one of our most important words to understand as we seek God. God says, "I have provision for you to see." (Isaac had curiosity about this when he wondered where the lamb was.) You will see and be provided for. Provision is linked with seeing, but this actually means that you can see beforehand or before the time that you have a need. Prevision and provision are the same thing.

The term *Roeh*—the prophet who sees and opens up provision—comes from this name. But location is also key for provision. Mount Moriah was the key place. The Lord said He would appear and provide at the place that He ordained and chose. This was where Solomon's Temple was eventually built. The substitute lamb was already waiting to be seen, and it was to be provided as the sacrifice for the future. This became the prototype of God's only Son (see John 1:29; 3:16; Rom. 8:32; 1 Pet. 1:18-19; Rev. 5:11-13).

Expect God to Perform His Word

The Lord is looking for a generation. He is looking for leadership. He is looking for individuals who will expect Him to perform His Word! When He finds such people and sees their leadership, He reiterates His plan for them to prosper. When His time is perfect, He will manifest His blessings. Here is what He said to Joshua, son of Nun, Moses' minister, when his time had come to manifest the promise:

> Moses My servant is dead. So now arise [take his place], go over this Jordan, you and all this people, into the land which I am giving to them, the Israelites. Every place upon which the sole of your foot shall tread, that have I given to you, as I promised Moses. From the wilderness and this Lebanon to the great river Euphrates—all the land of the Hittites [Canaan]—and to the Great [Mediterranean] Sea on the west shall be your territory. No man shall be able to stand before you all the days of your life. As I was with Moses, so I will be with you; I will not fail you or forsake you. Be strong (confident) and of good courage, for you shall cause this people to inherit the land which I swore to their fathers to give them. Only you be strong and very courageous, that you may do according to all the law which Moses My servant commanded you. Turn not from it to the right hand or to the left, that you may prosper wherever you go. This Book of the Law shall not depart out of your mouth, but you shall meditate on it day and night, that you may observe and do according to all that is written in it. For then you shall make your way prosperous, and then you shall deal wisely and have good success. Have not I commanded you? Be strong, vigorous, and very courageous. Be not afraid, neither be dismayed, for the Lord your God is with you wherever you go (Josh. 1:2-9, *AMP*).

Let me prophesy this portion of Scripture to you:

> *The time has come to get up and move into what I have for you. The last leadership has passed. You sat under their training and gleaned from them. However, there were things I wanted to do on their behalf that they never allowed Me to accomplish. You rise up. I will give you both the wilderness and richness of the territory. I will give you every enemy in your territorial boundary that I have promised.*

I have been waiting for you to enter these blessings. The blessings are in your blood. Your bones cry out for what I have to give you. Your heart is filled with desire for what I have promised you. Be confident in what I have done in you! Expect Me to work on your behalf. Align your desires with My desires for you. My desires are best. I have already promised your father and mother what I would do, so you expect Me to do this now!

Do not violate My boundaries. Walk wisely and circumspectly before Me and you will prosper. Meditate, chew My words to you, and you will succeed. You will see your way as a prosperous way and not one cursed and littered with death and destruction. You will have good success if you expect Me to move on your behalf. Let this word invigorate you. My vigor will dispel fear. Enter in now and daily allow Me to guide you. No enemy on your path can stop you. You will know when to stop and when to go! Expect to hear Me daily and feel My presence directing you. Expect Me! Now is your time to think like Me and occupy!

Choose Blessings!

Because we live in a fallen world, everybody has problems. There are things in everyone's life that are negative and unpleasant. But by God's grace, everyone also has some good and pleasant things in life. So everyone experiences both good and bad.

One way to determine if you are walking in God's blessing is to look to see which of these is increasing in your life. If you see the things that are good, positive and pleasant continually increasing in your life, then you are walking in what I call "blessed life"! On the other hand, if your life is marked by a continual increase of what is bad, negative and unpleasant, then your life is affected by the curse, and you need to overcome the "cursed life"!

God began His plan of blessing with Abraham. God came to Abraham with the promise: "I will bless you" (Gen. 12:2). Not only did God promise to bless Abraham, but He also promised to bless His offspring—and, ultimately, to bless the whole world through him. God's covenant with Abraham is often called the Covenant of

Blessing. This is a promise of all-inclusive blessing. Genesis 24:1 describes the kind of blessing Abraham received: "Abraham was old, well advanced in age; and the LORD had blessed Abraham *in all things*" (emphasis added). The *NIV* translates the last three words differently: "in every way." So the blessing Abraham received was not limited to a spiritual blessing. It was not just a promise of heaven when he died. It was a blessing in all things and in every way—a complete blessing in every area of life.

When you trust in Jesus, He links you in or grafts you to Abraham's Covenant of Blessing. Galatians 3:9 assures us: "Those who have faith are blessed along with Abraham" (*NIV*). If you trust in Jesus, you have the right to experience the same blessing Abraham did. This type of blessing is a complete blessing. You can expect to be blessed in every way!

Deuteronomy 7:12-15 describes the blessing of Abraham in this way:

> If you pay attention to these laws and are careful to follow them, then the LORD your God will keep his covenant of love with you, as he swore to your forefathers. He will love you and bless you and increase your numbers. He will bless the fruit of your womb, the crops of your land—your grain, new wine and oil—the calves of your herds and the lambs of your flocks in the land that he swore to your forefathers to give you. You will be blessed more than any other people; none of your men or women will be childless, nor any of your livestock without young. The LORD will keep you free from every disease. He will not inflict on you the horrible diseases you knew in Egypt, but he will inflict them on all who hate you (*NIV*).

That's the fullness of the blessing of Abraham! In a chaotic world like we live in today, you could lose sight of God's will for you to walk in blessing. However, as you read this book, I hope you see that blessing is not an idea thought up by some crazy biblical teacher who just wanted to prosper. Blessing is God's idea, and God's will is for His people to be blessed. We should expect to be blessed!

What We Need to Do to Experience this Blessing

The Old Testament gave clear instructions of what we need to do to experience this blessing: Obey the Law! In Deuteronomy 7:12, God says you will receive the blessing "if you pay attention to these laws and are careful to follow them" (*NIV*). He also pronounced a curse on those who do not fully obey: "But it shall come to pass, if you do not obey the voice of the LORD your God, to observe carefully all His commandments and His statutes which I command you today, that all these curses will come upon you and overtake you" (Deut. 28:15).

In the final chapter of this book, we will discuss the laws of blessing. To understand blessing, we need to see that God's Law reveals His boundaries for our lives. The area within those boundaries is called righteousness. As long as you live within those boundaries, you live in the realm of blessing! Within those boundaries, you find prosperity, security, joy, abundance, protection, health, fruitfulness and satisfaction. Those things are all God's will for you, and they are all found in the realm of righteousness.

When you violate God's boundaries for your life by choosing to sin, you leave the realm of righteousness. You are in sin! Because of that, you no longer live in the sphere of God's blessing, and you instead find yourself under the curse. The curse includes things such as poverty, sickness, fear, sorrow, hatred and betrayal. The Bible gives a detailed description of what the curse is like:

> However, if you do not obey the LORD your God and do not carefully follow all His commands and decrees I am giving you today, all these curses will come upon you and overtake you: You will be cursed in the city and cursed in the country. Your basket and your kneading trough will be cursed. The fruit of your womb will be cursed, and the crops of your land, and the calves of your herds and the lambs of your

flocks. You will be cursed when you come in and cursed when you go out.

The LORD will send on you curses, confusion and rebuke in everything you put your hand to, until you are destroyed and come to sudden ruin because of the evil you have done in forsaking him. The LORD will plague you with diseases . . . with wasting disease, with fever and inflammation, with scorching heat and drought, with blight and mildew, which will plague you until you perish. The sky over your head will be bronze, the ground beneath you iron. . . .

The LORD will cause you to be defeated before your enemies. You will come at them from one direction but flee from them in seven. . . . The LORD will afflict you with the boils of Egypt and with tumors, festering sores and the itch, from which you cannot be cured. The LORD will afflict you with madness, blindness and confusion of mind. . . . You will be unsuccessful in everything you do; day after day you will be oppressed and robbed, with no one to rescue you. . . .

You will build a house, but you will not live in it. . . . You will sow much seed in the field but you will harvest little, because locusts will devour it. You will plant vineyards and cultivate them but you will not drink the wine or gather the grapes, because worms will eat them. You will have olive trees throughout your country but you will not use the oil, because the olives will drop off. You will have sons and daughters but you will not keep them, because they will go into captivity. . . .

All these curses will come upon you. They will pursue you and overtake you until you are destroyed, because you did not obey the LORD your God and observe the commands and decrees he gave you. They will be a sign and a wonder to you and your descendants forever. Because you did not serve the LORD your God joyfully and gladly in the time of prosperity, therefore in hunger and thirst, in nakedness and dire poverty, you will serve the enemies the LORD sends against you. He will put an iron yoke on your neck until he has destroyed you (Deut. 28:15-48, *NIV*).

I call this being vexed. In *Time to Defeat the Devil*, I explain about vexation and how agitated and annoyed you can become if you are not seeing the blessings of God manifest.[1] I love that verse in the above Scripture that says God's goal for our lives is that we serve Him joyfully and gladly for the abundance of all things. That's blessing! The alternative is the curse. The curse involves being oppressed by the enemy; living in hunger, thirst and nakedness; and lacking all things. The curse imposes an iron (unbreakable) yoke of bondage on our lives that lasts until we are destroyed. Notice the differences between the blessing and the curse:

BLESSING	CURSE
Health	Sickness
Abundant provision	Poverty and lack
Success	Failure
Victory over your enemies	Defeat by your enemies

God's plan for your life is not the curse but the blessing! We want to see you break out of all vexation and expect God to bless you.

Escape the Curse and Receive the Blessing

God's plan for the blessing and curse is simple: He promises the blessing to anyone who perfectly keeps the law, and the curse to those who don't. Of course, that leaves us with a problem. By this standard, no one can be blessed! It's no use becoming legalistic and striving and recommitting yourself to try harder next time. The reality is that none of us will ever perfectly keep the Law. We will never be righteous enough to deserve the blessing. And because we don't keep God's Law perfectly, we actually deserve the curse instead of the blessing.

We must not expect that we can always do everything correctly. As I said earlier, I do not think God puts expectations on His children that are unobtainable. Therefore, we must know that God has a way to give us hope and a power to expect the best that He has. He has a way for us to receive blessing, even if we have made a complete disaster of our past.

As we study the Scriptures, we get a glimmer of hope. As we read about the life of Abraham, we learn that he didn't keep the Law perfectly. He messed up badly, yet he was still blessed. We look at David's life and discover that David didn't keep the Law perfectly either, yet he was also blessed. We see many examples in the Word of less-than-perfect people still being greatly blessed.

So there must be another route to receiving the blessing. I discuss God's Plan B in detail in *Redeeming the Times,* so let me just remind you that in Galatians 3:13 we read, "Christ redeemed us from the curse of the Law, having become a curse for us" (*NASB*). So Jesus redeemed us—He bought us, He paid our price—to bring us out from under the curse. He did this by taking the curse on Himself in order that the blessing of Abraham might come to the Gentiles (that's us!) and that we could receive the Spirit's promise through faith. This verse tells us that Jesus took our curse on Himself so that we could receive the blessing of Abraham. And we receive it by faith! This verse summarizes the divine exchange that took place on the cross!

This exchange is described throughout the New Testament. The history of our Lord's sacrifice reveals to us that His obedience on the cross to give up all, taking what we deserved, allowed us to have access to what He deserved. Wow! That is why blessings can become a reality. In the divine exchange, Jesus took our sins to give us His righteousness (see 2 Cor. 5:21). He took our infirmities to give us His health (see Isa. 53:4-5). He took our poverty to give us His riches (see 2 Cor. 8:9). And He took our curse to give us His blessing (see Gal. 3:13-14). That divine exchange is the heart of the Gospel!

The incredible truth is that Jesus was the only person who ever lived who actually deserved the blessing of Abraham. He lived a perfect life and always kept the Law. All of us deserve the curse. But on the cross, Jesus took the curse we deserve! And He took it "in order that in Christ Jesus the *blessing of Abraham* might come to the Gentiles, so that we would receive the promise of the Spirit *through faith*" (Gal. 3:14, *NASB*, emphasis added). That's how we gain access to the blessing of Abraham! We cannot work hard enough to gain the blessing. We can't become righteous enough.

Only by *faith* can we receive what has been paid for us already. Amazingly, that's how Abraham received the blessing also. He was not righteous enough to obtain the promise. But "Abraham believed God, and it was counted to him as righteousness" (Rom. 4:3, *ESV*). When God saw Abraham's faith, He was so pleased by it that He counted it as righteousness. He said, "Because of your faith, I will treat you as though you are righteous, even though you're not." And that's the same way God treats us! Galatians says, "So those who have faith are blessed along with Abraham, the man of faith" (Gal. 3:9, *NIV*). We enter the realm of blessing when we lay hold of the full work of Jesus on the cross by faith.

Here is a summary of the understanding that is needed for blessing:

- Jesus took on Himself all of the evil intended for us.
- Jesus purchased the full blessing of God for us.
- Jesus took all of the curse so that we could inherit all of the blessing.
- When we receive this inheritance by faith, the power of the curse is broken.

In the next few chapters, Robert Heidler and I explain the concept of timing. A key understanding for entering into prosperity is to be at the right place . . . at the right time! I think by now you can see that our inheritance from Abraham is to keep moving in time and crossing from blessing to blessing! We have one prayer for you: *"Cross over into a new level of prosperity!"*

Notes

1. Chuck Pierce, *Time to Defeat the Devil: Strategies to Win the Spiritual War* (Lake Mary, FL: Charisma House, 2011).

4

God's Desire for His People

Robert Heidler

God desires to prosper His people. That is His heart and nature. God is a good Father. He doesn't want His Church—His Bride—to be hindered by a continual lack of resources. He doesn't want His children so focused on "making ends meet" that they can't walk in overflowing thankfulness and generosity.

Many Christians have been hampered in their faith by the pagan philosophy of asceticism that crept into the Church during the Dark Ages. Asceticism subscribes to the belief that by being poor, a person could better concentrate on being spiritual. In the medieval church, monks had to take vows of poverty. Even today, many Christians have a mindset of poverty. But that philosophy is not found in the Bible!

Prosperity in the Bible

The Bible promises success and prosperity to those who walk in God's ways. Those with a poverty mindset try to argue against that, but they have a lot of Scripture to explain away! If you are not certain that God desires to prosper you, take a minute and meditate on the following passages:

- Deuteronomy 5:33: "Walk in all the way that the LORD your God has commanded you, so that you may live and prosper."
- Deuteronomy 28:11: "The Lord will grant you abundant prosperity."
- Deuteronomy 29:9: "Carefully follow the terms of this covenant, so that you may prosper in everything you do."
- Joshua 1:8: If you do what God says, "you will be prosperous and successful."
- 1 Kings 2:3: "Walk in his ways, and keep his decrees and commands . . . so that you may prosper in all that you do and wherever you go" (*NIV*).

- Psalm 1:3: "Whatever he [the righteous] does *prospers*."
- Psalm 34:9: "Fear the LORD, you his saints, for those who fear him lack nothing."
- Psalm 34:10: "Those who seek the LORD lack no good thing."
- Proverbs 28:25—"He who trusts in the LORD will prosper." (*NIV*).
- Jeremiah 29:11: " 'For I know the plans I have for you,' declares the LORD, 'plans to prosper you and not to harm you, plans to give you hope and a future.'"
- 2 Corinthians 8:9: "For you know the grace of our Lord Jesus Christ, that though he was rich, yet for your sakes he became poor, so that you through his poverty might become rich."
- 2 Corinthians 9:11: "You will be made rich in every way so that you can be generous on every occasion, and through us your generosity will result in thanksgiving to God."

If you have been taught a poverty mindset, these Scriptures may make you feel uncomfortable. Something inside you will want to argue against them. You may try to spiritualize them away. But these verses are the Word of God, and there are many other verses just like them.

The fact is, the Bible not only promises prosperity to those who walk in God's ways, but it is also filled with examples of people who experienced it. Most of the godly men and women you read about in the Bible were prosperous. Abraham and his offspring had great wealth. Job was one of the richest men in the land. Joseph rose to the top in every situation. David became king. Both Daniel and Nehemiah held high positions. The apostle Paul was incredibly successful and planted thriving churches all over the Roman Empire! Don't let a poverty mindset hold you captive!

But to experience the level of blessing these verses describe, we must allow God to reshape our thinking. We must receive a mind to prosper.

Aligning Our Lives with God's Ways

Prosperity comes as we align our lives with God and His ways. The process begins at salvation. When new Christians abandon their former lifestyles—alcoholism, sexual promiscuity, drug addiction or any other sins—the result is an increased level of prosperity. In times of revival, when large segments of a population are saved *en masse,* the adoption of godly lifestyles has often brought a measurable economic lift to the entire community.[1]

Perhaps the best illustration of how being aligned with God's ways results in prosperity comes from the Jews. The Jews have traditionally been called "the People of the Book." Even though most Jews are in unbelief with regard to their Messiah, their lifestyle and culture are saturated with the Bible in ways to which many Christians can't relate. So it's not surprising that when we study Jewish history, we discover that the Jews have often experienced lifestyles of blessing and prosperity far beyond that of the society immediately around them!

Author Steven Silbiger wrote a book titled *The Jewish Phenomenon,* in which he examines the prosperity of Jews in America. He points out that most American Jews arrived in the United States from Europe within the last two generations. They were driven out of Europe by persecution and came to our shores as poor immigrants. Yet within two generations, the Jews have achieved a level of prosperity unknown by any other ethnic group! The statistics Silbiger quotes are impressive. Even though the Jews make up only 2 percent of the U.S. population . . .

- 20 percent of professors at leading universities in this country are Jewish.
- 25 percent of American Nobel Prize winners are Jewish.
- One third of American multimillionaires are Jewish.
- 45 percent of the top 40 of the Forbes 400 richest Americans are Jewish.[2]

While not every Jew is wealthy, Jews in general have much higher average incomes than non-Jews. Dr. Thomas Sowell, in his book *Ethnic America,* writes, "Even where neither education nor age is a factor, Jews earn more."[3] Silbiger adds, "Among families headed by males with four or more years of college and aged 35 to 45, *Jews still earn 75 percent higher incomes* than the national average."[4] The success of Jews in America is not unique. Silbiger shows that in any society where their upward mobility has not been deliberately blocked, Jews have tended to rise into positions of wealth and influence in numbers far exceeding their percentage of the population.

How do we account for the incredible success of the Jewish people? In his book, Silbiger describes how elements of Jewish religion and culture have helped the Jews achieve financial success. The point of the book is that Gentiles could experience the *same success*—if they would do the same things! Interestingly, the elements of Jewish culture Silbiger describes are all based on the Scriptures. They are things God wanted His Church to live out as well!

The reason for the success of the Jews is found in the truths God taught the Jewish people thousands of years ago. God promised that those who observe His instructions *will* experience success: "Do not let this Book of the Law [*Torah*] depart from your mouth; meditate on it day and night, so that you may be careful to do everything written in it. *Then you will be prosperous and successful*" (Josh. 1:8, emphasis added; see also Deut. 28:1-14; Ps. 1:1-3). The Jews' commitment to honor these precepts, even in their unbelief, has given them the success God promised!

The promises of God are literally true, and they apply today. And they are just as valid for Gentile believers as they are for Jews. After all, we have been grafted into the root of Israel.

The problem is that while most of us Christians may say we believe the Bible "from cover to cover," there's a lot of God's Word we've been taught to ignore, rationalize and try to theologize away. As a result, we never experience the mindsets and understandings necessary to experience a life of prosperity.

For this reason, in this section of the book I want us to see how God imparted "a mindset to prosper" to the Jews, and how He wants to impart it to us as well.

Notes

1. Dr. Donald McGavran, of Fuller's School of World Mission, calls this phenomenon "redemption and lift." If you'd like to see some dramatic present-day examples of this, I encourage you to watch the video documentary *Transformations* by George Otis, Jr., which may be viewed at or purchased from Amazon.com.
2. Steven Silbiger, *The Jewish Phenomenon: Seven Keys to the Enduring Wealth of a People* (Atlanta, GA: Longstreet Press, 2000), p. 4.
3. Thomas Sowell, *Ethnic America, a History* (New York: Basic Books, 1981), p. 98.
4. Silbiger, *The Jewish Phenomenon*, p. 9 (emphasis added).

5

God's Cycle of Life

ROBERT HEIDLER

How do we align our lives with God's ways? We don't do so by reading a book or learning a list of doctrinal precepts. When God wanted to raise up a people who understood His ways, the first thing He did was teach them His cycle of life.

When Israel came out of Egypt, God commanded the people to begin meeting with Him at certain specific times every year. During these appointed times, they were to cease their regular activities, gather together and interact with God in specific ways. Over the course of time, these divine encounters shaped the Israelites' way of thinking and transformed their culture and lifestyle. They entered into what I describe as a God-given cycle of life, the understanding of which, I believe, is a crucial element in gaining a mindset to prosper.

Learning the Cycles of God

Let me explain how God began teaching me about cycles. In the fall of 2004, I sat at my computer one morning, reading the news of a monster hurricane approaching the coast of Florida. My computer screen was filled with a satellite image of this storm: a swirling circle of destruction!

When I finished reading about the hurricane, I switched to NASA's *Astronomy Picture of the Day* website. I usually check this site daily, because it often features majestic pictures of the universe taken by the Hubble Space Telescope. On this day, as the new picture filled the screen, I was amazed! The new image was almost identical to the picture of the hurricane! Instead of a swirling circle of wind, however, this picture revealed a beautiful disk of stars: a spiral galaxy.

The two pictures looked very similar, but there was such a stunning contrast! One was a circle of violent storms bringing terrible destruction, while the other was a spiral of billions of stars displaying the beauty of creation! As I switched back and forth between these pictures, God began to speak to me about cycles.

What is a cycle?

I like to define a cycle this way: A cycle is something that goes around, and moves to a destination. The universe is filled with cycles, and their movements range from causing destruction to bringing blessing.

Cycles of Destruction

There are many cycles of destruction in the universe. In nature there are hurricanes. They go around and around . . . and lead to devastation.

In people, destructive cycles include cycles of addiction, poverty, unbelief and defeat. Many people find themselves locked into these cycles and cannot escape!

A classic example of a cycle of destruction is found in the book of Judges, where we find Israel locked into a cycle of sin. The cycle looks like this:

1. The people rebel against God . . .
2. God allows their enemies to rise up and oppress them . . .
3. The people repent and turn back to God . . .
4. God raises up a deliverer to save the people from the enemy . . .
5. Once the oppression is broken, the people rebel against God.

In the book of Judges, the people of Israel go through this cycle seven times! If you want to see an outline of the book of Judges, look down into the toilet the next time you flush. In Judges, God's people go around and around the same cycle, getting lower and lower, until they end up in the sewer!

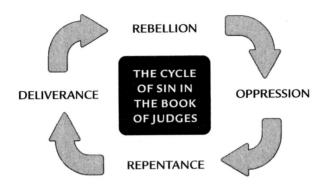

I've known people today who live in this same cycle. We've ministered to men and women who seek God with all their heart . . . when they are in jail! But when they are released, they quickly fall back into an old cycle of sin. So God makes sure they end up in jail again. Satan has many such cycles of destruction. He wants to lock us into cycles that will thwart God's plan and keep us in defeat.

Cycles of Blessing

The good news is that God also works through cycles. Like the beautiful spiral galaxy, there are cycles that reveal God's goodness and power!

In the natural realm, there is the cycle of sowing and reaping. When a farmer sows in good soil, he or she will reap much more than was sown. The result is multiplication and increase.

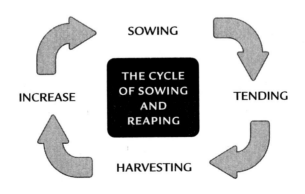

God uses cycles to bring us into new levels of His blessing and provision. An example of this is found in Joshua 6, where God instructed the Israelites to take the city of Jericho. At Jericho, God put Israel into a cycle of victory. As the Israelites walked in obedience around and around that city, God caused them to triumph over their enemy!

Cycles of blessing can also bring us from a lower place to a higher place. When I was much younger, I had a model railroad. It was like a miniature world, with towns and rivers and mountains. The railroad ran in a loop on ground level, but I wanted to have a branch line that would run across a trestle high in the mountains. But how could I get the trains from ground level to that higher level? My solution was to build a spiral of track inside one of the mountains. The trains would enter a tunnel and begin going around the spiral. Each time around the spiral they gained a little more altitude, until they emerged from a tunnel high in the mountains.

That's how God uses cycles of blessing in our lives.

God's cycles usually begin with a word of revelation. God says, "Do this!" When you obey what God has said, you may not notice a great difference immediately. But if you continue to walk in obedience, you will be led into a cycle. Each time around that cycle, you'll be just a little higher than you were before. By the time you've gone through the cycle several times, you begin to see major changes!

God wants to lock you into cycles of blessing—cycles of growth and increase. God has a cycle of victory for you today. God wants you to break out of Satan's cycle of destruction and into God's cycle of blessing.

Cycles in the Biblical Calendar

In the Bible, God established some important cycles for His people. These cycles were designed to break the power of the enemy and draw the people closer to Him, with an ever-increasing revelation of His blessing!

First, God established a weekly Shabbat cycle. He ordained this cycle at the creation of the world. God's design was that we work diligently for six days but take the seventh day as a Sabbath, a Shabbat. It was to be a special day, set apart to rest and enjoy God's goodness and blessing. God promised great blessing to those who keep His Shabbat.

Next, God established a monthly firstfruits cycle marked by a celebration the Jews call Rosh Chodesh. This is an important celebration, clearly taught in the Bible, yet most Christians never celebrate it. In fact, many Christians have never even heard of it!

Finally, God established a yearly cycle of feasts, or "appointed times" (Lev. 23:4). These were designed to take us through key steps to deepen our walk with the Lord, break the power of the enemy, and release the blessings of God into our experience. Repeating this cycle every year was designed to bring us into an ever-increasing experience of God's goodness and an ever-increasing victory over the enemy.

Discovering God's Cycles

Like most Christians today, I grew up in church knowing little or nothing about God's cycles. However, in 1997 Chuck Pierce gave an interesting word for our church: He said that God wanted us to celebrate three biblical feasts. From my studies in seminary, I knew that the Bible devoted a lot of space to a series of feasts, but I had never taken the time to study them. I had always assumed these feasts were just for the people of the Old Testament and had no relevance for Christians today. For the first time in my life, I began to seriously study the feasts.

I was amazed at what I found! As I began to study the feasts, I discovered that the biblical feasts were part of a God-given cycle of life that actually made up a biblical calendar. They were not just religious holidays or Jewish rituals. God called them His "appointed times." In a very real sense, these feasts are appointments with God: times set by God to meet with His people.

Feasts in the Old Testament

God's goal for these appointed times was to accomplish specific spiritual transactions with His people. Taken together, they form a yearly cycle designed to bring us into ever-increasing blessing. God gave many promises of blessing to those who would observe them. Deuteronomy 16:15 specifically links the celebration of these feasts with prosperity: "The LORD your God will bless you in all your harvest and in all the work of your hands, and your joy will be complete"!

As I continued to study the feasts, I discovered that these appointed times have not "passed away." The Word tells us that these appointed times are eternal and cannot be changed. One of the sins of the antichrist is that he would "try to change the set times" (Dan. 7:25, *NIV*).

I was also amazed to discover that these feasts were not just for Jews! Zechariah promised blessings for Gentiles who would observe God's feasts (see Zech 14:16-19).

Feasts in the New Testament

As I continued to study, I learned that Jesus and His apostles regularly observed these feasts. In fact, many important New Testament events occurred in the context of these celebrations:

- Jesus was crucified on the Feast of Passover.
- Jesus was raised on the Feast of Firstfruits.
- The Holy Spirit was poured out during the Feast of Pentecost.

When I saw this, I was stunned. I realized that God was keeping His feasts. Jesus could have been crucified at any time of the year, but God chose to have Him crucified at Passover to show that He is our Passover Lamb (see 1 Cor. 5:7-8). Jesus could have been raised from the dead at any time, but God chose to raise Him up on the Feast of Firstfruits to show that Jesus is the firstfruits of a new creation (see 1 Cor. 15:20-23). The Spirit could have been poured out at any time, but God chose to do it at *His appointed time*—the Feast of Pentecost (see Acts 2:1).

As I studied the book of Acts, I discovered that the Early Church considered these feasts to be very important. The Church not only observed these appointed times, but Paul actually planned the itinerary of his missionary journeys around them. Acts 20:6-16 tells us that Paul sailed from Philippi after the Feast of Unleavened Bread (Passover). But celebrating Passover in Philippi put Paul in a time crunch. Though he longed to spend time with the Christians in Ephesus, he was forced to sail past Ephesus in order to get back to Jerusalem in time for the Feast of Pentecost.

Paul's epistles also have many references to the feasts. Even when writing to Gentile churches, Paul assumed he was writing to people who celebrated these feasts. Writing to gentile Corinthians about purity of life, he says, "Get rid of the old yeast that you may be a new batch without yeast—as you really are. For Christ, our Passover lamb, has been sacrificed. Therefore let us keep the Festival, not with the old yeast of malice and wickedness, but with bread without yeast, bread of sincerity and truth" (1 Cor. 5:7-8, *NIV*). Writing about the resurrection in 1 Corinthians 15:20-23, Paul says, "Christ has indeed been raised from the dead, the firstfruits of those who have fallen asleep. . . . Each in his own turn: Christ, the firstfruits; then, when he comes, those who belong to Him." That statement would make no sense to someone who did not understand the Feast of Firstfruits. Paul had evidently taught these gentile Christians about that feast.

Feasts in Church History

As I looked into Church history, I found that the Church continued to observe these appointed times well into the fourth century, when they were finally outlawed by an act of the Roman emperor Constantine.

I concluded that God intended these celebrations for us! God's appointed times were not just temporary holidays to fill in until we got Santa Claus and the Easter Bunny. They are for all time! They are lasting ordinances for all generations (see Lev. 23:31).

During the Dark Ages, under pressure from the Imperial Roman government, the Church abandoned God's cycle of appointed times. In its place we adopted a paganized Roman "church" calendar.

What we need to understand is that we switched . . . God didn't! God is still waiting for us to keep His appointments. We need to heed God's call and be willing to meet with Him so that we can receive great blessing!

6

GOD'S GIFT OF SHABBAT

ROBERT HEIDLER

On the seventh day God ended His work . . . and He rested on the seventh day from all His work which He had done. Then God blessed the seventh day and sanctified it, because in it He rested from all His work.
GENESIS 2:2-3

As I mentioned in the last chapter, God placed great emphasis on establishing a "cycle of life" for His people. In this chapter, we will look at God's weekly cycle, the cycle of Shabbat (Hebrew for Sabbath).

Shabbat is foundational for gaining a mindset to prosper. It teaches us God's heart for His children—that God is a generous Father who wants His children to experience His goodness and enjoy His blessings! Interestingly, Shabbat was one of God's first commands to the human race. It was instituted, not at Mount Sinai, but at the creation of the universe (see Gen. 2:2-3).

Though many Christians today don't observe a Shabbat, it is probably needed more now than ever before in history.

Our Need for Rest

People today are probably the busiest people the world has ever known. Even though the twentieth century brought the invention of incredible labor-saving devices, the result has not been a life of leisure. In fact, the pace of life has escalated greatly. Wayne Muller describes our modern lifestyle this way:

> The more our life speeds up, the more we feel weary, overwhelmed and lost. Despite our good hearts and equally good intentions, our life and work rarely feel light, pleasant or healing. Instead, as it all piles endlessly upon itself, the whole experience of being alive begins to melt into one

enormous obligation. . . . To be unavailable to our friends and family, to be unable to find time for the sunset (or even to know that the sun has set at all), to whiz through our obligations without time for a single mindful breath—this has become the model of a successful life.[1]

Our labor-saving devices cannot produce a life of rest because work always expands to fill whatever time is available. The key to rest is not found in labor-saving devices. The key to rest is found in the Word of God. True rest begins with God's gift of Sabbath.

God's Intention for Sabbath

For many Christians, the word "Sabbath" has a negative connotation. We think of a Sabbath day as something oppressive, a legalistic burden, a day lived under rigid rules. That's the kind of Sabbath the Pharisees promoted, and Jesus had a lot to say *against* that kind of Sabbath.

The true picture of Sabbath is a day of celebration, a day to turn the burdens of life over to God and enjoy His goodness. God intended Sabbath to be a blessing, not a burden. In Mark 2:27, Jesus said, "The Sabbath was made for man, and not man for the Sabbath." God gave Sabbath as a blessing, as a gift. In Ezekiel 20:12, God said, "I also gave them My Sabbaths."

Sabbath was one of the first expressions of God's will in the universe. On the seventh day of creation, long before the Law of Moses was given, the Creator took a day off from His work and rested. He didn't rest because He was tired. He rested because He wanted to establish the Sabbath and set it apart as holy. He wanted the principle of Sabbath woven into the fabric of the universe.

Our problem is that humankind has generally refused to receive God's gift of Sabbath. We have been too fearful, worried and greedy to rest. We have ignored God's will and chosen to work seven days a week, trying to get ahead. So when God called Moses to the top of Mount Sinai, He gave a law to protect the Sabbath.

The way God chose to protect Shabbat is very significant: When God gave the law of the Sabbath, He didn't give it as a civil law for the nation Israel, nor was it one of the ceremonial laws governing Jewish religious ritual. It was given as part of God's moral law for humankind. God made the observance of Sabbath one of the Ten Commandments. That means it is just as much a violation of God's moral law to work seven days a week as it is to kill, steal or commit adultery.

By the time of Jesus, however, the law of Sabbath had been perverted. The Pharisees turned this gracious gift of God into a legalistic burden. They stood around with their clipboards, keeping watch over the Sabbath, condemning anyone who violated their rigid rules of prohibited activities.

Much of the New Testament teaching on Sabbath was designed to restore Sabbath to God's original intention. In Colossians 2:16, Paul sums up New Testament teaching on the Sabbath: "Do not let anyone judge you . . . with regard to . . . a Sabbath day" (*NIV*). Some have read that verse and assumed it means Sabbath is not for today and that we should not observe Sabbath. But Paul is not saying, "Don't observe the Sabbath." Rather, he is saying, "Don't judge each other on how you observe the Sabbath." He is prohibiting a pharisaical observance of the Sabbath and telling us to return to the Sabbath to God's original intention: to be received as a gracious gift of God.

Sabbath and "Church Day"

Some people get uncomfortable when we start talking about Sabbath. They think if they accept the idea of Sabbath, they will have to leave their church and go to one that meets on Saturday. That's a false understanding.

Sabbath has nothing to do with what day you go to church. The Early Church actually had Sabbath and "church" on different days! They rested on the seventh day to celebrate God as Creator, and then they met together to worship on the first day of the week to celebrate Jesus' resurrection.

Observing the Sabbath has nothing to do with going to church. We are free to worship God any day. In fact, it's good to worship God every day. The Sabbath was never meant to be primarily a day of public worship but a day of rest and enjoyment.

Which Day Is Sabbath?

On what day of the week should we observe our Sabbath? Through much of Church history, most of the Church has observed Sunday as a Sabbath. (If you've ever watched the movie *Chariots of Fire*, you've seen a good illustration of how the Church in an earlier generation honored Sunday as a Sabbath.)

Other Christians place great importance on observing Sabbath on Saturday. We know that biblically, Shabbat was observed from sundown Friday through sundown Saturday. That's a good pattern to follow, but I don't think choosing the "right" day of the week is as important as many suppose. God's instruction was simply, "Work for six days; then rest on the seventh."

I don't think the specific day is nearly as important as the fact that we *do* observe a Sabbath. (Many Jewish rabbis take their day of rest on Sunday, while many Christian pastors take their day of rest on Monday.) The real problem today is that most Christians do not observe any Sabbath at all.

In twenty-first-century America, we have chosen to ignore the biblical teaching on Sabbath. I recently heard a conference speaker address an audience about the need for commitment to Christ. To drive home his point, he shared that he had recently rebuked the assistant pastors in his church. These assistant pastors came to him asking if they could take a day off every week. His comment was that if the world works seven days a week to achieve their goals, shouldn't we be as committed as they are?

I was deeply grieved when I heard his statement. What this prominent Christian leader was saying, in effect, was "Because the world disregards the commandments of God to achieve their goals, shouldn't we do the same?" This, unfortunately, is a common attitude in the Church today. The result is, while we may go to church on Sunday, we do not seriously practice Sabbath on any day of the week. We have become the first Church in history that only teaches nine of the Ten Commandments.

My Personal Testimony

Several years ago the Lord convicted me to begin observing a weekly Sabbath. He impressed me to follow the biblical pattern, observing Sabbath from sundown Friday until sundown Saturday.

When the Lord first convicted me of this, I resisted. I said, "Lord, I can't do that." As a pastor, Saturday was often my busiest day of the week. Weekdays at our church office were so filled with appointments and administrative duties that Saturday was often the only day I had to prepare my Sunday message.

I said, "Lord, I'm too busy. I don't have time to take a day of rest." I thought, with horror, of having to stand up on Sunday morning with no message to give.

But the Lord answered, "To say you are too busy to rest on the Sabbath is like saying you are too poor to tithe. It means you have not yet learned My ability to provide. If I tell you to rest, you can rest."

So I chose to cast my concerns on Him and submit to His direction. I began to welcome Sabbath as a wonderful gift of God. There have been many times when Friday evening comes and my work is not done; and I have to place it, by faith, in His hands. But He has never failed to provide what I need.

And I have found in His Sabbath one of the greatest joys of life. Often my wife and I greet each other when we wake on Friday mornings with the joyful exclamation, "Sabbath starts today." It is something we look forward to all through the week. To think that it is God's will for me to rest one day a week and enjoy His blessings has given me a whole new level of appreciation for His goodness.

Seven Reasons for Observing Sabbath

I would like to give seven reasons why it's important to observe Sabbath. I believe Sabbath is important because:

1. *Sabbath honors God as Creator.* Sabbath observance is a tangible way of acknowledging God's greatness as Creator of the universe. Just as God created the universe and then rested, so too we celebrate His work of creation by entering into His rest.

2. *Sabbath is a celebration of God's provision.* The book of Hebrews teaches that Sabbath is a picture of Israel coming

out of the wilderness into the bountiful provision of the Promised Land. Sabbath is a celebration of God's blessing. The traditional Sabbath-meal prayer said over bread expresses wonder that God even brings forth bread for us from the earth!

3. *Sabbath reminds us of God's goodness.* One of the most difficult truths for Christians to accept is the goodness of God. Many people believe that God is righteous and powerful, but they have a hard time trusting in His goodness. Some Christians think of God as a harsh taskmaster who places excessive burdens on His people. Sabbath is an acknowledgment that God wants His people to experience and enjoy His goodness.

4. *Sabbath builds our faith.* Observing Sabbath teaches us to trust that God will provide, even when we rest. If God could create the universe in six days, He is certainly able to handle the concerns of our lives one day a week!

5. *Sabbath is a picture of salvation.* As we cease our daily labor and rest in God's goodness, we are reminded of the basis of our salvation. Salvation is not received on the basis of our own works but by God's grace. Salvation comes when we are willing, by faith, to rest from our own works and receive His blessings as a gift.

6. *Sabbath is a picture of heaven.* Sabbath is a God-given foretaste of eternity, an *anticipation* of that day when we rest from our works and enjoy Him forever.

7. *Sabbath releases God's blessing.* When done as a voluntary act of obedience, Sabbath releases God's blessing. A few months ago, I was praying for a greater release of God's blessing in our church, and God told me something very significant. He said, "If you are not experiencing what the Bible promises, it's because you are not doing what the Bible commands." Choosing to respond in obedience to God's revealed will releases blessing.

The Bible promises great blessing for those who will receive His gift of Sabbath. Notice the promises given in these verses:

> Foreigners who bind themselves to the LORD to serve him, to love the name of the LORD, and to worship him, all who keep the Sabbath without desecrating it and who hold fast to my covenant—these *I will bring to my holy mountain and give them joy* in my house of prayer (Isa. 56:6-7, *NIV*, emphasis added).

> If you keep your feet from breaking the Sabbath and from doing as you please on my holy day, if you call the Sabbath a delight and the LORD's holy day honorable, and if you honor it by not going your own way and not doing as you please or speaking idle words, *then you will find your joy in the LORD, and I will cause you to ride on the heights of the land and to feast on the inheritance of your father Jacob* (Isa. 58:13-14, *NIV*, emphasis added).

Interestingly, the promise in Isaiah 56 is not addressed to Jews but is specifically given to Gentile believers. That's most of us.

What to Do on a Sabbath

The Jews picture Sabbath as "a sanctuary in time." Just as a sanctuary is a holy *place* marked by the four walls of a building, the Sabbath is a holy *time* marked by hours and minutes in our lives. It is a time set apart from the rest of the week to enjoy God and His blessings.

God instructs us to sanctify, or set apart, the Sabbath day as holy. To sanctify something involves setting markers around it to distinguish it from the ordinary. When God told Moses that Sinai was His holy mountain, He instructed Moses to set markers around the mountain so that no one would stray onto it accidentally (see Exod. 19:12-13). So, the first step in observing Sabbath is to establish a marker to clearly distinguish when Sabbath has begun.

From their earliest history, the Jews have sanctified Sabbath with a special family worship celebration at sundown on Friday evening. This celebration begins with the wife offering a special prayer to welcome the gift of Sabbath, followed by the lighting of the Sabbath candles. The husband then offers prayer over the bread and wine, initiating the Sabbath meal. It is a special time when the husband prays a blessing over his wife, and the parents pray blessings over their children. It is a time to focus on the Lord and His goodness and to begin 24 hours of joy and relaxation as a family.

This special family worship celebration is not commanded in Scripture. For this reason we can choose to sanctify Sabbath in some other way, but the traditional Sabbath meal is an example that has proven helpful to many people. In fact, history tells us that the Early Church followed this pattern for several centuries.

Sabbath Activities

One question I am often asked is, "What do you do on a Sabbath?" My answer is that there is no legalistic list. Leviticus 23:25 tells us to enjoy Sabbath rest by avoiding our "regular" (*NIV*) or "customary" (*NKJV*) work. Sabbath is a day to avoid doing what you normally do to earn your living. It means you are freed from your normal responsibilities and given time to fellowship with God and enjoy His blessings!

I suspect that "proper" Sabbath activity will vary from person to person. If you are a farmer and work in the soil all week, you would not want to garden on Shabbat. But if you are chained to a computer six days a week, a few hours of gardening on a Saturday morning might be a wonderful way to rest and enjoy the Lord.

Although the Early Church did not have a proscribed list of activities for Shabbat, they did have one interesting prohibition: believers were not supposed to fast on Shabbat! Sabbath was not a day to be mournful or religious. It was a day for feasting. The primary purpose of the Sabbath is to enjoy God and His blessings, so whatever you do that promotes that goal is permissible.

This is how Wayne Muller describes Sabbath activity:

Sabbath is a time consecrated to enjoy and celebrate what is beautiful and good—time to light candles, sing songs, worship, tell stories, bless our children and loved ones, give thanks, share meals, nap, walk, and even make love. It is a time to be nourished and refreshed as we let our work, our chores and our important projects lie fallow, trusting that there are larger forces at work taking care of the world when we are at rest.[2]

So, Sabbath is a time to stock up on your favorite foods. Get together with close friends and family and plan enjoyable activities. Do those things that will fill your heart with thanksgiving and praise!

If you are able to hold Shabbat from sundown Friday to sundown Saturday, I believe you will find it is a wonderful experience. Begin with a Sabbath celebration on Friday night over your evening meal. Although the traditional Jewish Shabbat meal is often a formal affair around the dining room table, at our home we prefer to eat our favorite finger foods, sitting around the coffee table in the living room, and we often watch a good movie as part of the celebration. The key is to do whatever will fill your heart with thankfulness to God!

At the start of the meal, it is traditional to have the mother of the house light two candles and pray, welcoming God's gift of Shabbat. This doesn't have to be a formal, written prayer. Just offer a simple prayer expressing your thankfulness that God loves you enough to give you a time to rest and enjoy Him.

The father then prays a blessing over the wine and bread, acknowledging that all of our blessings come from Him. Another traditional part of Shabbat is for the father and mother to pray blessings over each child. If you do this, don't let it be a long, boring ritualistic prayer. Let it be an expression of your love for your children and an impartation of faith for their future.

The father can also pray a blessing over his wife, praising her in the presence of her children. On occasion, the father may want to read the section on the virtuous woman found in Proverbs 31 over his wife. Your goal is to make Friday night the most enjoyable time of the week and a time to thank God for His goodness. In a traditional Jewish home, this is the heart of worship.

On Saturday, Shabbat continues. This is a day to rest, read, go to the park or beach, or visit a museum. The precise activities depend a lot on whether you have children, their ages, and the things your family enjoys doing together. As you celebrate Shabbat, your focus should be on what you can do to experience God's goodness with joyful, thankful hearts!

As your heart is filled with praise and thanksgiving, don't neglect spending time with God! Have a relaxed time in the Word. Spend time in prayer and sing songs of praise. Enjoy God's presence and thank Him for all of His blessings! If you aren't sure if an activity is appropriate for Sabbath, ask Jesus. He is the "Lord of the Sabbath" (Mark 2:28).

Missing a Sabbath

What happens if you miss a Sabbath? Some weekends I minister at conferences and don't have the option of rest. What do I do if a week comes when I cannot celebrate the Sabbath? That's when I appreciate the grace of God. I remember that Sabbath is not a legalistic burden. When I miss Sabbath, I'm not filled with guilt. I'm filled with sorrow and disappointment. I have missed a blessing.

Let me emphasize that last point: Sabbath is not a burden to bear; it is a blessing we are privileged to receive! As Jesus said, "The Sabbath was made for man, and not man for the Sabbath" (Mark 2:27).

If you celebrate Sabbath as God intended, it will not be something you *have* to do; it will be something you *want* to do. Real Sabbath observance is addictive! God wants to make our walk with Him so enjoyable and so pleasurable that the world looks on with envy. Psalm 67:7 says, "God blesses us, that all the ends of the earth may fear Him" (*NASB*).

Shabbat is a time chosen by God to meet with you each week! As you celebrate Shabbat each week, you build a foundation of faith in your life. You are reminded every week that God is good and that He wants you to enjoy His blessings. That's the starting point for a mindset to prosper!

Notes
1. Wayne Muller, *Remembering the Sacred Rhythm of Rest* (New York: Bantam Books, 1999), quoted in "Remember the Sabbath?" *USA Weekend* (April 2, 1999).
2. Ibid.

7

THE CALENDAR OF GOD

ROBERT HEIDLER

There is a time for everything, and a season for every activity under heaven: a time to be born and a time to die, a time to plant and a time to uproot, a time to kill and a time to heal, a time to tear down and a time to build, a time to weep and a time to laugh, a time to mourn and a time to dance . . . a time to keep and a time to throw away.
ECCLESIASTES 3:1-6, *NIV*

The Bible teaches that God has a detailed plan for our lives. This plan includes key appointed times in which He desires to accomplish certain things for us. God has many kinds of appointed times. Some are one-time events: there is only one time to be physically born and only one time to die. Some are repeated events: every new year brings a new time to plant and a new time to reap.

Some appointed times repeat so regularly that they form a calendar. In the last chapter, we looked at God's *weekly* cycle of appointed times. In this chapter, we will examine God's *yearly* calendar of appointed times. God's calendar forms a yearly cycle designed by God to break off the oppression of the enemy and bring us into a fresh experience of His blessings every year.

Overview of the Biblical Calendar

The Bible gives us a great deal of detailed revelation about God's yearly calendar. There are three main appointed times in God's calendar. In Exodus 23:14-17, God states, "Three times a year you are to celebrate a festival to Me":

- "Keep the Feast of Unleavened Bread . . ." (Passover, celebrated in early spring: March or April)

- "And the Feast of Harvest . . . " (Pentecost, celebrated in late spring: May or June)

- "And the Feast of Ingathering" (Tabernacles, celebrated in the fall: September or October)

God concludes by stating, "Three times a year all your males shall appear before the Lord GOD."

Tri-dimensional Occasions

As we look at this yearly calendar, it's interesting to note that all of these celebrations have three dimensions:

1. *The Feast of Passover* begins the biblical calendar. It marks the first month in God's cycle of feasts. It is really a cluster of three closely related feasts: Passover, Unleavened Bread, and Firstfruits.

2. *The Feast of Pentecost* (or Shavuot) is held in the third month. It is a tri-fold celebration, thanking God for His blessings through the harvest (God's physical provision), the Word (the giving of the Torah on Mount Sinai), and the Holy Spirit (the outpouring of His power as recorded in Acts 2).

3. *The Feast of Tabernacles* is held in the seventh month and is a cluster of three closely related events: the Feast of Trumpets (Rosh Hashanah), the Day of Atonement (Yom Kippur) and the Feast of Tabernacles (Sukkot).

Celebration and Focus

Each of these three feasts has a different focus and is designed to accomplish some specific spiritual transaction in our lives. We might diagram them like this:

First Month	Third Month (Summer)	Seventh Month
Passover	Pentecost	Tabernacles
Focus: Redemption and Cleansing	Focus: Fullness of Provision	Focus: Dwelling in God's Glory

Passover focuses on redemption from sin and cleansing from impurity. These are always the first steps in approaching God! We must be "covered by the blood" of an atoning sacrifice and washed clean from impurity before we can enter into His presence.

Pentecost is a celebration of provision. It was initially the celebration of the wheat harvest, God's physical provision. Then, at Pentecost, God brought Israel to Mount Sinai and gave them Torah, which means "the teaching of God." That was God's primary spiritual provision for His people under the Old Covenant. Finally, in Acts 2, God chose the day of Pentecost to pour out the Holy Spirit. The Holy Spirit is our primary provision under the New Covenant. So at Pentecost, we celebrate the full experience of God's abundance.

After Pentecost comes the long, hot summer. Then in the fall, we move into the Feast of Tabernacles. Tabernacles is the celebration of the glory of God. When Israel was in the wilderness, God looked down from heaven and saw the people dwelling in tents, or tabernacles (temporary shelters). So God told Moses to have them make a tabernacle for Him as well, so He could come down and live among them (see Exod. 25:8). So Moses built the Tabernacle, and God's glory came down and was visibly manifested in the midst of the people. That's what the Feast of Tabernacles celebrates: the joy of dwelling in God's presence.

The Feasts and the Tabernacle
It's interesting that the three feasts in God's yearly cycle correspond to the three courts in Moses' Tabernacle. The Tabernacle might be diagramed like this:

Outer Court	Holy Place	Holy of Holiness
Focus: Redemption and Cleansing	Focus: Fullness of Provision	Focus: Dwelling in God's Glory

In the outer court of the Tabernacle were the bronze altar of sacrifice and the golden laver. The outer court was the place of redemption and cleansing. Before people could approach God, their sins had to be covered and their impurities washed away.

The inner court, or Holy Place, was a place to celebrate God's provision. The table of showbread was an acknowledgement of God's bountiful provision for the people's physical needs. The seven-branched menorah pictured the provision of the Holy Spirit, releasing illumination into their lives. The altar of incense pictured God's provision of access to His presence through prayer.

After the first two courts, there was a barrier: the veil. The veil was a thick curtain separating the innermost court from the Holy of Holies. Only the high priest could enter through this veil, and he could do so only once a year. On that one day, after careful preparation, the high priest would enter through the veil into the Holy of Holies.

The Holy of Holies was the place where God's glory dwelt in the midst of His people. God manifested His presence there in a tangible way, releasing His blessing into the earth.

If you were to put the two above diagrams side by side, you would see that the yearly cycle of feasts was like a walk through the Tabernacle. The cycle of appointed times was designed to transport people from the outermost court, through all the steps of preparation, and finally into the incredible experience of God's glory.

Why is that important? It's important because living in the world is like being on an escalator going down! We don't have to work hard to end up far away from God. Christians who end up far from God didn't wake up one morning and decide, "I'm tired of all this blessing! I think I'll go and sin."

No. In this world we are surrounded by temptations and influences designed to draw us away from God. In this world, if we don't make a conscious effort to draw close to God, the natural tendency is to drift farther and farther away.

But God's appointed times were designed to put you on an escalator going up! Every year they take you through the steps that draw you ever closer into His presence! If you have drifted away from God in any area of life, the feasts are designed to get you back on track.

The Feasts and Deliverance

The yearly cycle of feasts is not only designed to draw us closer to God; it is also designed to break off the oppression of the enemy. I believe the yearly cycle of feasts is designed to give us a fresh experience of *deliverance* each year.

Our church does a lot of deliverance ministry. In fact, I wrote a book on deliverance called *Set Yourself Free*, which is used by many deliverance ministries around the country. I wrote this book to show that there are certain things any individual can do that will help him or her gain and maintain freedom from Satan's oppression. *Set Yourself Free* is designed to give keys to getting free and staying free.

When I began to study the biblical feasts, I was amazed to discover that many of these key deliverance principles were included as part of the observances of God's appointed times. One of the first chapters I wrote leads people through the process of taking a spiritual inventory, asking God to show their sins to them, and consciously confessing each sin to God. That's one of the most important chapters in the book. Many people find that when they've done that, Satan's access to their lives is cut off. They are free! When I started to study the biblical feasts, I discovered that God had given His people a set time to do that kind of spiritual inventory every year. It's called the Day of Atonement. It's a day to confess every sin and make sure there is nothing to hinder your walk with God.

Another chapter of *Set Yourself Free* takes readers through the process of searching their homes and removing impurities. Sometimes we open ourselves to Satan's oppression when we bring objects into our homes that defile our homes with impurities. Searching out these objects allows our homes to be cleansed and shuts off that avenue of attack. Interestingly, God instructed Israel to do that very thing every year. At the Feast of Passover, even today, Jews still search their homes for leaven, symbolizing impurity, and remove every trace of it from their homes.

Those who observe these feasts, not as rituals but as times to meet with God, will be enabled to live free of Satan's oppression! When Satan's strategies are broken, you begin to prosper!

The Feasts and Revival

The yearly cycle of feasts also includes a roadmap to revival. When I was in college, my life was heavily impacted by the Jesus Movement in the late '60s, which was one of the great revivals of modern times. When you've been in a revival like that, it spoils you for "church as usual."

So I've become a student of revival. As I've traveled to places that were experiencing revival and studied the history of revivals, I learned that there are certain specific steps that are necessary to bring revival. Any group or individual that follows these steps will experience a measure of revival. Amazingly, these steps are included in God's yearly cycle of appointed times.

The seventh month in the cycle of feasts begins with a 15-day countdown to bring us into the presence of God. In doing so, it takes us through these four key steps of revival every year:

1. *The Feast of Trumpets*—a "wake-up call" from God! "Blow the trumpet in Zion, and sound an alarm on My holy mountain!" (Joel 2:1).

2. *The Days of Awe*—a time to seek God and allow Him to reveal any hindrances in our lives. "Then you will call upon Me and go and pray to Me, and I will listen to you. And you will seek Me and find Me, when you search for Me with all your heart" (Jer. 29:12-13).

3. *The Day of Atonement*—a time to confess any known sin and re-move hindrances to being in God's presence. "If we confess our sins, He is faithful and just to forgive our sins and to cleanse us from all unrighteousness" (1 John 1:9).

4. *The Feast of Tabernacles*—a joyful celebration of God's glory. "When Solomon finished praying, . . . the glory of the LORD filled the temple. And the priests could not enter . . . because the glory of the LORD filled the LORD's house" (2 Chron. 7:1-2).

As we will see later in this book, God designed these appointed times to bring us into the experience of revival every year.

Our Problem

When it comes to God's appointed times, we have a problem. We know all about our traditional holidays in the United States—such as the Fourth of July, Thanksgiving and Christmas—and how to celebrate them.

These holidays are an integral part of our culture and our lives. It's normal for us to have picnics and watch fireworks on the Fourth of July. No one needs to teach us to eat turkey and watch football on Thanksgiving! We all buy gifts and decorate our houses for Christmas.

But when it comes to God's appointed times, we are ignorant. We simply don't understand God's appointed times! Most Christians have never celebrated God's feasts. The few who have were often taught to observe them as legalistic rituals, and the true spiritual power was lost. Most of us have no idea how to celebrate them in a way that allows us to enter into the purposes of God!

To gain a mindset to prosper, I believe we must gain an understanding of God's appointed times. We need to see them not as legalistic rituals or as a new set of holidays or as traditional Jewish celebrations, but as they really are: appointments with God!

God's Heart for the Feasts

To put God's feasts in perspective, it's helpful to understand what the Bible means when it talks about a feast or festival.

In the Old Testament, several Hebrew words are used to designate God's appointed times. One word used is *mo'ed,* which simply means "an appointed time." It designated an occasion fixed by divine appointment to meet together for fellowship with God and worship.

Another Hebrew word used for one of these special days is *hag,* which is taken from the verb to dance and means "an occasion of joy or gladness."

A third Hebrew word used of a God-appointed time is *hagag.* This word has a variety of meanings:

- To celebrate a special day
- Rejoicing
- The festive attitudes and actions of celebrating a feast
- Wild and unrestrained actions, like the behavior of a drunken person (it's interesting to note that on Pentecost, the apostles

so overflowed with the Spirit that their actions appeared to be those of a drunken people)
- Festive dancing and celebrations, as of a victory over enemies in battle

From looking at these words, we can begin to get a sense of what holding a festival to the Lord, such as Passover or Tabernacles, was meant to be: a time of rejoicing and celebration with the kind of unrestrained joy you would experience when you were victorious in a battle!

This gives us real insight into the heart of God. God could have designed His appointed times to be times of sorrow. He could have made them times of severe fasting and repentance. That's how some view God! Greek Paganism taught that suffering makes a person holy. This belief, called "asceticism," still affects much of the Church today. Many Christians assume God wants them to show their devotion to Him by being miserable.

But that's not in the Bible! There are times for fasting and self-denial, but most of God's appointed times are times of feasting. God wants us to know that He desires for His children to enjoy Him and experience His goodness!

Avoiding Spiritual Drift

Why is God's cycle of feasts important? It's because God wants us to avoid what I call "spiritual drift."

Most Christians who are far from God didn't get there intentionally. They didn't choose one morning to rebel against God. They just drifted away. Over the course of time, they tended to accumulate things in their lives that hindered their fellowship with God. Then one day they realized they were no longer close to the Lord, and they were not sure how to get back. I've talked with many church members who look back longingly to times when they were excited about Jesus and sensed His presence with them.

Part of the solution to this "spiritual drift" is to allow our lives to be "linked in" to God's yearly cycle. As we meet with God in His appointed times, He is able to deal with the issues that would cause our hearts to grow cold. Each year the cycle brings us to a place where we experience God's glory anew.

Through the feasts, God wants us to enter in to the joy of meeting with God and experience the fullness of His blessing! May God bless you greatly as you enter into the cycles of God!

8

PASSOVER:
REDEEMED BY THE BLOOD

ROBERT HEIDLER

*Take a lamb . . . for each household. . . . [On] the fourteenth day of the
month . . . slaughter them at twilight. Then . . . take some of the blood and
put it on the sides and tops of the doorframes of the houses. . . . That same
night they are to eat the meat roasted over the fire, along with bitter herbs,
and bread made without yeast. . . . This is how you are to eat it: with your
cloak tucked into your belt, your sandals on your feet and your staff in your
hand. Eat it in haste; it is the LORD's Passover. On that same night I will pass
through Egypt and strike down every firstborn—both men and animals—
and I will bring judgment on all the gods of Egypt. I am the LORD. The blood
will be a sign for you on the houses where you are; and when I see the blood,
I will pass over you. No destructive plague will touch you. . . . This is a day
you are to commemorate; for the generations to come you shall celebrate it
as a festival to the LORD—a lasting ordinance.*
EXODUS 12:3,6-8,11-14, *NIV*

Passover is the first appointed time in God's yearly cycle. It's sad to say,
but most Christians today know very little about Passover. They don't
know what it is or how to celebrate it. If you are not familiar with
Passover, here's a one-sentence summary of what Passover is about:

Passover is a celebration of redemption and deliverance by the
blood of the Lamb.

For the Jews, Passover was (and is) a celebration of God's power in
setting them free from slavery in Egypt. They had been in bondage
under bitter oppression, but they cried out to God, and He delivered
them through what became known as Passover.

Christians also have a deliverance to celebrate. We have been in bondage under the oppression of a cruel enemy: Satan. Passover is a vivid picture of how God delivered us.

The Origins of Passover

The name "Passover" comes from the fact that the Israelites were passed over. The time had come for God's judgment to fall. It would have fallen on everyone in Egypt, but God gave the Israelites a way of escape. The key to their rescue was not an army or some great, heroic deed but a pure, spotless lamb. When the blood of that carefully selected lamb was placed on the doorpost of the home, God accepted the death of that lamb in place of Israel's firstborn. The angel of death passed over that house. Many things happened at Passover:

- By the blood of a lamb, Israel was redeemed.
- The judgment of God was turned away from the Israelites.
- The gods of Egypt were judged and their power broken.
- Israel was released from oppression and bondage.
- The Israelites were set free to enter God's promise.

God commanded the Jews in the Old Testament to observe Passover to teach them the importance of redemption by the blood. But it was also observed by Christians in the New Testament to remember God's redeeming work! The Bible tells us it is to be a permanent ordinance . . . a celebration for all time.

Many Christians don't realize that Passover is just as much a New Testament feast as an Old Testament feast! It is seen throughout the New Testament:

- Jesus and the apostles all celebrated Passover.

- The original Lord's Supper was a Passover meal!

- The apostles taught the Gentile churches to celebrate Passover. In 1 Corinthians 5:7-8, Paul wrote to a predominantly Gentile church, "Christ, our Passover, was sacrificed for us. Therefore let us keep the feast."

For hundreds of years, Passover was the most important yearly celebration in the Early Church!

The Battle Against Passover

Derek Prince once said that the most powerful faith declaration for deliverance is this: "I am redeemed by the blood of the Lamb out of the hand of the enemy!" He said that if we can make that declaration in faith and keep on making it, something will happen in our lives. We will be delivered from the power of the enemy!

That's really the message of Passover. The Feast of Passover is a faith declaration that we are redeemed by the blood of the Lamb. It does something in us when we celebrate Passover! When we come together to remember God's great works of redemption and declare the power of redemption in our lives, it always does something! That's why Passover is important to God. That's also why Satan hates Passover! Satan knows that when we lay hold of the blood of the Lamb by faith, his hold on us is broken. That's why Satan would always rather give us an Easter bunny than a Passover lamb. The power is in the blood!

Down through history, Satan has worked diligently to steal Passover away. There's always a battle for Passover.

In the fourth century, when the emperor Constantine tried to unify his empire by merging Christianity and paganism, he began by legalizing Christianity. That sounded like a good deal to many Christians. They no longer had to worry about being thrown to the lions if they attended a church service. But Constantine also demanded that the Church make some changes. He didn't mind Christians celebrating Jesus' resurrection . . . but he did have an issue with Passover! Constantine demanded that Christians *not* celebrate Jesus' resurrection at the time of Passover. At the Council of Nicea (AD 325), he declared, "This irregularity [observing Passover] must be corrected"![1]

So Constantine outlawed Passover and directed that Christ's death and resurrection be celebrated on "the Sunday following the first full moon after the vernal equinox," a time associated with the spring festival of the pagan fertility goddess Ishtar, also known as Eastre. This is why, in the Church today, we celebrate Jesus' resurrection at Easter instead of Passover. Constantine's goal was to remove the celebration of Jesus' death and resurrection from the context of Passover!

But many in the Church resisted Constantine's edicts, so for many centuries after Constantine, the battle for Passover continued. During the sixth century, Emperor Justinian sent the Roman armies throughout the empire to enforce the prohibition on Passover. In his attempt to wipe out the "heresy" of Passover, thousands of men, women and children were brutally murdered. The battle for Passover has had many casualties! Pressured by the government, the Roman Church joined in the attempts to stamp out Passover. At the Council of Antioch (AD 345), the Church officials stated, "If any bishop, presbyter or deacon will dare, after this decree, to celebrate Passover, the council judges them to be *anathema* from the church. This council not only deposes them from ministry, but also any others who dare to communicate with them." (The word "anathema" means cursed. The Church actually pronounced a curse on Christians who celebrated Passover.[2])

At the Council of Laodicea (AD 365), the Church officials decreed that it was "not permitted to receive festivals which are by Jews.[3] At the Council of Agde, in France (AD 506), Church officials said, "Christians must not take part in Jewish festivals."[4] So, for centuries, both the Church and the secular government did their best to wipe out Passover.

Satan's Attempts to Steal Passover

The battle against Passover is nothing new. Satan always tries to steal away Passover, because he knows the celebration of the blood releases power! We see the same thing occurring in the Old Testament. Just look what happened in Hezekiah's day.

Hezekiah did what was right in the eyes of the Lord. He repaired and cleansed the Temple, tore down the false altars, and restored the sacrifices and Davidic praise.

Then Hezekiah sent word to all Israel and Judah, inviting them to come to celebrate Passover. Couriers went throughout Israel and Judah proclaiming, "People of Israel, return to the Lord. "

The hand of God was on the people to give them unity of mind to carry out what the king had ordered. A large crowd of people assembled in Jerusalem to celebrate the Feast. They slaughtered the Passover lamb and celebrated the Feast for seven days with great rejoicing, while the Levites sang to the Lord every day, accompanied by instruments of praise.

The whole assembly then agreed to celebrate the festival seven more days; so for another seven days they celebrated joyfully. There was great joy in Jerusalem, for since the days of Solomon—son of David, king of Israel—there had been nothing like this in Jerusalem. The priests and the Levites stood to bless the people, and God heard them, for their prayer reached heaven, His holy dwelling place (see 2 Chron. 29–30).

We see pretty much the same thing happening in Josiah's day. Josiah did what was right in the eyes of the Lord. Then, in the eighteenth year of his reign, while the Israelites were repairing the temple, they found the Torah scroll in the Temple.

When the king heard the words of the Torah scroll, he tore his robes. He went up to the Temple with all the people. He read in their hearing all the words of the Covenant. Then all the people pledged themselves to follow it.

The king ordered them to remove from the Temple all the idols made for Baal, Asherah and the starry hosts. He tore down the quarters of the male prostitutes, which were in the Temple. Josiah then gave this order to all the people: "Keep the Passover to the Lord your God, as it is written in this Book of the Covenant" (2 Kings 23:21).

In the eighteenth year of King Josiah, the people celebrated this Passover to the Lord in Jerusalem. Not since the days of the judges who led Israel—nor throughout the days of the kings of Israel and the kings of Judah—had such a Passover been observed (see 2 Kings 22–23).

So we see a biblical pattern. In both of these passages, God's people had drifted far from the Lord and turned to idolatry. As a result, the blessing of God was lost. Then they turned back to God and sought Him, and the first thing God did was to restore Passover!

As the people turned from pagan idols and celebrated Passover, they were restored to God and experienced great joy and blessing. That's an interesting pattern! Over and over again in the Bible, we discover that Passover had been lost. Even during the Old Testament era, and even among the Jews, generations lived and died without celebrating Passover. Why had Passover been lost? Because Satan had *stolen* it away! Satan always wants to steal Passover! Then, as a new generation turned back to the Lord and began to study God's Word, they read about Passover for the first time. It seemed strange to them! They said, "We've never done this!" (That's exactly what we see in much of the Church today!) But as the Holy Spirit moved on their hearts, they celebrated God's feast of redemption, and God's power and blessing were restored.

Why Satan Hates Passover

Satan hates Passover because Passover is the celebration of Jesus. When the Church gave up Passover, it invented other celebrations of Jesus (that's how we got Christmas and Easter). Of course, it's not bad to celebrate Jesus on those other days—it's always good to celebrate Christ! But the celebration of Jesus that *God* gave us is called Passover.

The New Testament tells us that Jesus is the Passover Lamb. When John introduced Jesus, he said, "Behold! The Lamb of God who takes away the sins of the world!" (John 1:29). Paul said, "Christ, our Passover Lamb, has been sacrificed" (1 Cor. 5:7, *NIV*). In Revelation 4–5, we see all heaven joining together in what is essentially a huge Passover celebration honoring Jesus as the Lamb who was slain!

Celebrating Passover *is* celebrating Jesus. As the Passover Lamb, He shed His blood to redeem us from the enemy. When His blood is "on the doorpost" of your life, God delivers you from the destroyer. Everything in Passover is a picture of Jesus, and every element points to Jesus!

Picture in your mind what took place on the original Passover night: The father of the house took the blood from the Passover lamb and put it in a bowl. He went to the door of his home, dipped a branch of hyssop into the blood, and applied it to the doorposts of the home. Then he dipped the hyssop into the blood again and reached up to apply blood to the lintel as well.

Now stop and picture what is taking place. First, the father takes the blood-dipped hyssop branch and moves it from side to side to apply blood to both doorposts. He then lowers the hyssop down into the bowl and reaches up over his head to apply blood to the lintel. Can you picture in your mind what this Israelite father is doing as he stands before the front door of his home? It's a gesture you've probably seen Roman Catholics do! Every father in Israel stood in front of his house and made the sign of the cross in the blood of the lamb. What a dramatic picture of Jesus! God's deliverance always comes by His cross and by His blood.

Through Passover, the Jews were redeemed out of the hand of the enemy. But Passover is also how *we* were redeemed! Passover is the celebration of redemption.

As mentioned earlier, it was not by accident that Jesus died on Passover. God could have had Jesus die any time of year, but it was God's will for Him to die at Passover so that we would recognize Him as our Passover Lamb.

Consider this again: Passover is so important to God that He chose to have the most important event in history—the death and resurrection of Jesus—take place at this time. God went to great lengths to *connect* the sacrifice of Jesus to Passover. This is interesting, because Constantine's goal was to *separate* the work of Jesus from Passover, while God's goal was to *connect* Jesus' work to Passover! God wants us to think of Jesus in the context of the Passover celebration.

The Timetable of Passover

It's interesting to compare the timetable of Jesus' crucifixion with the Passover celebration. According to the Torah, at the time of Passover a number of events had to take place in a specific order, and at specific times.

The Passover Lamb Had to Be Selected on a Specific Day

Exodus 12 instructs that the Passover lamb had to be chosen on the tenth day of the first month. By the time of Jesus, only lambs from Bethlehem were considered eligible to serve as Passover lambs. So, a lamb born in Bethlehem was chosen and brought into Jerusalem from the east, down the Mount of Olives. The lamb entered the city through the sheep gate.

On the tenth day of the first month, Jesus, the Lamb born in Bethlehem, came down the Mount of Olives and entered Jerusalem through the sheep gate. (This is called the "Triumphal Entry.") As He entered, the people waved palm branches and shouted, "Hosanna to the Son of David! Blessed is He who comes in the name of the LORD!" (Matt. 21:9). By mass acclamation, the people designated Jesus as Israel's Messiah. The crowds had chosen their Passover Lamb!

The Lamb Had to Be Examined

The Torah instructed that once the priests had chosen a lamb, they had to carefully examine it for blemishes. Only a perfect, spotless and unblemished lamb would suffice for the Passover.

After arriving in Jerusalem, Jesus went to the Temple to teach. While there, He was approached by the Pharisees, Sadducees, Herodians and the teachers of the Law. Each group posed difficult questions, trying to trap Him. Essentially, they were looking for any blemish that might disqualify Him as the Messiah. But no one could find fault with Him. He was without blemish.

The Leaven (Impurity) Had to Be Cast Out

The Torah instructed that before the feast, all leaven (impurity) had to be cast out of every Israelite home. Each mother took a candle and searched for impurities, removing them from her house. This regulation is still observed today. Passover is a time to cleanse every house, and every observant Jewish family carefully cleans their house before Passover. Every trace of impurity is removed. After Jesus arrived in Jerusalem, He entered the Temple and cast out the moneychangers. In doing so, He was following the biblical instruction to prepare for Passover by cleansing His Father's house.

The Lamb Was Taken to the Altar for Public Display

On the morning of the fourteenth day of the first month, when all had been set in order, the lamb was led out to the altar. At 9 AM that morning, the lamb was bound to the altar and put on public display for all to see. On the morning of the fourteenth day of the first month, when all prophecy had been fulfilled, Jesus was led out to Calvary. At 9 AM that morning, just as the lamb was being bound to the altar, Jesus was nailed to the cross and put on public display at Calvary.

The Lamb Was Slain at a Specific Time

At exactly 3 PM, the high priest ascended the altar. As another priest blew a *shofar* on the temple wall, the high priest cut the throat of the sacrificial lamb and declared, "It is finished!" At 3 PM on that high holy day, at the moment the Passover lamb was being killed, Jesus cried with a loud voice, "It is finished!" (John 19:30) and gave up His spirit. In Greek, the words translated "it is finished" is *tetelistai.* It means, "The debt has been paid in full!"

Do you see how God chose to connect Jesus with Passover? It is no wonder that John introduces Jesus by saying, "Behold! The Lamb of God!" It is no wonder Paul writes, "Christ, our Passover lamb, has been sacrificed." Passover is all about Jesus!

Hiding the *Afikomen*

Even today, the Jewish celebration of Passover is all about Jesus. At the beginning of every Jewish Passover celebration, the father of the house performs an interesting ceremony called Hiding the *Afikomen*. This part of the Passover ceremony is very old, dating probably as early as the first century. No Jew today knows what it means; it is just "tradition." Yet it is done in millions of Jewish households, all over the world, every Passover night.

To perform the *afikomen* ceremony, the father of the house holds a prepared cloth bag called an *afikomen* bag (it's also called a unity bag). In that unity bag are three pockets. Before the feast, the father puts three sheets of unleavened bread (matzo) in the unity bag—one in each pocket. (The Jews have strict rules about how matzo is prepared. It has to be pierced, striped and bruised. If you hold a piece of unleavened bread up to the light, you will see light coming through the holes pierced in the matzo.)

At the beginning of the meal, the father takes the middle piece of matzo out of the bag. (This is the middle piece of the three matzos in the unity.) This piece of matzo is called the *afikomen*. Interestingly, *afikomen* is not a Hebrew word; it's Greek! It comes from the Greek word *aphikomenos,* which means, "He who is coming," or "the Coming One"!

So the father takes this bruised, striped and pierced *afikomen*—the middle of the three in the unity, the piece of matzo representing "the Coming One"—and he breaks it. Then he carefully wraps it in a white linen napkin and hides it out of sight until later in the Passover meal. At the close of the meal, the children are told to search for the *afikomen*, and the one who finds it gets a reward. When the *afikomen* is found, it is unwrapped and held up for all to see. Now, think about this—picture it in your mind:

- The *afikomen* being broken symbolizes Jesus' death.
- The *afikomen* being wrapped in linen represents the wrapping of Jesus' body in linen after His death.
- The *afikomen* being hidden from sight symbolizes Jesus' burial.
- The *afikomen* being unwrapped and held up for all to see represents the resurrection of Jesus!

That's the whole gospel story in the middle of a Jewish Passover celebration!

When the *afikomen* is found, it's eaten. (Usually each person gets a piece.) This is the point during the Last Supper when Jesus lifted the bread and said, "This is my body given for you" (Luke 22:19). Jesus was saying, "I am the *afikomen*! I am the coming One." He identified Himself with the Passover celebration!

After the *afikomen* is eaten, a cup of wine is poured. The Jews call it "the cup of redemption." This is the point during the Last Supper when Jesus lifted the cup and said, "This cup is the new covenant in my blood; do this, whenever you drink it, in remembrance of me" (1 Cor. 11:25, *NIV*).

This was the original context of the Lord's Supper! The Lord's Supper was given in the context of a Passover meal. Jesus clearly stated that He wanted to share this meal with His disciples (see Luke 22:15). I believe He still desires to share Passover with His people!

The Celebration of Jesus

Do you now see that Passover is all about Jesus? He came as the Lamb of God, and His blood redeems us. By His blood:

- Judgment turned away.
- The power of the enemy is broken.
- We are released from bondage and oppression.
- We are set free to enter into God's promise.

Passover is the "Jesus celebration." The more you understand Passover, the more you appreciate Jesus. Even more, if you don't understand Passover, you will have a hard time fully understanding what Jesus did for you! As you celebrate Passover, you are declaring your faith in the power of His blood and His redemption. That's why one of strangest things in world is that Christians have accepted Satan's lie that Passover is not a "Christian" thing. So instead, we get the Easter Bunny!

Satan has tried to steal away Passover because he knows the celebration of the blood releases power. When the celebration of Passover was stolen away from the Church, the power *left*. But when Passover is restored, the power *returns.*

The good news is that God is restoring Passover. All over the world, churches are again celebrating Passover—and the power is returning! So join with Christians all over the world in the restoration of Passover, and celebrate the power of Jesus' blood.

Passover was the first step in the Israelites' escaping the oppression of Egypt. Egypt was a place of absolute poverty for them, but Passover opened the door for escape. Passover allowed Israel to begin moving forward toward the abundant provision of the Promised Land. As you celebrate Passover, you will also begin to move forward toward abundant provision and begin to gain a mindset to prosper.

Preparing for Passover

As previously noted, there is a special time of cleansing in preparation for Passover. Every Jewish woman today still diligently searches her home, looking on every shelf, in every drawer and in every cabinet to find any trace of leaven (impurity). If any leaven is found, she must remove it before the Passover celebration can begin.

This would be good for us to do today. Before we can experience God's deliverance, we have to search our homes and remove all impurities.

Chuck Pierce and Rebecca Wagner Sytsema have written a helpful book called *Protecting Your Home from Spiritual Darkness*, which describes how to go through your home and remove defilement and impurity.[5] (You can also find information on cleansing your home in my book *Set Yourself Free*.) We have received many testimonies of how ridding a home of spiritual darkness has broken demonic oppression and released the blessing of God over the home.

God wanted this breaking of demonic oppression to be a yearly part of His cycle of life. So, to this end, here are some suggestions for preparing your home for Passover:

1. *Dedicate your home to the Lord.* Pray and invite the presence of God into your home. Ask the Lord to use your home for His purposes.

2. *Take a spiritual inventory.* Ask God to give you discernment as you look at what you own. Go through your house, room by room, and let the Holy Spirit show you any objects that should not be in your home. Particularly note:

   • Objects depicting false gods
   • Objects used in pagan worship, occult practices, or witchcraft
   • Objects exalting or promoting evil
   • Objects related to past sin
   • Objects that have become idols in your life

3. *Cleanse your home of ungodly objects.* Deuteronomy 7:25 says such objects should be destroyed by fire. Take what can be

burned and burn it in an appropriate place. If the object cannot be burned, pass it through the fire (as a symbolic act of obedience) and then destroy it by whatever means is appropriate, such as smashing or flushing. (Note: If you have a roommate or spouse, do not remove items belonging to them without their permission!)

4. *Ask forgiveness.* Once you have destroyed an object, renounce any participation you or your family have had with that object, and ask God to forgive you.

5. *Cleanse each room and cleanse the land.* Go through your house and repent for any known sin that has been committed in each room. Pray that the Lord would heal any trauma caused by the torment of demonic forces in your home. Pray over your property as well.

6. *Consecrate your home and property to God and His service.* Declare Joshua 24:15 over your home: "As for me and my household, we will serve the LORD" (*NIV*).

7. *Fill your home with glory.* Take communion at home as a family. Sing praises and pray in your home. Testify about the good things God has done for you. Speak the Word in your house. Read the psalms aloud. Play praise music. Keep your house bright. Cultivate a mood of hope in your home. Refuse any influence that would extinguish the brightness of God's glory.

When you have removed all spiritual defilement, speak a blessing over your house and invite the presence of God to fill it!

Suggestions for Celebrating Passover

There is no one "right" way to celebrate Passover. Some purchase a copy of a Messianic Jewish Seder and go through all the elaborate rituals.[6] It's wonderful to experience a Seder celebration in this way, but it is not required. You can observe Passover very simply by sharing a meal, telling the Passover story, and then taking communion to celebrate Jesus, our Passover Lamb. The primary goal is to remember the greatness of God's deliverance.

As you complete your Passover celebration, be sure to thank God . . .

- That you are redeemed out of every old cycle
- That bondage is broken
- That you are set free by the blood of the Lamb to enter the promise

If you would like some suggestions for celebrating Passover, see appendix 1 at the end of this book. You can also find an abbreviated Seder in my book *The Messianic Church Arising*, available from Glory of Zion International Ministries.

Passover Today—A Perspective from Israel

To conclude this chapter, I want to share a perspective on how Passover today is celebrated in Israel. Several years ago, Chuck Pierce had a huge gathering where people from more than 110 nations gathered in Denton (or by webcast) to learn more about the power of the blood and Passover. At that time, he heard the Lord say, *"The same God who visited Moses, who gathered the elders of His covenant, is now saying gather again to gain strategy and strength to advance past the enemy's tactics in the world."*

Chuck and his team had a tent brought in that held 4,000 people, and they filled it! Martin and Norma Sarvis, who write the Glory of Zion's "Prayer Update from Israel," arrived from Israel to participate in the event.[7] In March 2010, they wrote the following about Passover in Israel today:

I trust that the Body of Christ will once again learn the significance of joining in the Passover gathering. Passover occurs in the Hebrew month Aviv or Nisan. This is the First of Months for the Hebrews (see Exod. 12:2; 13:4; 23:15) and holds true with the religious calendar today (the numbering for the year changes at the Feast of Trumpets in the fall). The name Nisan has been used since the Babylonian captivity. Previously, it was called the month of the Aviv, the word originally referring to the stage in the growth of grain when the seeds have reached full size and are filling with starch, but have not yet dried. Today, Aviv survives in Israel as the Hebrew word for springtime.

On the tenth of the month of Aviv, a young lamb or goat was set aside for each Hebrew household in Egypt. At twilight on the fourteenth, the lamb was slain and its blood applied to the doorposts and lintels. When the Lord passed through the land at midnight, He would *skip over* the doors bearing the blood and not allow the destroyer to enter.

Passover is the grandest of the holy days in Israel. There is an excitement and sense of anticipation in the air—as near as Israelis are likely to come to experiencing something like the Christmas season in the West—yet it is, of course, also very different. School is out for several weeks; the stores begin either removing or barring with screens any foods containing leaven; and many Jewish homes, observant or not, choose this time for the removal of old leaven to do their spring cleaning.

Families begin planning and getting things together for the Seder night. "Seder" means "order" in Hebrew, and it is this word that has come to signify the order for sitting and recounting each year the mighty acts of the LORD in delivering Israel out of bondage in Egypt with His strong right arm (see Exod. 13:3-10).

For Messianic believers and Gentile Christians, the Passover lamb also signifies the sacrifice of the Lamb of God who carries away the sin of the world, who provides salvation for those who by faith find shelter under His shed blood. In New Testament times, Passover became a pilgrim festival. Large numbers gathered in Jerusalem to observe this annual celebration. Jesus was crucified in the city during one of these Passover celebrations. He and His disciples ate a Passover meal together on the eve of His death. Like the blood of the lamb, which saved the Hebrew people from destruction in Egypt, Jesus' blood, as the ultimate Passover sacrifice, redeems us from the power of sin and death.

On the third day, the day after the Sabbath of Passover when a sheaf of grain was waived before the Lord (see Lev. 23:11), we celebrate Yeshua's resurrection and priestly ascension on high to present Himself before the Father on our behalf as a firstfruits from the dead![8]

When we get in God's order and recognize the power of Jesus' blood, we enter into a time of cleansing and power. Ask the Lord to give you revelation on how to order your life in a new way. You will then be ordered for increase!

Notes

1. Dean Dudley, *History of the First Council of Nice,* fourth ed. (Boston: Dean Dudley & Co., 1886), p. 112.
2. Council of Antioch (ad 345), canon 1, second part.
3. Council of Laodicea (ad 365), canon 37.
4. Council of Agde (ad 506), canon 40.
5. Chuck D. Pierce and Rebecca Wagner Sytsema, *Protecting Your Home from Spiritual Darkness: 10 Steps to Help You Clean House, Place Jesus in Authority and Make Your Home a Safe Place* (Ventura, CA: Regal Books, 2004).
6. You can find an abbreviated Seder in the back of my book *The Messianic Church Arising.*
7. This update can be found at www.gloryofzion.org. It provides a direct line as to what is happening in Israel so that Christians can "pray for the peace of Jerusalem" on a daily basis (see Ps. 122:6).
8. Martin and Norma Sarvis, personal communication, March 23, 2010.

9

PENTECOST: CELEBRATING GOD'S PROVISION

ROBERT HEIDLER

The morning of the third day there was thunder and lightning, with a thick cloud over the mountain. . . . Moses led the people out . . . , and they stood at the foot of the mountain. Mount Sinai was covered with smoke, because the LORD descended on it in fire. The smoke billowed up from it like smoke from a furnace, the whole mountain trembled violently. . . . The LORD . . . called Moses to the top of the mountain.

EXODUS 19:16-20, *NIV*

When the Day of Pentecost had fully come, they were all with one accord in one place. And suddenly there came a sound from heaven, as of a rushing mighty wind, and it filled the whole house where they were sitting. Then there appeared to them divided tongues, as of fire, and one sat upon each one of them. And they were all filled with the Holy Spirit and began to speak with other tongues, as the Spirit gave them utterance.

ACTS 2:1-4

Several years ago, our friends John and Sheryl Price were driving to Middletown, Ohio, to attend a Global Harvest prophetic conference. As they were driving into town, they noticed a very strange cloud formation in the sky. It appeared to be a word written in Greek letters. John and Sheryl puzzled over this, so Sheryl got out some paper and attempted to draw what they were seeing. She brought it to me at the conference and asked me if it really was a Greek word.

When I saw what Sheryl had written, it really did look like a Greek word! I have a lot of Bible study tools on my laptop, so I looked up what Sheryl had written: *schizo. Schizo* is a Greek word that means "to rend, tear violently, open or unfold."

I know that when studying the Bible the first mention of a word is often important, so I looked up the first place *schizo* was used. I discovered that it was in Mark 1:10 when, at the baptism of Jesus, the heavens were "torn open" (*schizo*) and the Spirit descended as a dove. So, as John and Cheryl were driving into Middletown for a prophetic conference, God wrote *schizo* across the sky! What an incredible prophetic sign!

But what was God saying? I believe He was telling us that He is about to open the heavens. We are on the verge of a major move of the Holy Spirit! If that is true, then it means we live in days when Pentecost is important, because Pentecost is the feast of the open heavens. Just as Passover is God's time to deliver His people (see Exod. 3:8), Pentecost is the appointed time for the heavens to open!

If we want to understand and experience "open heavens," we need to understand Pentecost. Now, when most Christians think about Pentecost, they think about the outpouring of the Spirit described in Acts 2. But Pentecost didn't begin in Acts 2. Pentecost was a biblical feast instituted by God in the Old Testament.

The Feast of Pentecost is described in Leviticus 23:15-16, Numbers 28:26-31 and Deuteronomy 16:9-12. The Israelites were told to count off seven weeks (49 days) from the Feast of Passover, and then on the fiftieth day have a festival before the Lord. In Hebrew this feast is called Shavuot, which means "feast of weeks." In the New Testament it is called "Pentecost" which is Greek for "50 days."

Three Dimensions of Pentecost

There are three significant dimensions of Pentecost, and each represents a new expression of God's blessing. The three dimensions reflect the three things God wants to accomplish in our lives. Each involves a doorway we must pass through to enter into the full release of God's blessing. If we understand the three dimensions of Pentecost, then we will catch a glimpse of what God wants to do in our lives.

Provision

The first dimension of Pentecost is celebrating God's blessing of abundant provision—God's meeting our physical needs.

In ancient Israel, the farmers worked week after week to prepare the soil and plant the seeds in hope of harvesting an abundant crop. Yet they had no ability to make the earth produce. If the Lord did not open the heavens, there would be no crops. But as they trusted God, He opened the windows of heaven, and rain came forth. The result was that the earth brought forth harvest.

The Jews recognized that our physical provision is a wondrous act of God's grace. Every Sabbath, the father of the house lifts a freshly baked loaf of bread before the Lord and blesses (thanks) God for His bountiful provision: "Blessed are You, O Lord, our God, King of the Universe, Who brings forth bread from the earth!"

From the first sheaf of every new harvest, the Jews would bring a thanksgiving offering to the Temple, acknowledging that God opened the heavens to bring forth their bread from the earth. This was a praise offering—offered by faith before the full harvest was gathered. That offering was brought to God at Pentecost!

On Pentecost, the Israelites would express their praise by bringing burnt offerings, grain offerings, drink offerings, sin offerings, fellowship offerings and freewill offerings (see Num. 29:39). It was a massive outpouring of giving—every kind of offering imaginable!

It's interesting to note that this is what the disciples would have done the evening before "Pentecost morning." The night before the Spirit fell, they would have brought offerings to the Temple to thank God for His physical provision.

Pentecost is thus, first of all, a time to open our hearts to God through joyful giving and jubilant praise. As we do this, it positions us to receive! To prepare for Pentecost, we need to ask God how to express our thankfulness in a way that will open our hearts to Him.

Supernatural Revelation

The second dimension of Pentecost is supernatural revelation. Pentecost was the day God opened the heavens to reveal His Word.

When Israel left Egypt, God did not take the people directly to the Promised Land. He had some important things to communicate to them, so He led them southward down the Sinai Peninsula to Mount Sinai. Fifty days after Passover, God directed Moses to come up to the top of the mountain. There the heavens opened, and God gave him Torah.

What is Torah? Some call it the "Law" and picture it as a list of nasty "thou shalt nots." Some think it is just a big old scroll. But the word "Torah" really means "the teaching of God." Torah is the revelation of God's will, God's love, and God's character. Although the word "Torah" is most specifically used of the first five books of the Bible, in a real sense, all Scripture is "Torah."

On Pentecost, God revealed His heart to His people, and Pentecost celebrates the release of God's revelation. At the time Jesus lived, part of the celebration of Pentecost included staying up all night studying the Bible! It was a way of receiving God's Word anew.

In Acts 2:1 we read, "When the day of Pentecost had fully come, they were all with one accord in one place." When morning dawned on Pentecost, the disciples were already gathered together. What were they doing? As observant Jews, they would have brought thank offerings to the Temple the night before, and then gone to the upper room and stayed up all night studying God's Word!

Don't you wonder what they would have studied? We know that Jesus had recently promised the release of His power when the Holy Spirit would come. I believe, in light of that, they would have studied Scriptures about the outpouring of God's power. They might have read the passages about God coming down in fire on Mount Sinai, or Ezekiel's vision of the Lord coming in a whirlwind with darting flames of fire. They almost certainly would have studied the account of the Spirit's outpouring in Joel 2, where the end-time release of the Spirit was to be accompanied by prophetic utterance along with great signs and wonders.

As they filled their minds with God's Word, I believe God prepared them for the third dimension of Pentecost.

God's Power

The third dimension of Pentecost is being clothed in God's power. "When the day of Pentecost had fully come," the heavens were torn open! The power of God was released into the earth-realm!

Just as the fire had come down on Mt. Sinai, the fire of God's glory now came upon those who had gathered in the Upper Room. They were clothed with His power. The gifts of the Spirit were energized. The anointing of God equipped them to see the sick healed, the oppressed delivered, the gospel boldly proclaimed, and the world changed.

This is what the Church today longs for. The Church all over the world is crying out for a "new" Pentecost. However, because we don't understand Pentecost, we don't know how to prepare for it.

The apostles understood Pentecost. They knew how to enter into the blessing of an open heaven. They celebrated God's provision with thank offerings and praise. They acknowledged that He brings forth "food from the earth" (Ps. 104:14). When we come before God seeking new blessings, it's important to acknowledge the blessings we have already received.

As the apostles celebrated God's previous blessings at Pentecost, they positioned themselves to receive something new. They filled their minds with God's Word by devoting an entire night to studying and pondering the Torah. In the same way, as we meditate on the Word, we attune our minds to think the thoughts of God. Faith is released to receive all that God wants to give.

So, Pentecost is about three things: (1) God's abundant provision, (2) His supernatural revelation, and (3) the release of His power and authority "on earth as it is in heaven" (Matt. 6:10). All are available for us to receive when the heavens open. God is telling us to prepare for the open heavens!

Preparing for Pentecost

Here are three steps to follow to prepare for Pentecost.

1. Learn to Celebrate God's Provision

Don't take any blessing for granted! Marvel that God loves you so much that He brings forth bread from the earth! Be filled with praise! Praise Him with your testimony. Praise Him in singing. Develop a lifestyle of thanksgiving. Praise Him in thank offerings. Celebrate God's goodness through lavish giving. One mark of a poverty mindset is a lack of thankfulness. At our church, we give generously to the poor, but we've noticed something sad. When people who are in poverty come to us in need and we generously meet their need, the people hardly ever say thank you. That lack of thankfulness is part of what holds them in poverty.

Gaining a mind to prosper involves developing a thankful heart. That's what Pentecost is designed to do. It's a time set by God to joyfully acknowledge the blessings we have received. Our joyful praise opens heaven for fresh blessing to rain down!

2. Celebrate God's Revelation

The next step is to thank God that He has revealed Himself to you and that He wants you to know His mind and heart. Fill your mind with His Word! Psalm 1 promises that if you meditate on His Word day and night, you will prosper, so receive His revelation afresh. Allow the thoughts of God to reprogram your thinking processes. Memorize His promises. Observe how He worked in the lives of the men and women who trusted Him. Hunger and thirst for spiritual bread. Let faith arise!

3. Receive a Fresh Release of His Spirit

Finally, stay in step with God and obey His directives. Walk by faith. Meditate on His promises. God is about to rend the heavens! Be ready to receive.

Celebrating Pentecost Like the Apostles

In celebrating Pentecost, why not follow the example set by the apostles? Set apart an extended time to be with God. You can plan a private retreat to spend time with the Lord, or you may wish to gather with family and friends for a "Pentecost party." Get together with others who are seeking the Lord and spend time thanking God for what He has done. Sing praises to Him. Share testimonies. Prepare a thank offering.

Also, spend time in His Word. Study the accounts of God's power and miracles in the Bible. Read about the great revivals of history. Thank Him that He never changes! Pray for a fresh release of the

Spirit. If you are with friends, pray over each other for a fresh out-pouring and an increased experience of His blessing. Receive the fire of God and the energizing of His gifts. Praise God that He has released His power in the earth!

Pentecost is the second step in gaining a mindset to prosper. God designed it to give us a thankful heart. Each year, He wanted His people to set aside a day to acknowledge His blessing in the past, and welcome His provision for the future!

10

PREPARING FOR TABERNACLES

ROBERT HEIDLER

On the first day of the seventh month you are to have a day of sabbath rest, a sacred assembly commemorated with trumpet blasts. . . . The tenth day of this seventh month is the Day of Atonement, . . . when atonement is made for you before the LORD your God. . . . On the fifteenth day of the seventh month the LORD's Feast of Tabernacles begins.
LEVITICUS 23:24-34, *NIV*

Celebrate the Feast of Tabernacles for seven days. . . . Be joyful at your festival—you, your sons and daughters, your male and female servants. . . . For seven days celebrate the festival to the LORD your God. . . . For the LORD your God will bless you in all your harvest and in all the work of your hands, and your joy will be complete.
DEUTERONOMY 16:13-15, *NIV*

We've seen that there are three major "appointed times" in God's calendar. The year begins with *Passover*, which initiates God's yearly cycle. In the third month comes *Pentecost*, the feast of the open heavens. Then comes the long hot summer. When fall comes, God moves us into the climax of the yearly cycle, the celebration of His glory at the *Feast of Tabernacles*.

The Feast of Tabernacles (called Sukkot in Hebrew) is an appointed time to come boldly into God's presence, knowing that every hindrance is removed. It's a time to experience God's glory and have joyful fellowship with Him! Before the celebration of Tabernacles, however, God provided a series of events to prepare us to enter His presence. These events are often called the fall feasts.

Countdown to Revival

The fall feasts were given to create a pathway into God's glory. They give us a four-step countdown to bring us into His presence:

1. The Feast of Trumpets is designed to be a wake-up call.
2. The Days of Awe provide a time for seeking God.
3. The Day of Atonement is a day to be restored.
4. The Feast of Tabernacles is a week to experience God's glory.

These feasts have always been important, but I believe Tabernacles is the key feast for the Church today. We live in a day when God wants to draw us into His presence in a unique way. It is time for His power and blessing to be poured out. He wants us to experience His glory!

The fall feasts provide the pattern for revival for any individual or nation. By taking us through this countdown every year, God established a way to draw us closer and closer each year into His presence.

The starting point is the Feast of Trumpets.

The Feast of Trumpets

God gave a key commandment for this festival: All His people must listen to a blast of trumpets! The blast of the trumpets is a call to awaken! The Hebrew name for this feast, Yom Teruah, means, "The day of the awakening blast!"

We sometimes need a wake-up call. We need to be called to alertness. We need a call to enter the new season.

A wake-up call almost always comes before revival. This is true for nations as well as for individuals.

Many people have heard about the great revival in Argentina. Back in the '90s, many of us were thrilled at the wonderful accounts of what the Spirit was doing in that nation. Like many others, I was privileged to go to Argentina and visit that revival. That revival led many people in America to begin calling out to God in prayer and fasting so that our nation could see a revival like that here.

But the Argentinian revival did not come without a wake-up call! Argentina suffered a devastating defeat in the Falkland Islands War, followed by a crushing collapse of their economy. Alarmed at the devastation hitting the nation, pastors and Christian leaders began meeting together, praying in desperation for God to do something in their country. In the midst of that unified outpouring of desperate prayer, the Holy Spirit fell!

The Falkland Islands War was a wake-up call for the nation of Argentina. In the same way, many times a disaster or economic collapse will drive people—whether an individual or an entire nation—to seek God, resulting in revival. But God doesn't want us to wait till disaster strikes to enjoy His presence, so He invented a less painful wake-up call. It is the blast of the ram's horn.

Have you ever been startled by the sound of a loud noise? It does something inside you. You wake up! God designed the Feast of Trumpets to be signaled by the sound of a trumpet blast to pierce our souls to call us to attention. The sound of the trumpet awakens our spirits. When we hear the trumpet blast, we should ask God to show us anything in our lives that would hinder His work in us.

The Days of Awe

The 10 days after the Feast of Trumpets are called the Days of Awe. They are also called the 10 days of Teshuvah, which is a Hebrew word that means "to turn" and "to return." It means repentance, but it is also the word for springtime.

When God gives you a wake-up call, it's time to turn from anything that hinders your walk with God. It's time to return to God! Through these days of repentance, you enter a season of springtime. It's a season to experience a fresh release of the life and blessings of God.

You may have started the last year close to God but ended up drifting and getting off course. You may have neglected key appointments with Him. You may have become ensnared by sin. When the trumpet blast calls you to alertness, it's time to turn and return. It's time to again draw close to God and experience full restoration! It's time to seriously seek the Lord.

Here are some things for you to do during the Days of Awe.

1. Praise God and Read His Word

It's important during this season to spend some extended time alone with God. Open your heart to Him in praise. Spend time reading and meditating on His Word. While it's always important to seek God and spend time with Him, the Days of Awe are a time set by God when His Spirit is ready to meet you in some unusual ways.

I believe a key verse for the Days of Awe is Jeremiah 29:12-13: "Then you will call upon Me and go and pray to Me, and I will listen to you. And you will seek Me and find Me when you search for Me with all your heart." The New Testament equivalent is James 4:8, "Draw near to God and He will draw near to you." In other words, God says that if we will draw near to Him, seeking Him with all our hearts, He will draw near to us!

There are times when we need to make seeking God our most important priority! During much of the year, many people spend 20 minutes a day with the Lord, offering up a short prayer and reading a few verses of Scripture. While that is not a formula for spiritual health, it may get you by in the midst of a busy schedule. But we also need extended times with the Lord, times when we can open our hearts to Him and have Him open His heart to us. That's what these days are for!

2. Let God Reveal Old Cycles

As you spend time in fellowship with God and meditate on His Word, ask Him to show you any cycles of destruction in your life. Are you trapped in recurrent debt, infirmity or loss? Do you find that your heart has grown cold and that you no longer feel the closeness to God you once felt? If God shows you old cycles in your life, ask Him to show you His strategy for freedom!

3. Ask God to Reveal Any Sin in Your Life

All of us have blind spots, areas of sin we are not aware of. Those areas of sin hinder the work of the Spirit in our lives. So, during the

Days of Awe, ask the Lord to reveal hidden sin. When God reveals sin, He also gives us grace to gain victory over it.

4. Draw Close to God
Let God quicken your Spirit and awaken a new level of love for Him in your heart!

The Day of Atonement

When you have diligently sought the Lord during the Days of Awe, you are then ready for the Day of Atonement. This is a day to repent and be restored. It's a time to deal with anything in your life that would hinder fellowship with a holy God. It's a time to put all your sins under the blood of the Lamb and be fully restored to God and His purposes.

Hebrews 12:1 provides a perfect description of the Day of Atonement: "Let us throw off everything that hinders and the sin that so easily entangles. And let us run with perseverance the race marked out for us" (*NIV*). Isaiah 44:22 says, "I have wiped out your transgressions like a thick cloud and your sins like a heavy mist. Return to Me, for I have redeemed you" (*NASB*).

There are a few crucial steps to follow in observing the Day of Atonement:

- *Be sure you have accepted Jesus as your atonement.* If you are not sure you have trusted Jesus and received His atoning sacrifice for your sin, go to Him in prayer right now. Note that this is not a matter of joining a church or promising to do better, but accepting that Jesus has done it all! It is knowing your past is wiped clean and you are restored to God by the sacrifice of Jesus.

- *Be sure you are cleansed and restored to fellowship with God.* If you are aware of any sins in your life, confess them. I encourage you to set aside an hour to be with the Lord. Spend time in prayer and ask God to show you if there are any sins He wants you to confess. Write down anything He shows you. Then go through your list and confess each sin, agreeing with God about it.

• *Claim God's promise in 1 John 1:9.* If you have confessed these sins, they are forgiven! Tear up your list of sins and throw it away! Thank God that you are forgiven and cleansed by the blood of Jesus!

• *Know that all defilement is removed and that you can come joyfully into God's presence.*

The Day of Atonement is not a day for joyful celebration, but it does open the door for the most joyful celebration of the year, the Feast of Tabernacles.

11

TABERNACLES:
ENTERING GOD'S GLORY

ROBERT HEIDLER

The Feast of Tabernacles is the third of God's appointed times each year (see Exod. 23:16; 34:22). God's instructions for how to celebrate the feast are given in Leviticus 23:34-43. God told the people to go out into the countryside and cut down "palm fronds, leafy branches and poplars" (Lev. 23:40, *NIV*). They were to bring these branches back to their homes and use them to build tabernacles, or temporary shelters.

The Israelites were to feast in these shelters for an entire week and rejoice before the Lord: "Live in temporary shelters for seven days: . . . so your descendants will know that I had the Israelites live in temporary shelters when I brought them out of Egypt" (Lev. 23:42-43, *NIV*).

In Hebrew, the word for a temporary shelter is *sukkah*. Sukkot (the plural of *sukkah*) is the Hebrew name for this feast. (Sukkot can also be translated "booths," which is why this feast is sometimes referred to as the Feast of Booths.)

When God's people came out of Egypt, they lived in tabernacles. God told them to also build a tabernacle for Him so His glory could come down and dwell in their midst (see Exod. 25:8-9). The Feast of Tabernacles celebrated God's glory living with His people!

Experiencing God's Glory

To understand Tabernacles, we need to understand God's glory. Glory is the tangible manifestation of God's presence. God is always present everywhere, but there are certain times when He reveals His presence in a way that is discernible to our five senses.

In Moses' Tabernacle, God's glory manifested as a shining cloud. At Mount Sinai, it was revealed in thunder and fire. Sometimes

God's presence is evident through miracles and acts of power. Sometimes God's presence is heard in a gentle whisper, such as what Elijah experienced (see 1 Kings 19:12).

There are many ways God can manifest His presence. Most of us can remember times when we have experienced God's presence with us. If you ask people to share a testimony of God's work in their lives, they will almost always say things like this:

- "I knew God was speaking to me."
- "I felt I was surrounded by His love."
- "The room was filled with a strange light."
- "I had a strange sensation . . . I felt heat all over my body, my hands were tingling . . . I didn't know what it was."
- "I sensed God in a way I can't explain . . . I didn't see anything, but He was there, face to face."
- "I didn't understand what was happening. I couldn't stop weeping; tears were rolling down my cheeks, and God was there with me!"

These are all testimonies of people who experienced God's presence. At a given time and place, they heard God's voice, they saw a vision, and they had a physical response to His presence.

Anytime you sense God's presence in a tangible way, what you are experiencing is His glory. In His presence everything changes! In God's presence, we find salvation, repentance, empowering, healing, provision and fulfillment. Most of the significant experiences we have with God take place when His glory comes down.

But God doesn't want His glory to be a rare occurrence. He wants us to seek His presence, to dwell in His presence, to live with a continual experience of His power and goodness!

Celebrating God's Glory

The Feast of Tabernacles is a celebration of God's glory, and God promised a special blessing for those who would celebrate this feast. It's a time to remember past experiences of His glory. It's a time to seek His face and experience His glory now. It's a time to call out to God for a fresh outpouring of His glory in the new year.

Tabernacles is a time to enjoy the Lord and celebrate His goodness. Leviticus 23:40 says, "Rejoice before the LORD your God for seven days" (*NIV*). Deuteronomy 16:14-15 says, "Be joyful at your feast. . . . For the LORD your God will bless you . . . and your joy will be complete" (*NIV*).

Part of celebrating Tabernacles involves bringing an offering as an expression of thanks to God. Deuteronomy 16:16-17 says, "No man should appear before the LORD empty-handed: Each of you must bring a gift in proportion to the way the LORD your God has blessed you" (*NIV*). When we express our thankfulness in giving, we open our hearts to receive even more.

Tabernacles is a time to celebrate the fact that God tabernacles with His people. He wants His glory to be a normal part of our experience. He tabernacled with Israel in the wilderness, He tabernacled on earth in Jesus, and He continues to tabernacle with us today through His Spirit!

Finding Ways to Celebrate

As you celebrate Tabernacles, call out to God for His glory to come and dwell with you. Here are some ways to celebrate this feast:

- Set aside time to tabernacle with God and listen for His voice.
- Spend relaxed time in God's Word.
- Get together with family and friends and tell stories about the goodness of God.
- Plan to have a meal that consists of everyone's favorite food.
- Praise God and thank Him for all that He has done for you and everyone you know.

Building a Sukkah

Especially if you have children, you might want to celebrate this feast by building a sukkah. As discussed earlier, a sukkah is a tent or temporary shelter. Nehemiah 8:15-17 says:

"Go out into the hill country and bring back branches from olive and wild olive trees, and from myrtles, palms and shade trees, to make booths". . . So the people went out and brought back branches and built themselves booths on their roofs, in their courtyards. . . . The whole company . . . built booths. . . . And their joy was very great.

Although the sukkahs Nehemiah described were to be built of branches, a sukkah can be made of fabric, wood or some other material. However, it must be a temporary structure in order to properly reflect the temporary shelters the Israelites lived in when they left Egypt.

The sukkah represents God coming down and dwelling in a temporary shelter with them. Originally, God told the Israelites to live in sukkahs the entire week of Tabernacles. Today, many people simply spend some time each day in the sukkah, perhaps to eat a meal together as a family.

Building a sukkah offers a wonderful way to teach children what God has done for us. When our kids were young, there was nothing they liked more than to make a tent. They would make tents in the living room, draping sheets and blankets over the chairs. They would build forts outside with tree branches. Can you imagine how excited your kids would be to learn that God has set aside a special time for your whole family to make a tent? God wants you to "make a tent" and use it to teach your children about how God rescued Israel and how His glory came down and lived with them.

So why not build a sukkah? If you don't have room to build a full-sized one, you can build a model, or you can use sheets and chairs and build one in your living room.

Have the whole family get in the sukkah and have a picnic together as you tell the stories of God's tabernacles. As a family, you can decorate your sukkah, you can sleep in your sukkah, and you can even party in your sukkah. Whatever you do, remember these three things:

1. God tabernacles with His people.
2. He wants you to enjoy the fun of celebrating with Him.
3. He wants you to anticipate His glory.

Chuck D. Pierce and Robert Heidler

Ask God to tabernacle with you, and expect His presence to visit you as you seek Him!

Experiencing God's Presence

A few years ago during our Tabernacles celebration, I taught a course about the feasts of God. Eleanor, a friend of ours from Alaska, came down to attend the course. (Eleanor is an Eskimo and has an unusual sensitivity to the Lord and His Spirit.)

During the week, we invited Eleanor and some other friends to our home to sit with us in our sukkah. We had done this with other friends on previous nights, and it was always a joyful celebration. We would talk and laugh, just enjoying the fun of being in a sukkah together.

With Eleanor, though, the experience was different. She had just heard my teaching about Tabernacles and came with the expectation that the glory of God wanted to meet with her in the sukkah. As soon as she sat down in the sukkah, she closed her eyes and began to pray very intently for God's glory and presence to come.

We were amazed! Almost immediately the glory of God fell! The place was filled with His presence in such great power that we could hardly stand up. It was wonderful!

I learned an important lesson from Eleanor. I had been going into the sukkah as a ritual. It was the "thing to do" to celebrate the feast. It was a fun ritual—but still a ritual. I had not come into the sukkah seeking or expecting God's presence, and all I had experienced was a fun ritual. But when Eleanor came with an expectation of God's presence, that's exactly what she (and we) received!

As you celebrate these feasts, you can celebrate them as wonderful rituals, ways of remembering what God did in the past, and ways of identifying with the Jewish people today. They can be very meaningful. You can go away from them blessed and satisfied and yet miss the greatest blessing. If we celebrate God's appointed times only as rituals, we miss the incredible fact that God truly desires to meet with us during these celebrations.

I would encourage you, as you celebrate Tabernacles, to seek and expect nothing less than the awesome presence of God to meet with you!

Celebrating Jesus' Birth at Tabernacles

Here's another reason for Christians to celebrate the Feast of Tabernacles: This appointed time was probably Jesus' birthday!

Some people say we can't know when Jesus was really born, only when He wasn't born. We do know, for example, that Jesus wasn't born on December 25, because Israeli shepherds didn't keep their flocks out in the fields that time of year. But maybe we *can* know His birthday.

In Luke 1:5, Luke gives us an interesting piece of information. He tells us that Zechariah, the father of John the Baptist, was a priest of the order of Abiyah. He goes on to say that while Zechariah was burning incense in the Temple, an angel appeared and told him his barren wife, Elizabeth, would conceive and bear a son, and he would be called John. So Zechariah returned home, and nine months later John the Baptist was born! What's interesting is that Luke goes out of his way to tell us that Zechariah was a priest of the order of Abiyah. Most of us, when we read a phrase like that, just move on to the next verse. But everything in the Bible is there for a purpose. Why is it important that we know this detail?

Back in 1 Chronicles 24:7-18, we're told that the various priestly families took turns serving in the Temple, according to a fixed order every year. Zechariah's family, the family of Abiyah, was the eighth family in that rotation. Doing some calculations based on 1 Chronicles 24, we can determine that priests of Zechariah's order would have taken a turn serving in the Temple every year between the twelfth and the eighteenth day of the Hebrew month of Sivan. This chronology introduces an interesting chain of events:

1. Zechariah would have finished his week of Temple service on the eighteenth of Sivan and gone home to his wife, Elizabeth. Assuming Zechariah and Elizabeth got right to work on their assignment, it would not be unlikely to assume that Elizabeth conceived John the Baptist shortly thereafter, around the twenty-fifth day of Sivan.

2. If John the Baptist was conceived on the twenty-fifth day of Sivan, and Elizabeth had a normal pregnancy of 285

days, John the Baptist would have been born on the fifteenth day of the month of Nisan. That just happens to
be the Feast of Passover. (The Jews have long believed
that Elijah would come at Passover. Even today, observant Jewish families set an extra place at the Passover
table for Elijah. So it's very appropriate that John the
Baptist, who came "in the spirit and power of Elijah,"
would be born on Passover [Luke 1:17].)

3. Luke 1:36 tells us that Jesus was conceived in Mary's
   womb when Elizabeth was six months pregnant. If Elizabeth began her pregnancy on the twenty-fifth day of
   Sivan, she would have begun her sixth month on the
   twenty-fifth day of Kislev, the first day of Hanukkah.
   (Hanukkah is known as the Feast of Lights. What a perfect time for Jesus, the light of the world, to be conceived!)

4. If Mary conceived Jesus on the twenty-fifth day of Kislev
   and had a normal 285 day pregnancy, Jesus would have
   been born on the fifteenth day of the month Tishri, which
   just happens to be the first day of the Feast of Tabernacles!

This chronology certainly does not prove that Jesus was born
at Tabernacles, but it does fit with the New Testament accounts.
The apostle John chose an interesting word to describe the birth of
Jesus: "The Word [Jesus] became flesh and tabernacled [literal trans-
lation] among us and we beheld His glory" (John 1:14).

The birth of Jesus at Tabernacles would also shed light on the
traditional Christmas story from Luke's gospel. Luke 2:7 tells us
that Mary "brought forth" her child and "laid him in a manger."
That's the usual English translation, but the Greek word for
"manger" is *phatne*, which can be translated several ways, including
"manger, stall, stable, or temporary shelter."

The Hebrew equivalent of the word *phatne* is sukkah (temporary
shelter or booth), so you could also translate Luke 2:7 this way: Mary
"brought forth" her child and "laid Him in a sukkah." Of course,

during a feast time, every room in every inn would have been filled with pilgrims coming to celebrate the feast, but at Tabernacles, there would have been sukkahs everywhere!

So on that Feast of Tabernacles, the glory of God came into the sukkah as Jesus the Messiah was born!

Jesus' Promise for Tabernacles

Jesus gave us an important promise at Tabernacles. In John 7, we find the account of Jesus speaking during the celebration of this feast: "On the last and greatest day of the Feast, Jesus stood and said in a loud voice, 'If anyone is thirsty, let him come to me and drink. Whoever believes in me, . . . streams of living water will flow from within him'" (John 7:37-38, *NIV*). It is important to understand what Jesus was saying here: One of the key elements of Tabernacles is outpouring.

Every year at Tabernacles, the high priest performed a prophetic act. He would bring water from the pool of Siloam, carry it up to the Temple and pour it out beside the altar. This symbolized an appeal to God for the latter rain to fall on the land. It also symbolized an appeal to God for the outpouring of His Spirit, the spiritual rain spoken of in Joel 2: "I will pour out my Spirit on all people. Your sons and daughters will prophesy, your old men will dream dreams, your young men will see visions" (v. 28, *NIV*). The high priest's act of pouring out the water from Siloam was repeated every day of the feast, culminating on the last day, the "greatest day" of the feast. This was the climax of the Feast of Tabernacles, and the climax of the entire cycle of feasts.

As the priest brought water from the pool of Siloam and carried it up to the Temple, huge crowds would have accompanied him. The Temple court would have been packed with people anxious to watch this important ceremony. As the priest stood beside the altar and prepared to pour out the water, a hush would have fallen over the crowd. Then, as the priest began to pour out the water, Jesus stood and cried out in a loud voice, "If anyone is thirsty, let him come to me and drink. Whoever believes in me . . . streams of living water will flow from within him" (John 7:37-38, *NIV*).

That's the climax and the goal of all of the feasts! As we walk with God through His yearly cycle of life, He wants to bring us to the place where we experience His overflowing life! That's why God gave us His appointed times. He wants us to receive His life:

- He wants to remind us of His great deeds of the past to build our faith.
- He wants to remind us of His promises for the future to give us vision.
- He wants to accomplish spiritual transactions in us to break Satan's power.
- He wants to link us into His cycle of life so that we receive ever-increasing blessing.

That's why the Feast of Tabernacles is the third appointed time we need to celebrate in order to gain a mindset to prosper. Tabernacles is about receiving the overflowing life of God. It's about experiencing God's glory and dwelling in His presence!

When we experience God's river of life, everything changes. We gain fresh vision for the future. Our faith is increased. More than that, the outpoured life of God brings us an explosion of supernatural creativity!

As you study Church history, you'll discover that every great move of the Spirit brought a flood of new songs, new hymns and new creative expressions to the Church. That's what the presence of God does. All true creativity is from God, and the closer we get to Him, the more creativity we experience. In God's presence, we see things we've never seen before. We see new ways to overcome obstacles and solve problems. We gain strategies for increase. We receive new songs, new books and new inventions. The result is prosperity.

God wants to draw us into His presence and bring us into a higher level of prosperity each year.

12

ROSH CHODESH: GIVING TO GOD THE FIRSTFRUITS

CHUCK D. PIERCE

So far, we've looked at several of God's cycles. First was God's plan for Sabbath, a weekly cycle of rest, so that every week we are strengthened as we pause to celebrate God's goodness. Sabbath was designed to teach us God's goodness and release faith to walk in His blessing.

We next looked at God's yearly cycle of appointed times that are designed to draw us into God's presence throughout each year. God designed these times to break off Satan's oppression and cause us to dwell in His glory. Celebrating the feasts teaches us the ways of God so we can move forward and inherit His promises. Each feast is linked with the dimension of giving, worship and faith—actions that produce a threefold cord not easily broken (see Eccles. 4:12).

God also has given us a monthly cycle. Wouldn't you be excited to discover a new holiday you didn't know existed? For some of you, perhaps this chapter will do just that. While many Christians don't observe Sabbath and the biblical feasts, most do recognize that these observances are in the Bible.

Yet God has given us a monthly cycle of which most Christians are not even aware: what the Jews call Rosh Chodesh. This holiday is important to God, yet most churches never talk about or honor this cycle.

The Meaning of Rosh Chodesh

Because most Christians have never heard of Rosh Chodesh, we need to begin by defining what it is. Rosh Chodesh is Hebrew for "head of the month." It is a joyful celebration to the Lord, held on the first day of every month. It's a time to gather together to seek God and seek direction for the month ahead.

The Bible sometimes calls this celebration a New Moon festival (see Num. 29:6). That may sound strange to some Christians, because we know astrologers use the sun, moon and stars to predict the future. We don't want to have anything to do with that! So why would the Bible call this a New Moon festival?

Understanding the Signs in the Sky

Because of the prevalence of astrology, many Christians are frightened to have anything to do with the sky. Robert Heidler told me how, many years ago, he and Linda had a decorative globe in their living room but decided to get rid of it. Robert shared:

> One day, when we were looking at it, we noticed that it had the symbols of constellations printed on it. We recoiled in horror that we had allowed something related to astrology into our house. We immediately disposed of the globe. In studying history, I learned that many first-century synagogues had the signs of the zodiac imprinted on the floor in mosaic tiles. I was again horrified. Why would the Jews "dabble in astrology" when the Bible speaks so clearly against it.[1]

Of course, the real problem was a bad case of stellarphobia on their part! They had been taught to think that the constellations overhead were somehow bad, something occultic, and something to be avoided. The problem was, as Robert stated it, "I had never studied the Bible on the subject."

The Bible teaches that the sun, moon and stars were established by God and set in place to reveal His glory. In Psalm 8 we read, "O LORD, our Lord, . . . [You] have displayed Your splendor above the heavens! . . . When I consider Your heavens, the work of Your fingers, the moon and the stars, which You have ordained . . . O LORD, our LORD, how majestic is Your name in all the earth!" (*NASB*). In Job 9:8-9, we read, "[God] alone stretches out the heavens. . . . He is the Maker of the Bear and Orion, the Pleiades and the constellations of the south" (*NIV*). In Psalm 19:1, David wrote, "The heavens declare the glory of God; the skies proclaim the work of his hands" (*NIV*). So, according to the Bible, there is nothing evil or occult about the sun, the moon or the constellations!

It's true that the enemy has tried to pervert what God has made. Satan's plan to pervert the heavens is called astrology. It's an attempt to discern the future from the stars . . . to gain revelation without having to seek God and hear His voice! Astrology is a form of divination, and it's a sin. But some Christians have been so focused on avoiding astrology that they look at the heavens as something evil.

We've forgotten that God gave us the heavens. The heavens are not there to tell us the future, but God does want to use the heavens to give us revelation. In Genesis 1:14, God says, "Let there be lights in the expanse of the heavens to separate the day from the night, and let them be for signs and for seasons" (*NASB*). Notice that God uses two significant words to describe the heavens: "signs" and "seasons."

"Signs" is translated from the Hebrew word *oth*, which means a signal, omen or warning. God gives warnings and signals in the heavens. The wise men saw Jesus' star, a signal from God that the Messiah had come. The Bible says that in the last days there will be signs in the sky (see Matt. 24:30; Acts 2:19).

"Seasons" is translated from the Hebrew word *mo'ed*, which means an appointed time, appointment, a fixed time or season. *Mo'ed* is the same word used for a biblical feast or festival. God tells us that the stars are there to mark our seasons and are particularly used to remind us of the appointed times to meet with Him. So the heavens are a revelation of God's *times*.

The Jews understood this, and we need to understand it as well. God arranged the sun, moon and stars in the heavens to establish His times in our lives.

God's Clock in the Sky

The Jews saw the universe as a giant clock designed to reveal the appointed times of God. Our days are marked by the cycle of the sun, and the time of day is marked by the sun's position in the sky. As we count the passing days, we come into God's weekly cycle: *Shabbat!* God said, "Count off six days, and rest the seventh."

Then, 12 times a year, God arranged for the moon to go through a complete cycle. That divided our year into 12 months. The word "month" comes from the same root as the word "moon"! A month,

originally, was the time it took the moon to go through a complete cycle. Each new month began when the new moon appeared overhead,
beginning another lunar cycle. So every month, the Jews watched for
the new moon to appear. When they saw it, they knew a new month
had begun. (So a New Moon is really a new-month festival.) When the
new moon was visible in the sky, the Jews made the declaration, "The
new month has begun!" That was the signal to begin a joyful celebration to the Lord called Rosh Chodesh. It was a time to gather to the
prophets and gain God's revelation for the month ahead!

Rosh Chodesh and the Firstfruits Principle

Rosh Chodesh is an expression of the firstfruits principle (which is
something else many Christians don't understand). So, to understand
Rosh Chodesh, we need to understand firstfruits.

Deuteronomy 26 tells us that when Israel entered the Promised
Land and received their first harvest there, they were to put the first
portion of that harvest in a basket and take it to God's sanctuary. At
the sanctuary, they were to give the firstfruits offering to the priest and
publicly declare the goodness and faithfulness of God! God promised
if they would honor Him by giving Him some of the first of all the
crops they produced, He would set them high above all the nations for
praise, fame and honor; and they would be a people holy to the Lord.
That is an incredible blessing to receive for one basket of produce!

We see from this that there is something very important about
firstfruits. In fact, firstfruits is a major key to living in the favor and
prosperity of God. Why was firstfruits so important? That firstfruits
offering wasn't the largest gift of the year. When Israel brought in the
full harvest, one-tenth of the whole crop would be given to God as a
tithe. Firstfruits was much less than that—often just one small sheaf
of wheat! Yet it was key to a massive blessing!

The First Is Always Special!

To understand why firstfruits is significant, we must understand that
in all of life, there is something very special about the first! We've all
been to restaurants and businesses and seen a dollar bill in a frame

on a wall next to the cash register. In that frame is the very first dollar that business ever made. (Sometimes it's even labeled "Our First Dollar.") That business has brought in many more dollars since that one, but none of them was framed; only that first dollar was special.

We recognize that is true in most things. All of us remember who built the first airplane, but very few know who built the second airplane. We all know that Neal Armstrong was the first human being to set foot on the moon, but who remembers the name of the second human being on the moon? (Correct answer: Buzz Aldrin.) We all remember our first car, our first date and our first kiss! The first is special! God says an important way to honor Him is to give Him our first!

To understand the principle of firstfruits, think of the business owners with that framed dollar bill on the wall. Suppose those business owners give their lives to the Lord and are so overwhelmed with love for God that they look for ways to show it. The owners begin to tithe and give offerings but still feel as if they cannot adequately show God their appreciation.

Then one day, the business owners see that framed dollar on the wall—the first dollar the business ever made. It's very special. So, to honor God as the source of all their blessing, they take that dollar and give it to God. That is a firstfruits offering. You can give a firstfruits offering from every first in your life!

Robert likes to share, "At the beginning of every year, I try to write my first check of the year as a firstfruits offering to God. It may be $10. It may be $100. It may be $1,000. We have learned through the years to always try to seek God on what our personal firstfruits offering should be. When we get income from a new source, we try to give the first portion of that income as a firstfruits offering. When our garden produces its first vegetables, the first ones I pick I give as a firstfruits offering."

Firstfruits is honoring God by giving back to Him the first and best of all He has given us! The amount of the gift is between you and God. It can be a little or a lot. The key is that you have chosen to put God first.

Firstfruits and the Tithe

Many assume that if they tithe, they are giving the firstfruits. That is not the case. Tithing is one kind of giving, but firstfruits is something very different! The Bible actually describes three categories of giving. We see these clearly presented in Nehemiah 12:44: "Men were appointed to be in charge of the storerooms for the contributions [or offerings], firstfruits and tithes" (*NIV*) Nehemiah 10:35-39 describes these in more detail:

1. *Firstfruits*—Verses 35-37 tell us to "[bring] to the house of the LORD each year the firstfruits of our crops and of every fruit tree . . . the firstborn of our sons and of our cattle, . . . the first of our ground meal, of our grain offerings, of the fruit of all our trees and of our new wine and oil" (*NIV*).

2. *Tithes*—Verse 37 tells us to "bring a tithe of our crops to the Levites, for it is the Levites who collect the tithes" (*NIV*).

3. *Contributions (offerings, or voluntary expressions of thanksgiving)*—Verse 39 tells us to "bring . . . contributions of grain, new wine and oil" (*NIV*).

Sometimes people will ask, "I tithe, so why don't I see the full level of blessing the Bible promises?" Part of the answer to that question is that tithing is just part of the picture! The tithe is 10 percent of your income, given in obedience to God. It is something God has claimed as His own. Strictly speaking, you don't give a tithe; you pay a tithe. The tithe is like a tax you pay as a citizen of God's kingdom.

The contribution, or offering, is anything given as an expression of thanksgiving to God. It is an act of worship in acknowledgment of God's blessing. The firstfruits offering is a special way to honor God. By giving God the first of what you receive, you acknowledge that He is truly first in your life and is honored above everything else you hold special. Specific blessings are promised for every kind of giving, but the fullness of blessing is released when we worship Him with all three!

The Significance of Firstfruits

What does firstfruits giving accomplish? Let's look at four things

First, firstfruits giving honors God as your source. It is a declaration that your blessings come from God!

Second, firstfruits giving sanctifies (makes holy) the rest of your income! Romans 11:16 tells us, "If the . . . firstfruits is holy, then the whole batch is holy" (*NIV*).

Third, firstfruits giving releases the fullness of God's blessing. Ezekiel 44:30 tells us, "Give . . . the first portion . . . so that a blessing may rest on your household" (*NIV*).

Fourth, firstfruits giving opens us to receive God's overflowing provision. Proverbs 3:9-10 promises that if you "honor the LORD . . . with the firstfruits of all your crops; then your barns will be filled to overflowing, and your vats will brim over with new wine" (*NIV*).

The Blessing Released by Firstfruits

There are many biblical examples of firstfruits releasing incredible blessing. Isaac was the son of promise, the firstfruits of Abraham's offspring. But before the rest of Abraham's blessing could be released, Abraham was tested. Would he be willing to put Isaac on the altar, giving God his first and best? When he passed this test, all the promised blessings were released to him!

God promised Israel all the cities of Canaan, with the first city being Jericho. God said they could keep the plunder of all the other cities, "but all the silver and gold [in Jericho], and vessels of bronze and iron, are consecrated to the LORD" (Josh. 6:19). Jericho was the firstfruits of the Promised Land. When the spoils of Jericho were given to the Lord, the entire land was sanctified, and the rest of the plunder was Israel's to enjoy.

Later, when Hannah gave her first son, Samuel, to the Lord, God blessed her with more sons, with the bonus that the entire nation was transformed. When God gave His firstborn Son, Jesus, the result was bringing "many sons to glory" (Heb. 2:10)!

Firstfruits and Rosh Chodesh

God wants us to develop a mentality of firstfruits in every area of life, and that includes giving God the firstfruits of our time. Again, remember that giving God the firstfruits is *always a key to releasing His blessing.* Just as giving God the firstfruits of our money releases His blessing on our finances, so giving God the firstfruits of our time releases His blessing on our time.

A key expression of the firstfruits is Rosh Chodesh, which is why the Jews celebrated a special feast at the start of the month. They sought God's *favor* by dedicating the firstfruits of the month to Him! They would gather in the Temple to watch for the new moon, and when it appeared, they would hold a special praise celebration!

In holding this new-month celebration, they were declaring that the very first thing they would do with their time that month was joyfully celebrate to the Lord. That firstfruits principle still applies today. As we honor God with the first of our time, all of our time is set apart (made special, or holy), and we are positioned to walk in blessing all month!

Rosh Chodesh in the Old Testament

The Old Testament mentions a number of people who observed Rosh Chodesh. Here are a few examples:

- David (see 1 Sam. 20:5)
- Solomon (see 2 Chron. 2:4)
- Nehemiah (see Neh. 10:33)
- The Shunammite woman (see 2 Kings 4:23)

As we read the Old Testament, we find that the Rosh Chodesh celebration was characterized by some specific things:

- It was to be a joyful celebration (see Ps. 81:3-7; Hos. 2:11).
- It was to be a day of rest—businesses were closed (see Amos 8:5).
- It was a day to offer special offerings to God (see Num. 28:11-15).
- It was a day of worship (see Num. 10:10; Isa. 66:23).
- It was a day of celebration and feasting—no fasting was permitted (see 1 Sam. 20:5).
- It was a day to seek the prophet, to gain revelation for the month ahead (see 2 Kings 4:23).

Rosh Chodesh in Jesus' Day

By Jesus' day, Rosh Chodesh had become one of the most important celebrations for God's people. It began with the sighting of the new moon. Sumptuous meals were prepared in the Temple courts, and people crowded in. Everyone eagerly searched the sky for the first glimpse of the new moon. When two witnesses confirmed that they could see the new moon, the Sanhedrin leaders stood and declared: "The new month is sanctified!" and a jubilant celebration before the Lord began!

Unfortunately, there has been some bad teaching in the Church concerning biblical feasts. This teaching has even affected the way some have translated the New Testament! Many are taught that Christians are not supposed to celebrate things like Rosh Chodesh. *The Living Bible* translation is one of the worst offenders. When you look up Colossians 2:16-17 in this version, what you find is this:

> Don't let anyone criticize you . . . for not celebrating Jewish holidays or feasts or new moon ceremonies or Sabbaths. For these were only temporary rules that ended when Christ came. They were only shadows of the real thing—of Christ himself.

In reading this passage, our natural response would be, "I must not celebrate a New Moon!" But *The Living Bible* gives a bad paraphrase and actually adds words that drastically change the meaning of the passage. If you were to read this verse in the original Greek (or in a good translation), you would be shocked at the difference. Colossians 2:16-17 does not say, "Don't let anyone criticize you . . . for not celebrating Jewish holidays or feasts or new moon ceremonies or Sabbaths." It does not say that "these were only temporary rules that ended." Those words are not even suggested in this passage!

What does Colossians 2:16 really say? A literal translation of this verse is, "Let no one sit in judgment on you with regard to a New Moon or a Sabbath." This verse is not teaching against observing the feasts; it's teaching against a legalistic attitude!

The Pharisees had tried to turn the joyful celebration of Rosh Chodesh into a legalistic burden and had developed all sorts of rules about what should and should not be done. They sat in judgment on everyone to make sure it was all done "right." In Colossians 2:16, Paul is warning the Church not to fall into that trap! This verse is a warning about pharisaic legalism. Paul is saying: Don't judge each other by how you celebrate this feast. Rosh Chodesh is not a legalistic ritual where someone needs to judge you on whether you do it 'right.' "

The monthly firstfruits celebration is to be a joyful time to experience the Lord. It is designed to give us a picture of a wonderful spiritual reality. I love the way the *Amplified Bible* translates these verses:

> Therefore let no one sit in judgment on you in matters of food and drink, or with regard to a feast day or a New Moon or a Sabbath. Such [things] are only the shadow of things that are to come, and they have only a symbolic value. But the reality (the substance, the solid fact of what is foreshadowed, the body of it) belongs to Christ.

Notice that it says that New Moons have "symbolic value." They point us to the reality of what we have in Christ.

The *Amplified Bible* really describes Rosh Chodesh in terms that are similar to the way we describe the Lord's Supper. The Lord's Supper is a celebration that has incredible symbolic value. At the Lord's Supper, the elements themselves can never save you. You can drink all the grape juice (or wine) you can hold, and you can eat all the communion wafers your stomach can hold, but those acts will not bring you salvation. The Lord's Supper is not the reality. It is a picture—with great symbolic value—that points to what Jesus accomplished on the cross.

In the same way, Rosh Chodesh is a picture of what Jesus came to do. It was designed to teach us about Jesus by picturing the reality of the new beginning that is found in Jesus. As Rosh Chodesh celebrates the beginning of the new month, it gives a reminder that Jesus brings life out of death!

Reasons for Celebrating Rosh Chodesh

Why would believers in Jesus want to celebrate Rosh Chodesh? Here are three reasons:

1. It gives us an opportunity to honor, praise and thank God for what He has done for us in the previous month.

2. It is a time to worship God, to inquire of Him about the month ahead and to feast with Him.

3. By giving God the first of everything, we sanctify our whole month and are positioned to receive His blessings throughout the month.

At Glory of Zion, we have a monthly celebration we call our Firstfruits Harvest Gathering. It's our new-month celebration. We come together at the start of every Hebrew month for a time of praise and worship, to give firstfruits offerings, to fellowship, and to gain prophetic perspective on the month ahead. This gathering is one of the most popular things we do. As people come and see the blessings released in their lives at this celebration, they want to come back and celebrate every month.

People see that when they honor God by giving Him the first and best of their income, time and abilities, the result is a great outpouring of His blessings. When you gain a mindset for firstfruits, you truly have a mindset to prosper.

We Must Keep Going

Many of us never move fully into God's promises because we quit moving forward. Unless we continually renew our minds and embrace a mindset to prosper, we can be captured in old ways of thinking and fail to move forward in God's cycle of blessing.

There are many elements and circumstances that influence our times and seasons in the earth. Adverse circumstances may come into our lives, blockades may arise on our path, or our vision may get blocked. We must never forget that what we see in the natural must be processed in the spiritual. We must continue to grow and mature spiritually. We must keep going!

Jesus called all of His disciples and those He was teaching to follow Him. In the process of time, if we keep our face set like a flint—just as Jesus demonstrated to us when He walked the earth realm—we will reach our destination.

It was over a period of three years that Jesus taught His followers what they needed to know so that history would be affected and God's kingdom would be advanced. God stepped out of time and came to the earth to save us. Jesus was the perfect image of God the Father, and He taught us how to walk "in time."

Here are some time-sensitive events that I note in *Interpreting the Times* to which we can all relate:

1. We Must Go Beyond Our Current Levels of Celebration and Religious Ritual

In John 2, Jesus and His mother were invited to a wedding. His disciples attended with Him. Weddings in Jewish culture were events of celebration. The celebrations were meant to last seven days. Prophetically, a wedding represented the Feast of Tabernacles. During the wedding ceremony, the vows would be exchanged midweek, and then they would celebrate until the Sabbath. In the wedding at Cana, the celebration was coming to a close too early. The wedding party had run out of wine, which was a disgrace. Mary said to Jesus, " 'They have no wine.' Jesus said to her, 'Woman, what does your concern have to do with Me? My hour has not yet come' " (John 2:3-4).

Timing is so important when beginning a new thrust or season of life. Mary continued by encouraging the servants to do whatever Jesus told them to do. Jesus then asked them to bring water pots that were normally used for religious purification ceremonies. Once those pots were filled to the brim with water, He turned the water into wine.

Then the wedding host exclaimed, "Every man at the beginning sets out the good wine, and when the guests have well drunk, then the inferior. You have kept the good wine until now!" (v. 10). The wedding party had advanced to the next level of celebration. What had been used for religious ritual now was used for festive celebration. This was a picture of what was to come. Jesus said He did this because this act was the beginning of the revelation of His glory, so that His disciples would believe.

At first, this does not appear to be the beginning of the next phases of Jesus' life and teaching. Jesus could do nothing but what the Father told Him to do. Evidently, the Father told Him, "Begin now to reveal Your glory." Once He started revealing His glory, He knew He would have to go all the way until that revelation became complete in the fullness of time.

2. We Must Go Beyond Our Poverty Way of Thinking and Enter into a Harvest-Multiplication Thought Mode

First Kings 17 is the story of the prophet Elijah coming on the scene to deal with the spiritual atmosphere of idolatry that had overtaken Israel. He began by making a spiritual decree and legislating the heavens. He declared the heavens would produce no dew or rain except at his word. This decree affected him along with everyone else. He left where he was and went to the brook called Cherith, which eventually dried up because of no rain.

To find a supply of water, he had to keep moving. The Lord told him to go to Zarephath, where he would find a widow at the gates of the city. The drought that he had proclaimed had affected the entire region.

When he arrived at Zarephath, he saw a widow who was picking up sticks and preparing for her last meal. This was the woman who God said would take care of him. However, this woman was filled with a poverty mentality and with despair. He instructed her to go home, take whatever she had left in her cupboard, and prepare him a meal *first*. By faith, she did this. Her obedience created enough supply for them to be sustained over the next three years. Once she broke through her poverty and gave her *firstfruits* to the prophet, supply did not run out.

3. We Must Also Go Beyond Our Debt Mentality and Know that the Lord Can Free Us to Accomplish His Purposes

In 2 Kings 4, Elisha had his own experience with a widow. This widow was in terrible debt. The debtors were coming to take her entire inheritance, including her children. She went to the prophet and explained her situation to him. In verse 2, Elisha says, " 'What shall I do for you? Tell me, what do you have in the house?' And she said, 'Your maidservant has nothing in the house but a jar of oil.' "

If we understand the *law of use,* we can get past our debt structure. The prophet told her to go to all of her neighbors, borrow all their vessels, and then pour all her available oil until all of the vessels were filled. Upon selling the oil, she would have enough to overcome her debt. Do not allow debt structures to put you into debt. God will give you a strategy to break the debt structure that has come to control your times and future.[2]

See Past a Spirit of Poverty

In my book *Time to Defeat the Devil,* I note the following about how to see past a spirit of poverty:

> The church is in an incredible season of change, and I believe we are all sensing those changes in us and around us. There is a growing awareness for how the Lord longs to see His people prosper—even in times of hardship. I can hear the Lord saying to us, "What you seed will begin to produce great fruit." There is a grace for our offerings to multiply—thirty to a hundred-fold—if we are obedient with what we have been given to steward. We can gain victory through giving in order to break the curse of robbing God in our generational bloodline. This is a time to bud! Our giving returns in multiplied form. Everything that we have seeded we can see multiply, blossom, and bud! Proverbs 11:24 says, "There is one who scatters, yet increases more; and there is one who withholds more than is right, but it leads to poverty."
>
> One cycle that I feel we must break to come into a new level of increase is linked to the spirit of poverty. In a materialistic society, this spirit tends to blind us from seeing the will of God. We must declare victory over the spirit of poverty! This spirit has violated God's perfect order and produced instability in many individuals. I feel that the Lord is saying that we need to take a violent and passionate stand on behalf of the Body of Christ concerning this spirit—that we must press through difficulties and storms to force an atmospheric change.
>
> Poverty creates an atmosphere. This spirit encircles you or your sphere of authority to create lack. No matter how much this spirit attempts to find a foothold in your life, this atmosphere can be invaded with the atmosphere of blessing and

glory from heaven. We can see His glory in our lives. Noah found favor in His eye. The heavens and earth realigned during his day. We can find favor and heaven can come into our atmosphere and defeat poverty. Glory and wealth are synonymous.

The Body of Christ needs to see restoration in our provision! Restoration is always linked with multiplication. Debt and past financial defeats in our lives need to reverse. A spirit of poverty that has held our generational bloodlines in captivity, keeping us from the fullness of the prosperity that God has for us, must be broken. The Lord is breaking begging off His people. He is making us a people of faith. He will change the identity of His people from beggars to kings! Ask Him to reveal poverty now. See how poverty works in your life.

In Joseph's life in Genesis 45:11 we find: "There I will provide for you, lest you and your household, and all that you have, come to poverty; for there are still five years of famine." Many individuals are afraid of leaving the familiar to receive their provision for the future. The famine in Canaan created a move to Egypt for all of God's covenant people. Egypt was not the promise, but was the necessary place of provision for a season. . . .

If you are sent to war but lose the battle, you wear a reproach until you gain a subsequent victory. Many in the body are afraid to war. But war is necessary in order to conquer our enemies and take possession of what has been promised to us. War is receiving grace to fight (see 1 Tim. 6:12; 2 Tim. 2:3-4). War is receiving the necessary armor for victory (Eph. 6:11-17). War produces an opportunity for us to enter into victory (Rev. 3:21).

The Lord used armies to bring His people out of Egypt (Exod. 12:51) with a trumpet sound and a battle cry. Later, He brought them out with the Ark, the presence of God (1 Sam. 4:5-6). He used forces of nature when necessary to help them defeat their enemies (Josh. 10). God always releases strategies that enable us to plunder the enemy's holdings, to prosper and to stand. (See Matt. 10; Eph. 6.) He has a banner of victory over us. While Jehovah Nissi puts a banner over us to cover us, the Lord Sabaoth sends the hosts of heaven to help us. He is God of the armies of Earth (1 Sam. 17:45), and God of the unseen armies of angels (1 Kings 22:19). He is the Lord of the armies (see Rom. 9:29). He already has victory for you! See your victory over poverty.

We must hear how poverty speaks and operate in the opposite spirit. We are required to combat poverty by being kind and generous to others. Like Ruth in Boaz's field, we combat poverty by allowing people to glean in our vineyard and provide them with access to our excess (Ruth 2). We combat poverty by developing strategies to help those who have been ravaged by systemic poverty. In other words, we help others gain wisdom on how to break out of the system that Satan is using to hold them captive financially. We are also required to develop reaping strategies (Amos 9:13). When we do this, we overcome, and our increase will go from multiplication to multiplication. . . .

Prosperity is linked with finding help along your road. As children there were several Bible passages that many of us were taught. Psalm 23 was one we memorized and was used for comfort in distress and affliction. However, most of us never realized this psalm really says, "I will lead you in your path of prosperity through paths of righteousness for MY name's sake."

In Hebrew, the word path is `agol, which means, "to be round or a cycle." The Lord guides us in the cycles of righteousness. The enemy hates the thought of us staying on a path of righteousness because he knows that we will see the fullness of God's plan for our lives. God already has our path of prosperity in place. This path or cycle is linked with the yearly return received from the Feasts of Yahweh.

The Hebrew word *chag*, or festival, means to make a cycle. If we understand the feasts, then we understand cycles. We can be led properly, begin to prosper, move into abundance, and have no lack when we stay in the timing of God. "The Lord is My Shepherd, I shall not want because He leads me in the cycle of prosperity. I will see My blessings wherever I walk. Even through the Valley of the Shadow of Death, I can celebrate Him and not get out of time, and see my blessings!"[3]

Celebrating Firstfruits Keeps Us Seeking

In previous chapters, Robert Heidler gave an explanation of God's cycles and feasts, so now let's see how firstfruits is a part of each feast and how we can build on it. In *Time to Defeat the Devil*, I wrote:

> By understanding the timing of the feasts you go from harvest to harvest until increase becomes a way of life. Each feast celebration has a firstfruits dimension, and as we have shared, there are great blessings that come from heaven when we participate each month in giving God our best. By understanding, celebrating and giving at firstfruits, you gain momentum in the Spirit, and eventually God's blessings overtake you. This produces a kingdom mentality in you. You learn to give your best each month. This is different from tithing. This concept builds within you the call to seek His kingdom first and then watch all else be added.
>
> When we quit seeking Him first, we lose momentum. This is a time to gain kingdom strength and momentum. Matthew 11:12 says, "And from the days of John the Baptist until now the kingdom of heaven suffers violence, and the violent take it by force." This was the statement that the Lord made to John the Baptist's disciples. John, who had chosen not to move with Jesus in his three-year ministry of revolution, was now imprisoned. During this time, he had begun to question the One for whom he had paved the way to produce the redemption of mankind. Jesus' ministry was gaining momentum, and John's ministry was coming to a close.
>
> Jesus had just finished His charge to His twelve disciples and left to teach and to preach in some Galilean cities. Only Philip and Andrew had left John's wineskin to follow the Lord and seek the kingdom. When John heard about the activities of the Lord, he sent some of his remaining disciples to question Jesus by asking, "Are You the One Who was to come, or should we keep on expecting a different one? And Jesus replied to them, Go and report to John what you hear and see: The blind receive their sight and the lame walk, lepers are

cleansed (by healing) and the deaf hear, the dead are raised up and the poor have good news (the Gospel) preached to them. And blessed (happy, fortunate, and to be envied) is he who takes no offense at Me and finds no cause for stumbling in or through Me and is not hindered from seeing the Truth" (Matt. 11:3-6, *AMP*). In other words, "John, at least remember, and believe and *see* what you prophesied in the past manifesting now. Follow hard! Do not get offended and stumble over something that I am doing differently."

It is the same with us. This is a time that many prophecies from the past season are manifesting. We must not look away and quit following because they are coming about in ways we did not expect. We must not get offended by the changes coming into our methods, messages, and worship structures. We must keep seeking first and not get shaken and lose momentum.

You are in a kingdom that cannot be shaken (Heb. 12:27-28). Unspiritual and carnal man cannot understand or see this kingdom. We become carnal when we lose the process of seeking Him first. Jesus taught and imparted an understanding of kingdom—kingdom manifestation has a perfect timing.[4]

A More Excellent Sacrifice

God has a redemptive plan for each of us—we just need to learn how to think like He thinks and appropriate His promised blessings. By doing what His Word and His Spirit tell us to do, giving Him the sacrifice of worship, and staying in the glory of His presence no matter what is happening around us, we will be rightly aligned and positioned for advancement in His time.

Hebrews 11:4 says, "By faith Abel offered to God a more excellent sacrifice." Abel brought his firstfruits. If you go back and study this in the Hebrew, you will find Abel bringing his firstfruits, his best, to worship and honor God. This angered his brother because Abel obtained God's favor. Abel's sacrifice of worshiping God became more excellent than Cain's. This sacrifice of worship was a display of faith linked with righteousness.

The moment you transfer your life to God, you become the righteousness of God in Christ Jesus. The book of Romans says that through the worship and sacrifice of bringing your firstfruits to God, He can bless the remainder of what you have.

Cain killed his brother and he was sent out from the presence of God. As a result, Cain and all of his generations wandered. To get back on track, you have to acknowledge your need to understand your positioning and become realigned with firstfruits giving. Once you take that step, you enter into the more excellent sacrifice wherever that might be. The power of Abel, whose blood still speaks, is reconciled through you as you display the same type of worship that Abel displayed by giving your firstfruits to the Lord.

This faith principle is one that few ever enter into. We must understand how faith is related to positioning and timing. Learning how blessings follow and overtake us will ensure that we are not caught in the same structure that many others will be caught in.[5]

Redeeming Our Time

We must always remember that our times are in God's hands. One of the things that foul up many of us is trying to order our own times. In the earth realm, Satan tries to change times and laws (see Dan. 7:25). Therefore, if our flesh does not submit to God's time, we give access to Satan and that moves us out of time. That is where we start losing our blessings. I've learned that if I move in the timing of Rosh Chodesh, I can restore and redeem time.

In my book *Redeeming the Time*, I address how to obtain redemption and restoration. I recently did an Internet search and learned there are only two books on redeeming time. One is by Jonathan Edwards, from the 1700s, and the other is the book I wrote a few years ago. I was amazed to see how Edwards's perspective leaves off with the same viewpoint God gave me to write in *Redeeming the Time*. The Lord is attempting to show us that we can enter in with Him to not only reverse what the enemy has done in our lives but also to set the course to accelerate God's purposes in the earth.

Without understanding time, you leave yourself open for the enemy to try to stop you from advancing. Numerous Scriptures will help you understand how redemption works. The Scripture that changed my life when I was 18 and caused me to get on course was Proverbs 3:5-6: "Trust in the LORD with all your heart, and lean not on your own understanding; in all your ways acknowledge Him, and He shall direct your paths." With this Scripture, God gave me the faith that He could redeem all of what had been lost in our family. When you look at these verses in the original Hebrew, the meaning indicates an intimate relationship and communion that you can enter into with the Lord that equips you to defeat the devil.

Listen and Declare Your Path

Many people don't understand Proverbs 3:5-6. They reason that if they just think right, they'll be okay; but there is more to this verse than that. God spoke this to me: *"There is a path of freedom and a path of deliverance for you."* If you enter into what this verse is saying and learn to listen, He will direct your path. In effect, He will make your walk upright, and by doing so, He will untwist the iniquity in your path and make the way straight before you. You will then know where you are going. Declare that you will know where you are going, and your children will know where they are going. Declare that your children's children will know where they are going.

Proverbs 3:7 says, "Do not be wise in your own eyes; fear the LORD and depart from evil." God will define "evil" for your life, and you're going to have to leave that evil behind. There are many definitions of "evil" in the Word of God, but some "good" things might be evil for you too. You must allow the Lord to define His parameter of evil and, with that, set the course for your life.

The Lord goes on to say in verse 8 that if you'll do this, "it will be health to your flesh." I like the wording for this verse in the *Amplified Bible* better: "It shall be health to your nerves and sinews." There was a generational iniquity in my bloodline resulting from generations of fathers going outside their boundaries; in the process, their nerve structures were damaged severely. The Lord spoke to me and said, *"You can redeem that damage. All you have to do is depart from evil and not think your own way through things."*

Verse 8 goes on, "And strength to your bones." Your blood will be energized. Your navel structure will be realigned. What that means is that the iniquitous structure that was passed on through your DNA can be untwisted, and the blood that you have can be purified by the Spirit. Then your blood will start functioning in God's way. There is more to it than "strength to your bones." In other words, the thing that was connected to your navel can be re-ordered. The key to this is to honor the Lord with your possessions and with the firstfruits of your increase.

In the case of Abel and Cain, Abel gave honor to the Lord with his firstfruits. If you will do the same, you will be blessed with healing and restoration. Rosh Chodesh is the path to the next move of healing. We keep crying out for a move of healing; but as long as we allow mammon to rule us in the present Church structure of America, we will not see the next move of healing.[6]

Reverse Bloodline Iniquity
If you are born again, Satan will try to remove your hope for the future. To do this he has to break through your life cycle in some way to divert the blessings God has planned for your family. Once he accomplishes that, an iniquity begins to form in your bloodline. That's why the Lord spoke to Cain as He did.

Genesis 4:6 says, "The LORD said to Cain, 'Why are you angry?'" In Ephesians 4:26, we find this explained a little differently: If you don't deal with your anger in time or if you let the sun set on your anger, the result is that you become fair game for the enemy to take you out of time. A Christian who won't deal with his or her anger within a given time frame opens the door to demonic oppression. This doesn't mean you can't be angry, but if you don't deal with your anger within the given time frame God allows, you sin and a root of anger develops, which gives the devil a foothold, in your land.

"Why are you angry? Why has your countenance fallen?" In other words, why is your face reflecting your emotions wrongly? "If you do well, will you not be accepted?" If you decide to give your firstfruits offering, you'll be accepted. That's what Genesis 4:6 means. In other words, God says, "If you decide to worship Me the way I'm worthy to be worshiped, you'll be accepted, just as Abel was." This issue involved firstfruits. God explained iniquity and how understanding Rosh Chodesh and firstfruits giving can reverse iniquity.

Some of you have roots of rejection because your family had God-robbing ties. Those ties are the reason why you can't get the root of rejection broken in your life. If your family has God-robbing in its bloodline, iniquity is deeply rooted as well. At the very point you try to step into freedom, Satan gains access to knock something out of place. This usually comes through rejection and rebellion, which always work together. Suppose you rebel through some circumstance the enemy puts in your path and your response is "I'm just not going to give." You pull out of your giving cycle, and you remain in rejection and continue to act out your rebellion. You can become as religious as you want to be, but you're still in a lawless state. When you're operating in lawlessness, you can't submit and you can't align. Your gift won't find its place in time. Then Satan will reactivate that iniquitous structure and cause you to wander again, right at your time of deliverance.

Satan comprehends time better than we do. He knows exactly how to destroy unity. He is a legalist. He has expert knowledge of law structures and knows how to use them against us. You must recognize the fact that "religion" interpreted in a ritualistic way is dead works. God's intent is for us to move from blessing to blessing when we celebrate Rosh Chodesh and firstfruits giving. God said to Cain, "If you do well, will you not be accepted? And if you do not do well, sin lies at the door. And its desire is for you, but you should rule over it" (Gen. 4:7). (Desire was the iniquity in Cain's mother, Eve. Her desire got shifted when she sinned.) If you don't worship right and don't know how to practice the concept of worship through sacrifice and time, the iniquity that flows through the desire of your bloodline overtakes you. That's what happened to Cain.[7]

Are You Willing to Prove God's Faithfulness?

I was meeting with some of our younger generation recently and read aloud Proverbs 3:9-10: "Honor the LORD with your possessions, and with the firstfruits of all your increase; so your barns will be filled with plenty, and your vats will overflow with new wine." I said to them, "This makes up my spiritual DNA. I have meditated on verses from Proverbs 3 since I was 18. That's 40 years." When you meditate on a passage of Scripture for that long, the Word becomes a part of your life. You fully understand the truth that then flows through your veins.

Let's add a verse to build on this understanding. Daniel 7:25 warns that our enemy, the devil, "shall speak pompous words against the Most High, shall persecute the saints of the Most High." That means he will wear down your thinking. The verse continues: "And shall intend to change times and laws." He can't do that if you stay in time and if you're honoring God with your firstfruits. You simply must make sure that you're moving in God's time.

Malachi 3:8 says, "Will a man rob God? Yet you have robbed Me! But you say, 'In what way have we robbed You?'" At this point in history, the people had fallen into what is called obsession. They believed only on what they were fixated. They were religious, but they were obsessed. The whole book of Malachi is about this: "You've robbed Me!" The people ask, "How have we robbed You?" And God answers, "In tithes and offerings." He could have said, "You haven't understood firstfruit offerings" or "You haven't understood the concept of tithing."

These key Scriptures from Proverbs, Daniel and Malachi will help move you back into the place of God's ordered time. I am blessed to help the Body of Christ move forward in this process, because nobody's bloodline was more scavenged and ravished than mine. I have watched the Lord sovereignly restore my bloodline by the obedience of operating in both firstfruits giving and Rosh Chodesh. That's what will restore you too and make you holy.

Then we move to the New Testament where the Lord Jesus Christ says to the Pharisees, "At least you have tithed" (see Matt. 23:23; Luke 11:42). God is saying there is so much more than just tithing. Because of being captured by money, many of you will go to war, saying, "Well, I'm not even sure we have to tithe." I'm saying this with as much grace as God has given me, "At least tithe!"

Then Jesus says, "This affects your nation." Pay attention to the teaching in this book if you want to know why our nation is messed up! Because we have not celebrated Rosh Chodesh as a nation, we have left our root of ordered time and celebration, and as a result the nation started going astray and suffered a financial crisis. Jesus told us that that would happen!

In November 2010, President Barack Obama began trying to make an alignment with India, because India had no recession. We cannot make that claim for the United States. India is an ally of ours, but we have to be careful, because we can't just seek India like Israel sought Egypt and expect India to get us out of a mess. If we don't return to the principles of God, we will still be in a mess or be owned by someone else. Remember when the 12 tribes went down to Egypt during a severe drought? After Joseph died, the Israelites lived as slaves in Egypt for 400 years, until God intervened. Pharaoh owned them.

Going back to Malachi 3, God says, "You have robbed Me . . . in tithes and offerings. You are cursed with a curse, for you have robbed Me, even this whole nation. Bring all the tithes into the storehouse, that there may be food in My house" (vv. 8-10). This same thing is repeated over and over again by the prophets. "And try Me now in this" (v. 10). "Prove Me now and see if I won't do what I said in Proverbs 3." That was the turning point of my life. God is no respecter of persons. Honor Him with your possessions and the firstfruits of all your increase, and watch Him prove Himself in your life as well.[8]

Notes

1. Personal communication, September 13, 2012.
2. Chuck D. Pierce, *Interpreting the Times: How God Intersects with Our Lives to Bring Revelation and Understanding* (Lake Mary, FL: Charisma House, 2008), pp. 73-76.
3. Chuck D. Pierce, *Time to Defeat the Devil: Strategies to Win the Spiritual War* (Lake Mary, FL: Charisma House, 2011), pp. 132-35.
4. Ibid., pp. 135-136.
5. See Chuck D Pierce with Robert and Linda Heidler, *A Time to Advance: Understanding the Significance of the Hebrew Tribes and Months* (Denton, TX: Glory of Zion International Inc., 2011), pp. 103-104.
6. Ibid., pp. 104-107.
7. Ibid., pp. 117-118.
8. Ibid., pp. 107-109.

13

REORDERING YOUR MIND
TO PROSPER

CHUCK D. PIERCE

I made this statement once: "The need to profit should be a foundational core value of every person's life, especially every Christian." The feedback from God's people over this statement was astounding, astonishing and quite shocking. Most people in the Body of Christ do not have the proper mindset to profit, prosper and succeed!

When the Holy Spirit was left in the world, God released the power for us to become "children of God" (John 1:10-13). God is the most creative, the best steward, does exploits, and multiplies and blossoms seeds that have lain desolate. If He is like this, then so should be His children. First Corinthians 12:1-7 says, "Now concerning spiritual gifts, brethren, I do not want you to be ignorant.... There are diversities of gifts ... differences of ministries ... diversities of activities, but it is the same God who works all in all. But the manifestation of the Spirit is given to each one for the profit of all." When we are properly aligned with the Lord and with each other, we profit! The Holy Spirit, the third person of the Trinity, gives us diverse ways to profit.

In this chapter, I want to discuss how we are uniquely made by the Creator to adapt in ways to gain wealth, be successful and profit. If the Holy Spirit is central in our lives, profiting should be one of the main manifestations of God within us.

You Are Uniquely Equipped to Profit

I believe that we humans are unique and special! Daily we solve many problems without even the cognitive awareness that we are problem solving. We can have our arms full and use our noses or chins to open a door! We can see patterns in most animals that we do each day, but then no animal can uniquely solve problems the way we have been equipped to do. I believe that many mammals are brilliant, but we alone are at the top of the food chain.

We are made in the image of God. "Now may the God of peace Himself sanctify you completely; and may your whole spirit, soul, and body be preserved blameless at the coming of our Lord Jesus Christ. He who calls you is faithful, who also will do it" (1 Thess. 5:23-24). If we submit our entire being to the One who created us and uniquely knit us together, then we can do things like Him (see Ps. 139). We can be just as creative and do exploits (see Dan. 11:32)!

We are a supernatural people. We are beyond magicians and diviners. We are made like God, the Father of our spirits. Remember Moses! The magicians were successful to a point in replicating and reproducing the miracles he did when he represented God. But after a certain time, only God's power could do through Moses what God wanted, and the supernatural dark powers of the mind and the demon powers were limited in operation. We are unique, powerful, supernatural, creative and special, and we are meant to profit. The enemy can do miracles and prosper in certain dimensions. But with God, we are limitless!

Think Change

There is one requirement in our uniqueness: we must always think change. One thing that differentiates us from other mammals is that we attempt to form concepts about imperceptible situations in the physical, biological and psychological arenas around us, and we try to explain an effect as having been caused by something. We question and reason to come up with hypotheses and conclusions. However, because of our emotional state, we can make errors in our reasoning, and these errors can lead to mistaken beliefs. This can cause us to enter a realm of loss. This can also make us lose the power we need to acquire wealth.

In our thinking processes, there are non-conscious and conscious actions going on. Therefore, if we are unaware of spiritual laws, we can easily violate one of those laws and not make accurate, decisive actions that lead to prosperity. How information or a perception enters our consciousness is how we develop our thinking.

If we allow faith revelatory-principles based upon the Word of God to develop in our base of power thinking, we are assured of developing and being successful as we walk in life. If we embrace negative thoughts sent to oppose our unique success, we will get hindered in our prosperity. If these thoughts that are contrary to our covenant destiny enter deep into our thinking consciousness, blockages will begin to form. These are called strongholds. In *How to Minister Freedom,* I describe these blockages this way:

> The enemy builds strongholds within our mind to protect his resources. When we are confronted with a truth and our mind seems to go blank, it is often a good indication that a demon is at work, because demons don't want truth to go in like an arrow and shatter strongholds that are there. That's how truth works. When a spirit of truth is inside of us and a godly revelation comes in, it's as if a battering ram hit that stronghold, causing its destruction.[1]

These structures can hide the blessings that were intended to prosper us and establish the portion that we have in God's covenant plan while we are here on the earth.

You Have a Pipeline of Connectivity in Your Brain

I worked during summers on pipelines in the oil and gas fields of East Texas. I know this might surprise many of you, but I learned so much from the Lord as I worked out in the fields seeing how oil and gas resources in the earth would get to their destinations. I worked within a 150-mile radius. In that field, many lines were necessary to funnel gas and oil flows to their recording stations and on to the necessary selling point, where the prosperity of the resource was received, recorded and acknowledged. We had to walk the lines to see if there were construction blockages on the right of way of passage.

We also were responsible for keeping the path of the line clear. One of us had to detect any leaks that were stopping the ultimate prosperity of the field from occurring.

In cognitive processing, your mind is like a field. In the Bible, your mind is equated to land. The mind can be a rich resource, or it can be a minefield filled with dangers. Obstructions can build up in your mind that stop the necessary thoughts of prosperity that you need to connect from connecting. These obstructions can build dams that prevent knowledge in one area of the brain from connecting to the necessary wealth in any area. When that happens, you lose strength and the hypotheses that you work with are shortsighted or delayed from producing the ultimate overcoming power that produces wealth.

This is one of our enemy's goals. When he sees that a Kingdom person is on the verge of diverting resources into God's kingdom plan, he must interject thoughts, temptations and even wrong knowledge into our fields. This is how he develops strongholds.

Lots of different aspects of the brain must kick in for us to make the key decisions we need to prosper. Therefore, if a stronghold develops in one area of our thinking, a blockage occurs that prevents the connectivity necessary for our whole thought process to operate properly. This stops success!

We must keep changing our thoughts until they are fully aligned with God's. We must embrace new methods of thinking. However, we must do this carefully. Here are some principles that will help you adapt to changes in your thought processes:

- Embedded in God's promise is both stability and change! We must not change just to change.

- Understanding what is essential and what is not allows you to effectively master the infiltration of new revelation versus just conforming to the shifting world around you.

- The whole concept of repentance is based around the changing of your mind. Therefore, when you make mistakes or when you resist revelation, you must repent to advance. Repentance must include your intellect, will and emotions all realigning.

Chuck D. Pierce and Robert Heidler

- Out of stability, change comes.

- Change produces opportunity.

- Don't fear change. You must learn to turn change into an ally.

- Business success depends on change! Zebulun, the business tribe and the tribe of Israel that was linked with wealth, was always adapting and changing, so Israel had the necessary supply and provision to advance.

- You must change and adapt to changing times without shifting your core values and the boundaries assigned for your prosperity.

- To profit should be a core value in you that never changes.

Bind the Strongman to Overcome Strongholds

Let's talk more about the enemy of our prosperity. The enemy sets up idolatrous, stubborn spirits to work against us so that we develop strongholds and resist change. In *The Future War of the Church,* Rebecca Wagner Sytsema and I wrote an entire chapter on how to unlock the wealth that Satan holds:

In Matthew 12:22-29, our Lord addresses the Pharisees concerning the deliverance of a man who had been blind and mute. The Pharisees accuse Jesus of being part of the ruling demonic structure that had blinded the man. But Jesus reminded them that a kingdom divided against itself cannot stand. If Jesus were of Satan's kingdom, then by casting out demons Satan's own kingdom would be made powerless. Jesus' works, He explained, demonstrated that, in fact, the kingdom of God was among them.

Then He sets forth an interesting principle in verse 29: How can one enter a strong man's house and plunder his goods, unless he first binds the strong man? And then he will plunder his house. Jesus' illustration is tied in with prosperity and wealth. First, He tells us there is a strong man who rules

Satan's kingdom in any territory. This is where we see the Lord beginning to define the hierarchical structure of Satan's kingdom. He also tells us that if we bind the strong man then we can plunder his house and take his spoils.

As apostolic authority arises throughout the earth and aligns with strategic prophetic intercession through spiritual warfare, I believe we will plunder the enemy's kingdom and unlock the wealth necessary to reap the harvest for the Kingdom in the days ahead. We must learn to bind and loose in order to build God's plan from season to season. When we have God's blueprint from heaven we are assured to prosper. However, we are required to forbid what needs to be forbid in our field and bring and loose new methods into the field to overcome the strongholds that are blocking resources from coming to their ultimate Kingdom destination.[2]

Satan Operates Cyclical Iniquity

Idolatry and strongholds develop from misplaced power and affections. Worship is linked with prosperity. This is obvious in the story of Abel and Cain. The sons of Adam and Eve had been taught to worship and present their firstfruits offerings from their fields.

While Abel presented his best to God, Cain presented what he didn't want from his field and kept the best for his own decision-making. This created a major breach, which led to murder and caused a door of iniquity that was linked with idolatry to open in the earth. The Bible records the first city in the history of society being built by Cain. All of the structures of that society were built out of this iniquity. Iniquitous patterns and ways built up in these cities until God decided to wipe away the societal manifestations of these iniquities and begin again by releasing a new blueprint from heaven to a man named Noah.

However, cyclical iniquity seems to operate from generation to generation. We read in the Bible that people began worshiping what they could see—the moon, the stars, and so on—instead of pressing in to know and communicate with our holy God. Satan empowered this type of worship through his demonic hordes. Then a god or goddess, depending on its manifestation, would be worshiped to ensure fertility, agricultural prosperity and material stability (see Jer. 7:18; 44:17). Such worship has long been a major influence in holding people captive to the devil's system.

Satan Hoards the Spoils of the Kingdom

A biblical example of wealth being held captive involves God's promise to Abraham concerning the Promised Land of Canaan. We have discussed this in other chapters, but let me add some things here. It wasn't until 470 years after the Lord spoke to Abraham and promised him total victory within his field, or territorial boundaries, that the Israelites entered the region to appropriate the promises. There was a long process in the earth while the Lord developed a group of people and the leadership for this group. Led by a man named Joshua, this group would ultimately overtake, bind the strongman of the promise, and take the field of promise. The assignment, or mission, that Joshua and the tribes of Israel were to accomplish was a transference of the wealth from the inhabitants of that region for the fulfillment of God's covenant kingdom plan.

To do this, Joshua and God's covenant people needed daily strategy concerning how to advance and possess God's inheritance promised to Abraham. If the Israelites were going up against a city, they sought and received their instructions from the Lord as to how to take the spoils of war. We need to do likewise. We need to meditate on God's covenant vision that He has given each of us to accomplish. God promised the Israelites success if they would listen, receive and chew on what He sent from heaven before proceeding in the field. We will also have success if we follow that same pattern.

Jericho, the invincible city, was blocking the children of Israel from their promise. This stronghold had to be torn down to advance into the riches that God had been waiting for hundreds of years to release to His people. To overcome this stronghold, Israel had to be ordered with a strategy. Once they obeyed God's strategy, the stronghold fell and they advanced. Jericho was a firstfruits offering of the strongholds of the land and needed to be fully presented as an offering to the Lord who was giving them the whole land.

However, the very next stronghold, Ai, was perceived casually. There had also been a violation in the original strategy God had given. Once that occurred, error multiplied, and Israel was not clear in its perceived advancement. They did not properly connect the strategy of their last victory to their thinking process in the conflict with Ai, and for this reason they did not overtake that enemy. Defeat occurred and loss resulted. Wealth was postponed. This is a great example of how the strongman hoards his spoils.

Remembering God's Portion

I come from a family that had much potential to prosper. My dad was a creative, self-made man who probably felt the lack of money was the root of all evil. It seemed that whatever he touched met with success. He really didn't care about an impressive resume; he just felt that whatever you put your hand to should prosper and multiply. Yet he never really mastered the power of money.

Money and wealth have inherent power; if you do not bring that power under the subjection of the Holy Spirit, it will overwhelm and ensnare you. My father fell into the covetousness and the strife of wealth. His ability to succeed drove him to forget God. In forgetting God, he forgot God's portion. I believe this was his downfall.

You can read my testimony in *Possessing Your Inheritance*, a book about restoration. My dad allowed money to become his god, and the abundance that had been given him to steward was lost. When God showed me that He could restore what had been devoured by the enemy, He revealed to me the power of giving. I believe that giving of your resources—your money, your time, your mind, your heart—can unlock your destiny.

No matter what the generations of your family before you have done with their money, you can break the cycle of the sin of greed by confessing the sin of your bloodline and by the determination to no longer be ruled by the god of mammon. This will release the power for you to secure God's inheritance for your future.

Harvesting in Your Canaan

God is giving us a strategy for reaping in the harvest fields. We have discussed how apostolic authority can overthrow the powers and principalities that are holding back the supply necessary to advance God's covenant purposes. God spoke this principle to His people as He prepared them to enter into the land He had promised them: He would give them the power to get wealth so that they could advance His covenant (see Deut. 8:18).

God knew they would be in for a spiritual war with the gods of the land of Canaan. Joshua and the tribes of Israel had to take the wealth from the inhabitants of that region for the purposes of God's covenant plan. Therefore, the gods of the land had to be defeated and their wealth plundered. As Rebecca Wagner Sytsema and I share in *The Future War of the Church*:

> Just as there are two competing kingdoms in the heaven-lies—God's and Satan's—there are two economic systems competing for the earth's wealth: God's and Satan's. Psalm 24:1-2 says that the earth and its fullness belong to the Lord because He, and He alone, is the sovereign Creator. Individuals, corporations, banks, lending institutions, markets, governments and international organizations are called to be stewards of God's resources in order to glorify Him and to demonstrate His righteousness and justice in the earth.
>
> Jesus said, "You cannot serve God and mammon" (Matt. 6:24). "Mammon" was a figure of speech in Jewish literature, a way of personalizing inanimate wealth and riches. But this figure of speech points to a deeper truth. "Mammon" is an accurate description of the demonic personalities behind economic injustice and misery in the world.
>
> The Scriptures teach that Satan is a usurper, a thief and, ultimately, a destroyer. Satan uses economic systems—individuals, corporations, banks, lending institutions, markets and governments—to subvert God's rule as part of his plan to get people to worship anything other than God. If Satan can get people to worship money or monetary systems, all

the better. As "prince of this world" (John 12:31, [*NIV*]), Satan has a great deal of power he can exercise on earth. But we must always remember that his power is limited, that it is nothing compared to the power of God and that Satan is ultimately an eternal loser. Nevertheless, Satan uses demonic forces, deception and human proxies to administer and control supply and distribution of wealth according to his agenda. Satan is a Machiavellian prince, not just of religions but also of economics. . . .

In every generation it is important to have apostolic leaders who understand the purposes of God and who know how to seek the Lord for revelatory strategy. Joshua led God's covenant people into the territorial boundaries declared in Genesis 15. Joshua received daily strategy for advancing the Lord's armies and possessing the inheritance that had been promised. He was God's leader for the season. If we are going to successfully overcome every obstacle—a city, a people or whatever—we must have individuals who inquire of the Lord and receive instructions from Him about how to advance. And we must know what we are to do with the spoils of war.

Deuteronomy 8:18 tells us: "And you shall remember the LORD your God, for it is He who gives you *power* to get *wealth*, that He may establish His covenant which He swore to your fathers" (emphasis added). "Power" means vigor, strength, force or capacity (whether physical, mental or spiritual). But what does the Bible mean when it speaks of wealth?[3]

If we are children of God, then we have access to the power to gain wealth.

A Proper View of Wealth

In *The Future War of the Church*, Rebecca and I write that the Bible has many things to say on the subject of wealth. Here are just a few:

- Wealth is a blessing from God (see Prov. 10:22).
- Wealth is a reward for obedience (see Deut. 7:12,13; Prov. 3:9,10).

- Wealth is a reward for wisdom (see Prov. 8:18,21).
- Wealth is a result of enterprise and useful work (see Prov. 10:4; 12:14; 14:23).
- Wealth is taken away from sinners and given to those who please God (see Prov. 13:22; Eccles. 2:26).
- Wealth is imperfectly distributed in this world, and it is sometimes gained through oppression and injustice (see Prov. 22:16; Amos 2:6; 4:1; 8:4-6).
- Wealth is not an end in itself (see Prov. 23:4; Eccles. 4:8).
- Wealth is potentially a deadly snare (see Eccles. 5:10,13; Matt. 6:24; Luke 16:13).
- Wealth is not guaranteed to believers at all places and all times (see 1 Sam. 2:7; Pss. 69:33; 82:4; 2 Cor. 8:2; Rev. 2:9).
- Wealth is to be shared with the needy (see Prov. 14:21; Eph. 4:28; Jas. 2:15,16; 1 John 3:17).
- Wealth is sometimes to be given away completely (see Luke 12:33; 18:22).

Wealth is generally acknowledged to be a blessing from God. All the patriarchs became very wealthy. Solomon's wealth was seen as God's favor. Job had wealth, lost it and then regained a double portion. Jesus' parable of the talents complimented the servants who multiplied their master's wealth (see Luke 19:11-27). However, He did warn us that the pursuit of riches and pleasure can keep our faith from maturing. Jesus warned us not to let money become a rival to God for our affections.

Christians should view wealth as a resource intended for the advancement of God's kingdom. With the approach of one of the greatest spiritual harvests ever, this is a season when wealth needs to be channeled into ministries that serve people and spread the gospel.

We must not fear the concept of wealth. We must not fear the idea of reaping what God has given us to harvest. We must not fear increase, for money in itself is not bad. The Bible says it's the love of money that is the root of all kinds of evil (see

1 Tim. 6:10). We must never confuse the abundance or lack of money with the attitude of our heart.

We must also resist the idea that to be poor is spiritual. This teaching has its roots in gnosticism, which states that matter is bad and the mind is good. Gnosticism has caused many problems in the Church, including the separation of the sacred and the secular.

We must also separate our worth from our possessions. That is, we must realize that we are worth far more to the living God than the monetary value of our wealth and possessions. What is important is our willingness to be good stewards of what God has given to us, to take appropriate risks and to make our possessions available to God to do with what He wants. Once we understand this, we are free to go forth into the harvest field that we are a part of and ask the Lord how we can best reap the harvest of that field. As faithful stewards, we will be given the vision and focus to overthrow anything that sets itself against the call of God on our life in our field. . . .

As we consider matters of wealth, there are very real traps we must avoid. We must detect and repent of any of these patterns in our own lives, and we must stay in God's covenant timing.

When we go up against the enemy to fight for the transference of wealth into the kingdom of God, we must guard ourselves against the love of money. The Greek word *philarguria* in 1 Timothy 6:10 refers to avarice (the insatiable greed for riches) and covetousness (to desire the possessions of others).

We must also be wary of the deceitfulness of riches (see Mark 4:19). This can include the perceived power that comes with having money. Money can produce an attitude of heart that seeks to manipulate through false pretenses and appearances.

Money is good when it is made a servant to us. However, when we become a slave to its dominion, we are in trouble. Lot, Esau, Achan, Gehazi, Judas, Ananias and Sapphira are among those in the Word who were cursed by wealth and trapped by their own impure desires. As we prepare to move against the enemy, we must renounce every issue of covetousness that is tied to mammon.

The Lord says, "Take heed and beware of covetousness, for one's life does not consist in the abundance of the things he possesses" (Luke 12:15). The sin of covetousness is linked with uncontrolled, selfish emotional desire. The enemy attempts to lead us into illicit forms of idolatry because they misdirect our desires from a holy God toward flesh-filled, demonically inspired forms of lasciviousness. James 4:1 asks, "Where do wars and fights come from among you? Do they not come from your desires for pleasure that war in your members?" . . .

Provision is necessary for building God's plan. In the book of Exodus, God remembered the children of Israel and raised up a deliverer to lead them into His covenant plan. However, God didn't just free the people and send them into the wilderness with nothing to show for 400 years of hard labor. Not only did He save His people, but He also provided for them! As the Israelites prepared to depart from Egypt, God prompted the Egyptians to give them all kinds of riches and goods: "And the LORD had given the people favor in the sight of the Egyptians, so that they granted them what they requested. Thus they plundered the Egyptians" (Exod. 12:36).

The Lord still wishes to give miraculous provision to His children today, as He breaks us out of the system we are in and points us toward the covenant blessings He has set aside for us throughout the earth.

God gave Moses a detailed plan for building His tabernacle in the wilderness, and we can surmise that some of what He had given the Israelites from the Egyptians would be used to fulfill that plan. God wanted them to build a tabernacle, or dwelling place, for Him so that they could worship Him and receive His vision for their future. Even as God was giving the plans for the tabernacle to Moses, the supply was already there to provide for its building.

Moses waited on God for every detail that was necessary for the future prosperity of his people. Unfortunately, the people did not wait on Moses. While he was on Mount Sinai receiving the plans, the people grew impatient. They took the provision that had been given them, and in their discouragement they wandered back to the very gods from whom they had been liberated:

> And [Aaron] received the gold from their hand and he fashioned it with an engraving tool and made a molded calf. Then they said, "This is your god, O Israel, that brought you out of the land of Egypt!" (Exod. 32:4).

Not only was this molded calf a familiar god of Egypt, but the calf was also worshiped in Canaan through the religious system that had been erected there. When we are discussing wealth, I don't think provision is the only issue in regard to God's covenant people and plan. There is provision all over the earth. However, worship and devotion to a holy God and His purposes do become an issue in the release and stewardship of wealth.[4]

Launch Out for a Transfer!

Just as there were enemies to overcome for the successful conquest of the land of Canaan, so too you have enemies attempting to stop you from advancing. However, sometimes the greatest enemy to your prospering will be the big "I"—yourself. Your natural, or carnal, mind can resist wealth.

Let's look at how your brain operates to gain a simple understanding related to wealth and prosperity. The brain has two parts—left and right. The left hemisphere is made for intelligent thinking, and the right for episodic memory connected with emotions, feelings and desires. The two should integrate properly and work together, not competing, but synergizing thoughts to gain the power to succeed.

One of my favorite stories in the Word of God concerns an incident in the business world, when Jesus' disciples had been working hard for their sustenance. They had fished all night and caught nothing. Fishermen in Jesus' day would take a circular net with weights attached to the perimeter and cast it out on the water. After the net sank, they would pull a drawstring and haul in the catch. But this time, Simon Peter and the other disciples had been doing this all night and had caught nothing (see Luke 5:5).

Jesus then gave Peter a direction that would have been contrary to his way of thinking: "Launch out and go deeper!" (see Luke 5:4). Peter probably doubted that Jesus could really understand his daily situation and the time-honored method of gaining the supply he needed. Furthermore, what he had done the night before was firmly implanted in his memory. He remembered the effort from the night before, that they had caught no fish, and he undoubtedly felt all the frustration and emotions linked with lack.

Furthermore, Peter and the others were likely tired. Nevertheless, the disciples obeyed Jesus and hauled in an overwhelming catch that supplied not only their needs but their partners' needs as well (see Luke 5:7). Then the Lord said, "From now on you will catch men" (Luke 5:10). After this demonstration of power, the disciples went forth evangelizing. It had taken a miracle for them to overcome their doubt.

There was another time when a similar incident occurred. This was after Jesus' death, when Peter's emotions of following the Lord for three years and seeing his hopes dashed would have been raw within him. So, instead of following an idea for the future, Peter returned to fishing.

Jesus, who had resurrected and overcome death, hell, poverty, sickness and lack, appeared to the disciples in the midst of their toiling and told them to cast the net to the right side of the boat instead of the left. I have always equated the sides of the boat to the two sides of the brain. The disciples' intellect was ruling them in their business, but the Lord seemed to say, "Shift to the right side of your thinking process—your call, your emotions, your future, your deep desires. Cast your net there, and you will open up the way for the next season." The disciples did, and miraculously had a full net.

Today, God is saying to His people, "Launch out!" The word "launch" means to send off, to send forth with force, to set in operation, to start on a new course, or to throw oneself into an enterprise with vigor (power). The Lord wants to do miracles in our everyday lives. These miracles will cause supply to be released that will meet our needs. These miracles will cause faith to be released that will propel us forward to achieve God's purposes in our homes and our cities. As we see Him move in our lives, we can have faith that an entire region can be freed from the clutches of mammon and the power of covetousness.

Align Yourself Under the Flow of Fullness

There is a perfect time for us to launch out and be open to miracles in the future. There is a moment when all of the elements align and breakthrough for our future happens! Matthew 1 lists the genealogy of Jesus, and once we get through most of the "begots," we come to the following lines:

> And Jacob begot Joseph the husband of Mary, of whom was born Jesus who is called Christ. So all the generations from Abraham to David are fourteen generations; from David until the captivity of Babylon are fourteen generations [fourteen is the number of deliverance], and from the captivity in Babylon until the Christ are fourteen generations (Matt. 1:16-17).

There is a timing element that is so important for us to understand if we want to see heaven breakthrough into earth. When the three cycles of 14 aligned, God's redemptive plan from heaven entered the earth. This allowed us to have the power to reverse the process of loss that attempts to hold our fields captive.

God Gave His Firstfruit to the Earth

When the three sets of 14 generations aligned, God came to earth! Not particularly how humans expected, but He came! He grew! He was favored! He accomplished His purpose to realign humans back to God's heart! The Father gave His best—His only Son—so that we might see Him! In seeing Him, we could see us! Right now, we're in a similar time of alignment between heaven and earth, and this timing is so important. Time does not bind God, but we are in time and must respond from our time frame to His sovereign way of thinking. He never changes. We must change. We must operate in His laws and principles in our time frame.

He gave His best—His firstfruit—to redeem the earth. God came down to earth, as a man, and suddenly we had the fullness of who God was right in front of us so that we could see Him. God, the Father, allowed us to see what He looked like through the Son, at a point in time. You have to understand that now He continues with the remnant that is always looking to see Him in a greater fullness. If we stay in time, we will see Him in time again.

Here is what I've learned about applying the concepts of firstfruits: If I stay in God's time, I will remain under the portal of blessing. You will have to meditate on this next statement: When the fullness of blessing enters the earth realm, between heaven and earth, I am aligned under that flow of fullness. This is how time works, so you must learn how to stay in time.

In previous chapters, Robert taught us about firstfruits from the Scriptures to show us why we should fully participate in that celebration, which has never been removed from God's appointed times. Even Jesus participated in firstfruits. If God, Himself, came into the earth realm and fully participated in firstfruits, doesn't that explain the importance of why we should fully participate in it as well?

We Can Operate in a New Way

We don't celebrate the feasts the same as people in biblical days celebrated the feasts through time. We celebrate the feasts "in" time. We don't observe the rituals the way the 12 tribes did them in Egypt, or the way they did in Babylon, or the way the Church observed them in Jesus' day. However, what we do is stay in time because of the feasts. We celebrate the feasts in the sanctified way God tells us to celebrate them.

The Jews didn't forget time when they moved from place to place. This means that if you aren't here to celebrate firstfruits with us, you will not have lost your salvation. When Robert and Linda Heidler were ministering out of the country during one of our firstfruits gatherings, they gave as their firstfruits gift the monetary gift they were blessed with while ministering out of the country.

Participating in firstfruits giving isn't about giving your tithe; rather, it's about you doing several things that make you enter into a flow of blessing. First of all, God has predetermined your times and boundaries: God "determined their appointed times and the boundaries of their habitation" (Acts 17:26, *NASB*). This isn't Old Testament but New Testament.

Let me try to explain this from a religious standpoint. There was a covenant that became full. The covenant was brought into its fulfillment from one dispensation to another. That's what Old and New "Testament" means—Old and New Covenants. The people didn't change the way they operated, but they were freed to operate in a new, more excellent way. Here is what you need to understand: We don't do away with the Law; we fulfill the Law. Go out and murder someone and see if the law still exists. Do you see what I'm saying? Nations developed their civil law structure from God's Torah, but nations are much like the Pharisees. They add law upon law to the point that eventually no one knows what they're doing. We have to realize there is a time of fulfillment.

Humans are the most unique and dangerous creation in the world. Only a supernatural God can be the source of such creative creatures. Humans have been given wills and playbooks that allow them to operate beyond any other creature. The Jewish people were unlike any other people. They were humanity and Torah . . . the teachings of laws and the grace of God. So law and grace meet as we multiply and profit in the earth.

In the next chapter, we will discuss what law is, and also address the spiritual laws that will make us profit.

Planting and Reaping Have Perfect Timing

Robert and Linda Heidler used to minister frequently in the former Soviet Union. One of the things they learned there is that the people thought that the most efficient way to do everything was to have everything controlled centrally by a bureaucrat in Moscow. That was a kind of false apostolic appointment.

For example, the people decided that the bureaucrats in Moscow should set the dates for planting and harvesting for the entire Soviet Union. So, when the order came down from Moscow, the people planted their seeds, no matter what time the order came down. Often when the order came down, the farmers knew the ground was too wet and the seeds were going to rot, but they had to follow the order, so they planted their seeds.

Then, when the order came from Moscow to go out and harvest the crops, they went out and did so. They could not go out and harvest until the order came. If the timing was wrong, they sat and watched the crops rot in the field, because they hadn't gotten the okay from Moscow to do it. The Ukraine used to have some of the most productive farmland in the world, but because the farmers were not allowed to operate in the right timing, the entire area suffered a massive famine.

There is a timing we must be in if we want to reap the harvest. That's why God is speaking to His Church about alignment. To experience harvest, we need to be aligned. We need to be positioned. We need to come into alignment with His leaders, with His people, with His timing, and with His glory.

When God brought the Israelites out of Egypt, they were not much above being a rabble. The Bible says they were a "mixed multitude" (Exod. 12:38). They were free from Egypt, but they weren't ready to move forward as God's people. They were not ready to accomplish God's purposes, and they weren't ready to receive the harvest.

So, instead of God taking them directly to the Promised Land, He took them down to Mount Sinai and spent a year teaching them. During that time, He aligned their camp physically. He aligned them correctly with His leadership. He aligned them with His timing, and He aligned them with His glory. God spent a year saying, "People, I have a great harvest for you. I have a great promise that I want to bring into reality in your experience, but I cannot do that until you get aligned." God is saying this same thing to His Church today.

Biblically, God's goal for us is harvest. We see this all the way through the Bible. God wants our barns to be filled with plenty and for our vats to overflow. He wants us to experience the fullness of His promised blessing. That's what harvest means. Harvest is what we've been working for and praying for. It's the promise that God has held out before us, that we have been pressing into, and the time does come when we will receive the harvest. Harvest is not "pie in the sky by and by." Harvest is the reality of the promise coming into our experience.

God not only wants us to harvest in the natural realm but also to see a harvest of righteousness. He wants us to experience a harvest of souls. But there is a time for harvest. Psalm 1 tells us that God wants us to be like a flourishing tree that brings forth its fruit in its season. Ecclesiastes 3 tells us that there is a time and a season for everything. There is a time to plant seeds, and there is also a time to reap the harvest.

We need to be in God's timing. God wants us to have an abundant harvest, but if we aren't in the right season, we will not get a harvest. Too often, the Church goes out to harvest in the wrong season, and instead of getting grain, it just gets snowed on. If you're not in the right season, you won't get a harvest. That's a basic principle.

I have a prayer for us:

Lord, we want to be aligned with You, to experience Your power and Your blessing. Lord, open our eyes, open our minds, open our hearts to receive what You have for us so that You can move us into areas we're not familiar with but that are dear to Your heart, areas that will move us forward into the harvest You have for us. Amen.

There Is Power in Alignment

Why is alignment important? Robert discussed alignment in chapter 4, but I want to emphasize the fact that there is power in alignment. God even shows that in the natural realm. In the physical world around us, there is power that comes in alignment.

Here is an example: Suppose you have an iron bar, just a cold piece of inert metal, and you also have a magnet. The magnet can be the same size and weight as the iron bar. It can even be made out of the same material. Chemically, they're identical, but the magnet has a power that the iron bar lacks. What makes the difference? Scientists tell us that what makes the difference is that in the iron bar, the molecules are not aligned. They're all in there and have their own magnetic fields, but they're all just doing their own thing. They're all going their own way.

The result is that there is no power! However, the amazing thing is that the iron bar can become a powerful magnet. If you take the iron bar and put it, for a season, in a strong magnetic field, the molecules will align with that magnetic field. When they come into alignment, they gain the power of alignment and, suddenly, you have another magnet! God even uses the physical universe to teach us these things.

God took His people down to Mount Sinai, and for a year He put them in the strong, magnetic field of His glory to get them into alignment. He also aligned them physically. He put the Tabernacle in the center and positioned the tribes around it. On the east side, He put Issachar, Judah and Zebulun. On the north side were Dan, Asher and Naphtali. On the west, He put Ephraim, Manasseh and Benjamin. On the south side were Reuben, Simeon and Gad.

Each of the tribes was given its own position, and each was in alignment with the other. God knew all the tribes were different and that each tribe had its own call and its own destiny, its own gifts and abilities. Issachar was the tribe that understood timing; Judah knew warfare and worship; Zebulun knew how to prosper in commerce. God took the tribes and aligned them with each other in such a way that all of them could prosper.

Not only were the tribes aligned with each other, but they also were all aligned with the Ark. They each had to learn how to relate to the glory of God. When everyone was aligned, it created a place for the glory of God to come down and dwell in their midst.

God not only aligned them physically—around the Ark and with each other—but He also aligned them with His timing. When they were camped at Sinai, God began to teach them about His times and His seasons. It could have been during that time that God began to give Moses the book of Genesis, where He described how He created the world. (Remember that it was in Genesis 1:14 that God said, "Let there be lights in the expanse of the sky to separate the day from the night, and let them serve as signs to mark seasons and days and years" [*NIV*]. God was so concerned that we align ourselves in His timing that He put signs up in the sky where we can easily see them.)

God wants us to know He's given us markers—He's given us very easily discerned ways to know His days and His seasons and His years. That's how important this is to God. God said, in effect, that our aligning ourselves with His timing is so important to Him that He has actually structured the whole physical universe to be a revelation of that. Just as God arranged in groups of three the 12 tribes around the Ark, so too He arranged in groups of three the 12 months around the year. Those are called seasons. God sovereignly arranged the physical universe to give a revelation of His times and seasons.

Understand God's Seasons

God has seasons, and we need to understand them. A person doesn't just blunder through life and say, "Well, I think I'll do this now." A person doesn't say, "Oh, it's a nice day; I think I'll go out and plant some seeds." A person needs to plant in season so he or she can reap the harvest. What's interesting about seasons is that although God never changes, His seasons do, so what worked last season will not always work this season.

As a teacher, Robert sometimes can get in a rut, wanting to do the same thing month after month, year after year. However, I often can tell when we need to shift our focus so we will stay aligned with God's season. What worked last year will not necessarily work the same way this year. If we want to prosper in life, we need to know God's seasons.

We again can see this at work in the natural realm. God has given us clear seasons. In one season you can walk around in shorts and a T-shirt and be very comfortable, but when the seasons change, you'd better get out your coat. In the physical realm, God's seasons constantly change. Spring turns into summer, which becomes fall, which turns into winter, which turns into spring—and the cycle of seasons begins again. You can prosper in any one of these seasons, but you'd better know what season you're in.

Each Season Is Different

Springtime is the season to plant. When you are in a spring season, you put off what you'd like to do, because you know you've got to get the seeds in the ground. You say, "I have to plant now, if I want to reap at a later time." The Bible says spring is also a time of war. That doesn't mean you won't war at other times, but it means spring is an opportune time for war.

Summer is a time to tend your crops. There are some crops harvested in the summer, but it's primarily a time to work and wait in expectation for the harvest that's to come.

Fall is a season of fulfillment. It's a season to bring in the harvest. It's a time for joy and thankful celebration.

Winter is the time to enjoy the fruit of your labor. It's also a time to prepare for planting again.

Each Month Has Its Own "Flavor"

Each of the four different seasons is made up of three months. Although the months are grouped in threes, each month has its own flavor, or mood. This becomes clear as you go through the Bible. Every month of the year has its own prophetic significance. God grouped the months into seasons so that as we walk with God from month to month, we can move into our destinies.

At our monthly firstfruits festival, we gain understanding of that particular month. It's a time to talk about where we are and what's happening in the spiritual realm and a time to discern what God is saying over the month. If we want to walk in God's blessing, we need to recognize that every month has its own meaning.

Some people might say, "It sounds strange that every month has its own meaning. What do you mean by that?" If that sounds strange to you, remember the same thing is true of our earthly calendar. Every month in the world's calendar has its own meaning, its own character, its own climate and its own significance. Part of the character of the month is the manifestation of the season. That's why we say, "March winds bring April showers. April showers bring May flowers."

October, the Halloween Season

There are also key events in certain months that give a special flavor to the month. For example, in October we have Halloween, so this month has become the Halloween month, and the whole month sort of has that flavor. All through the month of October when you go through the stores, you see decorations of witches, ghosts and skeletons. People buy pumpkins and make jack-o-lanterns. Television stations broadcast gruesome horror movies. It seems as if everyone thinks it's a good idea to celebrate fear, death and witchcraft, and our whole culture joins in the celebration. But then the month closes, and we move into November.

November, the Thanksgiving Season

In November, we have Thanksgiving, a whole different season. At Thanksgiving, people make plans to be together with their family. They eat a big meal together. They go outside and play touch football in the backyard. They watch the Thanksgiving Day parades and their favorite football games. The whole month of November is focused on that celebration.

Interestingly, Thanksgiving is probably the most biblical holiday we have. A lot of people don't realize this, but it originated with the Pilgrims, who came over on the Mayflower. They barely survived their first year in the New World, but with the help of some Native Americans who taught them how to fish and farm the land, they did survive. At the end of the year they held a big harvest feast to give thanks to God and say, "We made it!"

The Pilgrims were devoutly religious and seriously committed to the Bible, even though legalistically so many times. They would not celebrate Christmas, and they refused to celebrate Easter (they believed these were man-made feasts and weren't in the Bible). When they fled persecution in England, the New World wasn't the first place they went. The first place they tried was over in Holland where they found refuge among some Sephardic Jews, and they lived there several years before they came to the New World. When they lived among the Jews, they learned about a biblical festival called The Feast of Tabernacles to celebrate the harvest. So our original Thanksgiving was patterned after a biblical feast. It's not at the exact time of Tabernacles, but at least it has a little of that flavor.

December, the Christmas Season
After Thanksgiving, we move into the Christmas season. The whole month of December—the "flavor" of the month—comes from the Christmas celebration. In our culture, Christmas is really a celebration of family. Think about it: Christmas is a time to be sentimental and nostalgic. It's a time to be home for the holidays (many people who cannot get home for Christmas—or don't have a home to go to—can get seriously depressed at this time of year).

Christmas is a heartwarming holiday. We like to watch movies like *It's a Wonderful Life*. It's a time to watch the joy of little children as they open their Christmas presents, and in the background is the wonderful family scene of Mary, Joseph and baby Jesus. We know December 25 is not when Jesus was born, but it's always good to celebrate Jesus. It's always good to have a good time with your family, and there's nothing wrong in celebrating Christmas. When it's over, we move into January.

January, the New Years' Season
January starts off with New Year's Day. On New Year's Eve we stop and think for maybe 30 seconds about what happened in the past year, and we make some resolutions of things we ought to do in the new year (even though we know we're likely not going to keep them). We watch the ball drop at Times Square at midnight, we make a lot of noise. Then we listen to "Auld Lang Syne" and get teary eyed, even though we have no idea what the words mean! Then the rest of the month is spent either trying to keep the resolutions we made on the first day of the month or feeling guilty that we already broke the resolutions.

Even in our culture, every month has a different purpose, and every month has different celebrations. They are even marked by different colors. We decorate with different colors, we have different fragrances, and we eat different kinds of food. They bring different emotions in our lives. The emotions we feel at Halloween are different than the emotions we feel at Christmas. The different months also usually involve different activities. For example, the things we do at a Thanksgiving dinner are not the same things we do at a New Year's Eve party.

God Has an Order!

So, as we see, God has an order in His months, and the world does as well. If you don't align with God's order for the months, you will be aligned with the world's order. That's one of the ways the world will control your emotions, your activities and your values. That's one of the ways the world will press you into its mold. The cycle of months in the world will set an order in your life.

The problem is that the world's yearly cycle is not in sync with God's yearly cycle. The world's yearly cycle will not lead you anywhere. It will not draw you closer to God. God's yearly cycle has three key celebrations—three appointed times with God—that give a flavor to each month of every season through which you move. These celebrations are designed to set God's tone for the seasons of our lives.

The first of the three major celebrations is Passover, in the early spring. It is a commemoration of bringing in the barley harvest, but it's also a celebration of redemption by the blood of the Lamb. The second celebration is Pentecost (or Shuvuot), in the late spring. It's the celebration of God's bountiful provision in every area of life. It's when the first fruit of the wheat harvest is brought in. The third celebration is the Feast of Tabernacles, in the fall. It's the major ingathering of the harvest, and it's a celebration of God's glory.

God has a purpose for this yearly cycle. As you walk with God from month to month, understanding the meaning of what God is doing each month, you are positioned to grow ever closer to God every year, until you experience the fullness of His blessing.

When you align your life with God's times, you will suddenly find you are aligned with God Himself and all the forces of His creation. When you align with God's timing, you are positioned to be in sync with

His timing, and you will not miss windows of opportunity. The result will be that you will plant in seed time and reap a bountiful harvest.

As you continue to prayerfully read through this book, let God bring you into alignment and experience the fullness of His harvest mentality.

Atmospheres Are Changing

I once wrote an email in which I said, "LeAnn will be leading worship in the first service, and Aaron in the second service, and John will be sitting with me." This is a picture of where we all are. John is a gifted psalmist and worshiper as well as an incredible historian. He knows not only the history of our nation and the world but also the history of the sound of the Word of God.

However, the Lord had said to John, *"Wait a minute. Over the next six weeks, I'm repositioning you."* This was hard for all of us to hear, because we had gotten used to hearing the same way we've heard in the past. We were used to doing the same things we had done in the past. But when God says, "Here's your new position," you have to acknowledge that change *will* happen, and you have to move to the next place.

John was used to doing worship, and he was a great leader. But that was not going to be his role for the next six weeks. Instead, he would be listening to the message over a cup of coffee. If he hadn't shifted positions as God instructed, he would have missed the interaction of God's glory in that new position.

What happened to John is just an example of our needing to be aware of and take note of changes in the atmospheres. We all are coming to a new place. Some of you are being repositioned in your vocation. It's important to watch for that. Some of you are being repositioned in your gift. Right now, you are trying to operate in your gift as you did in the last season, because you've become comfortable with the way the revelation comes to you. But you can't settle for that now!

The wind of the Spirit is blowing. The heavens are changing. That means that when you stand up and walk outside, the first realm you're walking into is changing. That is the first heavenly realm.[5] The earth is shifting, and it's a totally different concept. The heavens are changing, because the wind of the Spirit is blowing. Remember, the Lord says, "You don't know which way it goes" (see John 3:8). You have to know how to sense the wind of the Spirit!

This is a season where the Spirit will be like the aperture of a camera, which opens and allows light into our spirits so we have insight. This will come quickly, so we must keep our consciences, the eyes of our hearts, clear and aligned with the Lord. An aperture can also be used to experiment: Changes in the light settings can achieve a variety of effects. This will be a season of experimentation—much like what occurred in the Early Church. By following the biblical laws and patterns, you will be able to keep the window of your conscience clean and your spirit free from vexation.

As you read earlier, I believe that we can interpret the times. I always look at the season we are moving in from a Hebraic perspective. I believe we have entered a new spiritual season in the history of the world. This nation has now made a shift into a season of change and consequence. This historical time and the actions you see by governments in the earth are creating a call for God's people to return to a Day of Deliverance. When we get in God's order and recognize the power of His blood, we will enter into a time of cleansing and power.

I believe we are to call out louder than before to the Lord. We are to reach up, and He will either reach down or send revelation to us that will cause us to build the future. No longer will we remain stuck in the hard places of the last season.

The anointing is like a spring. New springs are opening up in you. You are gaining insights on how to take new ground. Where you could not break ground in the last season, you can now! The river of life from your inner person can flow in a new way. You must know that God is watching over you as you become a watchman for Him. Ask the Lord to give you revelation on how to order your life in a new way. You will then be positioned for increase!

The atmospheres in the heavens and earth continue to change rapidly. This is a season of looking beyond. We are learning to war with not only the Word but also with our testimony! Sense the wind of the Spirit and be ready to move!

Chuck D. Pierce and Robert Heidler

God's will is that you will extend the testimony from your testings of the last season into the next season. This is a time to go deeper into the things of God. You will seek a matter and find that you understand more deeply what you have been seeking to understand. You will find the missing link or puzzle piece of the vision you are carrying in your heart. You will gain understanding in the circumstances of the past season that left you perplexed. This will produce a new hope and strength in you.

Notes

1. Chuck D. Pierce, *How to Minister Freedom: Helping Others Break the Bonds of Sexual Brokenness, Emotional Woundedness, Demonic Oppression and Occult Bondage,* Doris M. Wagner, general editor (Ventura, CA: Regal Books, 2005), p. 42.
2. Rebecca Wagner Sytsema and Chuck Pierce, *The Future War of the Church: How We Can Defeat Lawlessness and Bring God's Order to the Erath* (Ventura, CA: Regal Books, 2007), p. 175.
3. Ibid., pp. 182,188-189.
4. Ibid., pp. 182-186.
5. For more about this, see my books *The Worship Warrior, The Future War of the Church* and *As It Is in Heaven.*

14

FOLLOWING THE LAWS OF GIVING AND MULTIPLICATION

CHUCK D. PIERCE

We have discussed many things in this book in an attempt to help you break into a new level of prosperity. Remember that the opposite of prosperity is poverty, and in a changing world, poverty attempts to rule. In the days ahead, new economic structures will arise. As in the days of Joseph, many new pharaohs will come into rule, each attempting to stop God's covenant from coming into fullness.

Many have asked me, "Will the Body of Christ pull aside and create their own economy?" I don't see Christians creating their own economy, but I do see biblical patterns and laws in operation that will favor us. God's original intent was for us to prosper. Let me explain some of the patterns that I see that are important for us to understand.

1. *The Storehouse Principle:* In the midst of drought and famine, Joseph, a deliverer and dreamer, was positioned by God to save an entire nation of people. His ability to bring supernatural revelation into hard, natural circumstances was the key to a whole people surviving hard times. He created a system of survival in Egypt. People brought their harvest during 7 good years to the 12 distribution centers that had been created for storage. During the next 7 years, when a severe drought took place, these distribution centers gave out what had been stored. No one perished. (This is a precursor to the last pattern I will discuss.)

2. *The Egypt Escape Pattern:* Four hundred years of trial and oppression had created poverty for God's Chosen People. But God had a plan. He had destined a place of promise different from the place of maintenance, oppression and poverty that

was holding His people. God caused a deliverer, Moses, to rise and confront the powers and principalities that were holding the people in wrong boundaries and keeping them from being positioned in a new place of promise with new resources. When the ruling powers were broken, the people escaped with the wealth that had been taken from them. This is a great pattern of recovering what had been stolen and guarded by a strongman.

3. *The Wilderness Maintenance Pattern:* Though I do not feel this is the best model, it is a valid one. When we resist the ultimate plan that our holy God destines for us, He is still faithful to help us maintain and sustain ourselves. Out of fear of the future and the unwillingness to war for their inheritance, the Israelites were left captive in a wilderness state. God sustained them daily with manna and quail to eat, and their shoes and garments did not wear out but lasted 40 years. However, creativity and direction were stifled. They existed but never prospered.

4. *The Transference of Wealth/Warring for the Promise:* God has boundaries and laws to prosper us. When we find our place of inheritance, we are to war for the stewardship of the resources connected to the place. We are to demolish strongholds and overthrow the strongmen that hold our resources captive. The book of Joshua is a pattern of the transference of wealth. The riches came under the rule of God's people who had created laws and structures to deal with the riches. God's leadership was in place to rule the riches aligned with the promised boundaries of the people.

5. *The Cyrus Principle:* Government officials can uncover decrees and legal documents linked to the wealth and purpose of God's Kingdom people. In this way government would favor God's people and position them to build the future. This is a rare but valid pattern.

6. *The Coin in the Mouth of the Fish Model:* The Messiah did not attempt to create a new structure separate from the world structure around Him. What He did do was move supernaturally in the world structure. He entered the tax offices and found people who understood the world system. As the tax structures and religious structures threatened to control His mission, He did not shy away from governmental controls but found ways to meet their demands. He sent His people into their work spheres and told them to find the tax payment. Peter, a fisherman, was sent to fish and find the fish that had a coin in its mouth, and then the money was used for tax payments (see Matt. 17:24-27). God has ways to favor us in our jobs to meet governmental controls and demands.

7. *The Early Apostolic Model:* In Acts 4, we find a new model of bringing all that we have under apostolic rule. Only Kingdom laws were applied to the resources of Kingdom people. The apostolic leadership who had been fully taught to multiply and distribute resources was in authority over the resources of the people. They distributed as they saw fit, and no one was left wanting. This seemed to be a modern adaptation of the Storehouse Principle (see above).

I want to encourage you: God has a plan. When you learn His laws of prosperity, you will be sustained in times of drought, and you will prosper in times of trial. Let's discuss those laws of God that will help you to overcome poverty.

The Laws of God

A law is really just a picture of reality. It's a description of how things *work.* For example, the law of gravity is a description of how objects behave on planet Earth. On this planet, when you let go of an object, it falls. That's the law of gravity.

God has established many laws. For example, the one that most of us are familiar with is the law of the harvest, which says that a person will reap what he or she sows. That's a description of how the universe operates and is like the law of gravity. If you want to have a bountiful harvest, you must first sow your seed. When you understand the law of the harvest, you are enabled to prosper.

Similarly, God's moral laws describe spiritual reality. Torah, the law of God, is not an arbitrary list of rules; rather, it's a description of spiritual reality. God's Law is a picture of what God is like and is a window into His heart. If you want to know what God is like, look at the Law.

God's moral laws tell us that God is a God of righteousness and justice. He is also a God of covenant. God's moral laws reveal the boundaries between what pleases and what displeases God. When you live in a way that pleases God, you stay within God's boundaries and experience God's favor and blessing. If you violate the boundaries, you leave the realm of God's favor and experience the wages of sin. When you violate God's laws, there must always be a penalty.

The bad news is that all of us have violated God's boundaries. All of us bear the consequences of violating God's Law. The good news is that we don't have to pay the penalty ourselves. Jesus came to pay the penalty for us. He took on Himself the wages of our sins so we could experience the blessing of righteousness. That's the gospel!

Many Christians assume God gave us His moral law to enable us to live lives that please Him. That is false. Because of our sinful nature, we no longer have the ability to stay within the boundaries of the Law in our own power. The Bible teaches that God gave us the Law to show us our sin problem, not to cure it. Trying to use the Law as a means of becoming righteous is called legalism, and it never works.

God's provision for staying within the boundaries is called grace. Through grace, the Holy Spirit dwelling within us produces the fruit of the Spirit in our lives (see Gal. 5:22-23). The result is that as we walk in the Spirit, our lives are characterized by the fruit of the Spirit—love, joy, peace, patience, kindness, and so forth. When our lives are characterized by the fruit of the Spirit, we find ourselves automatically living within the boundaries that the Law describes. As Paul says in Romans 8:3-4, "What the Law could not do, weak as it was through the flesh, God did: sending His own Son in the likeness of sinful flesh and as an offering for sin, He condemned sin in the flesh, so that the requirement of the Law might be fulfilled in us, who do not walk according to the flesh but according to the Spirit" (*NASB*).

How a Poverty Mindset Develops

Satan uses times and laws to stop God's people from advancing and manifesting His grace and power. As mentioned earlier, Daniel 7:25 says that Satan tries to wear down our minds or ways of thinking to capture us and consequently capture the blessings and promises God intended for us. Once we agree or fall prey to Satan's ways, we begin to decrease rather than increase. The enemy's plan of devastation takes effect, and we begin to lose the war of resisting.

This is when we move from operating in the laws of prosperity and begin to embrace poverty. Satan overtakes our minds with a flood of thought that starts this reversal. Instead of thinking prosperity and meditating on the covenant that God has with us, we develop a poverty mindset. We must remain alert as to what is happening in our field or the enemy will attempt to get his hand on what belongs to us. When we grow passive and are not aware of the enemy's scheme to rob our supplies and assets, he maneuvers and manipulates his way into the storehouses meant for us. When the enemy gains an upper hand over our inheritance, we lose our stewardship ability to multiply. When we fail to capitalize on the opportunity to bring in our harvest, he steals the field.

We can plant, watch our crops grow and have breakthrough, but if we do not take the opportunity to gather and steward the spoils, a strategy of poverty will begin to develop against us. Remember the story of Gideon. Every year at harvest times, for seven years, the Midianites would let Israel grow the harvest and then come to steal, rob and plunder. When we increase without developing storehouses to contain our spoils, we eventually lose the spoils, and poverty begins to work.

Refusing to become what God created and destined you to be causes poverty to work in your life. Not believing that the Lord can branch you into the fullness of His plan is just as bad as refusing to become what He intended and created you to become. Not just experiencing lack but also having a fear that you will lack is a poverty way of thinking. When you conform to your circumstances or come into agreement with the blueprint of the world, the prince of this world will use you until he has fully captured your strength for his purpose. Here are some areas in which the enemy attempts to conform us to his pattern:

- Greed—in a world where debt rules, he attempts to get us to align with structures that cause our interest rates to go beyond a godly mentality of interest (see Prov. 11:24)
- Gluttony (see Prov. 23:21)
- Indolence or laziness (see Prov. 24:30-34)
- Hastiness (see Prov. 28:22)
- Fear or unwillingness to face our enemy (see Prov. 22:13)
- Succumbing to persecution of faith (see Prov. 13:18)

The Law of Love and Giving Combats Poverty

God is kind and good. His method of change was giving. He gave us out of poverty—by His stripes, He took our poverty upon Him (see Isa. 53:5). He spoke, He gave, and we entered into a law called redemption. Therefore, we have the ability to give our way out of poverty. (As you read further in this chapter, you will understand better what we mean by the law of love that has no bounds or poverty, and the law of grace that has no ability to be hindered.)

God is kind, so our acts of kindness and generosity toward others combat the power of poverty as it attempts to root itself in our lives. When we allow others to glean from our vineyard and have access to our excess, God honors and creates a field of prosperity around us that protects and prevents poverty from working. When we develop strategies to combat the systemic poverty that is ruling a territory or group of individuals around us, we prosper. When we do not hold back what God has entrusted to us, our portion will always increase, not decrease.

God has ways to increase the seed we have to give us more seed. Let's begin by looking at this Law of the Seed.

The Law of the Seed

One key law to understand is that of the seed. There is a seed, and the seed has to grow. This is how the Lord looks at everything—in every area of our lives we have to understand this concept of "seed," because it's the seed that's going to advance. In Ephesians 4:7-11, Paul shows how God's kingdom expresses the understanding of "seed":

> To each one of us grace was given according to the measure of Christ's gift. Therefore He says: "When he ascended on high, He led captivity captive and gave gifts to men." Now this, "He ascended"—what does it mean but that He also first descended into the lower parts of the earth? He who descended is also the One who ascended [a seed had to die, then be resurrected and exploded, and you're a product of it] far above all the heavens, that He might fill all things.) And He Himself gave some to be apostles, some prophets, some evangelists, and some pastors and teachers.

Yeshua, our Messiah, is at the right hand of the Father and is available to each of us. He is in the process of loosing now what has been stored in the heavens. He is sowing. This passage doesn't say "just in the church," for God is giving these gifts to society so that society will prosper! Anytime we give back a seed that He put into our care, that seed prospers. As Paul writes:

> [God gave these gifts] for the equipping of the saints for the work of the ministry, for the edifying of the body of Christ, until we all come to the unity of the faith and of the knowledge of the Son of God, to a perfect man, to the measure of the stature of the fullness of Christ; that we should no

longer be children, tossed to and fro and carried about with
every wind of doctrine, by the trickery of men, in the cunning
craftiness of deceitful plotting, but, speaking the truth in
love, may grow up in all things into Him who is the head—
Christ—from whom the whole body, joined and knit together
by what every joint supplies, according to the effective working by which every part does its share, causes growth of the
body (Eph. 4:12-16).

This is a growth principle, though it is not usually looked at as a
growth principle. Most of the time this statement is viewed as a foundation principle but not a growth principle.

Seven Aspects of the Law of the Seed
The Law of the Seed has seven aspects:

1. *The seed lives, produces and reproduces.* That is the whole concept of seed. Consider a river in relation to seed. "River"
   and "seed" are both life-giving words. Psalm 46:4 says,
   "There is a river whose streams shall make glad the city of
   God, the holy place of the tabernacle of the Most High."
   In contrast to the raging environment, there is a peaceful
   river of supply in God's sanctuary that produces life.
   Though Jerusalem had no such literal river, it is believed
   by many that there is a subterranean supply that is the
   source of various fountains and pools in Jerusalem. The
   unseen river becomes a symbol of the inner life, grace and
   joy that only God gives. God, the Father (see Jer. 2:13);
   God, the Son (see Zech. 13:1); and God, the Holy Spirit
   (see John 4:14; 7:38) are all referred to as a river. In Psalm
   46, the river refers to the ministry of the Holy Spirit, which
   flows to and brings life to every member of the Church
   (the city of God). As the streams of the river make glad the
   city of God in a context of calamity, these streams may
   also refer to the ministries of the Holy Spirit that are given
   to members of the Body of Christ, especially in times of

trouble and that produce joy (see Acts 13:52; 1 Thess. 1:6). This law of the seed in the river is linked to that whole concept of the life-giving substance that carries the seed. It's linked to the procreative, whole reproductive type of thought process.

2. *Like produces like.* This is a principle of the seed. If you cross seeds, they will produce a hybrid, and then you're dealing with a totally different mixture of development. That's where we're going in the economic structure today. Hybrids involve a different concept of either warfare or prosperity.

3. *The seed is in the fruit.* What is produced has the seed in it.

4. *The seed has an enemy.* Every seed has an enemy structure that wants to capture the increase of that seed. Remember that God said He would put enmity between the seed of the woman and the seed of the enemy, and her seed would begin to rise up and put its foot on the serpent's head (see Gen. 3:15). In whatever you are working with, you have to factor in this Law of the Seed and realize you are dealing with an enemy. If you don't factor that in, your seed can literally be overcome.

5. *The seed is filled with identity.* The identity of the seed is expressed through being chosen. The seed was filled from identity from the beginning. We talk about identity all the time, but it came in the form of a seed, and until the seed comes into fullness, the identity isn't expressed. When you study the Hebrew, the concept of identity is linked back to the seed, and it involves a supernatural force of being chosen. For example, the seed of Adam was in both Abel and Cain, but Abel was the one chosen and favored. Therefore, there is certain seed that will be favored because of its reaction—the seed searches the light to go back to where it was sown. The same was true of Jacob and Esau, and Jesus taught the same. You see this principle all through the

Word of God. So it is this supernatural factor of being chosen that causes our identity to come into its fullness.

6. *There are seeds in all things that can prosper* (see Col. 1:17). Everything—visible and invisible—has seeds. Once you begin to see and understand this Law of the Seed, you will move forward into a whole new level of prosperity.

7. *God is now decoding seeds to produce our future.* This principle of resurrection and power in the seed is important, because it brings us to the whole concept of DNA. This concept operates in the same way in our national industries as well as in our local businesses. God is untwisting some things and bringing a touch of His power, His DNA and His holiness into what we're about. When He does this, we can go to the next level of financial prosperity. That's what we're seeing in the financial industry right now. In 1988, certain economic decisions were made that began to produce an iniquity in the national debt structure and the way prosperity was occurring in this nation. What God is doing now is letting things fall and decoding them—unwrapping that iniquitous structure—so He can begin to recode them. He's looking for people like you and me who have His seed and His Word hidden in us so He can send us into these industries and businesses and recode them.

The Word of God Is the Seed

When you look at the concept of seed, you find a progression of understanding. You need to get this progression built into your logic and core value. You must look at your seed. What has been sown in you has been placed there to profit as you mature in life. You need to understand this from a Hebraic point of view, because most of us do not have a mindset to prosper.

1. *The seed is the Word of God, and all seed is linked with the Word of God* (see Matt. 13:1-23). The first basis is that the seed is

the Word. God knew you from the foundation of the earth. He knows that seed that created you, knit you together, and formed you. He *can* cause your uniqueness to prosper!

2. *The Word of God was from the beginning* (see John 1:1-5). The seed has always been there. It has already been built into what you are for you to use to prosper this season. All of your thought processes—especially your covenant alignment back into prosperity—are built from the concept of the Word. I don't mean just the Bible. Rather, I mean the Word and how it is structured moving in you, through you and around you. The revealed Word of God is constructed from 22 fundamental letters, or parent roots, so every word that you're carrying has a parent root in it. If that parent root is not flowing from a godly perspective, whether it's the vision of your business or your life or your family—no matter what you're operating in—it will not produce good fruit.

When we're talking about the Word, we're talking about how you can wake up with an idea that to you is a new idea. But that idea was already seeded in you from God, and it is built and constructed from the life-giving Word of God. The idea has a root system that can produce fruit. (This is how we think Hebraically.) Suppose you have an accounting background. Accounting makes you happy, you love doing it, and other people love you doing it. Your feeling about accounting (from the Hebrew word for "order and reconciliation") was built into you from the beginning, and now it has sprung forth. Do you think you came up with all this yourself? That you just happen to like doing certain things? No! Rather, it's amazing how the parent root that caused your seed to come alive had already been encoded in you.

3. *The beginning produces the end* (see Isa. 46:9). If the seed is in the Word and the Word was from the beginning, then the

beginning produces the end. In other words, based on how
you write your vision, and make it plain and keep that vision refocused and rewritten, is how your end is going to
be produced. That the beginning creates the end is a biblical principle.

4. *The agricultural principle of the seed begins in the beginning and is
scattered throughout every concept of the life-giving word that prospers* (see Gen. 1:11-12). When God decided to redo the
earth and break through the darkness on the third day, He
created the seed principle. He spoke it into everything in
the earth realm in the beginning. If you don't understand
this concept, then you won't see the realm of prosperity.
You may say to me, "Well, then where's the seed of trans-
portation?" The seed was spoken into the ability to follow
and move from one place to another. Through that seed
God would give ways—creative ways, from age to age to
age—to advance what was put into action from what was in
the beginning. You then have the capacity of moving
things around and using the seed that had been scattered—
the seed principle from the third day—to move everything
in this age. This extends to your generation and to the industry to which He has called you and it includes a whole
new level of growth. The seed's already there!

It is important to remember that every seed that began in the beginning got scattered. The principle of scattering is most obvious in the story of the Tower of Babel
(see Gen. 11). You need to understand this principle of
scattering so you will recognize times when your own seed
is scattered. Look also at the descendants of Ham and
Canaan. You will see their seed reproduced and became
wealthy in the Promised Land. God had scattered it there
because it was fertile ground. He allowed the enemy to
create great riches there—riches that would be transferred
to the Israelites. He scattered the seed there and said to
Abraham, "Until the iniquity that was in that seed comes

into fullness, I'm not going to transfer it over to your stewardship" (see Gen. 15:16). It took 470 years before He could transfer it.

A Tree that Prospers

The Word of God, the seed, was in the beginning (see John 1:1). The Word of God is also equated with a living tree:

> Blessed is the man who walks not in the counsel of the ungodly, nor stands in the path of sinners, nor sits in the seat of the scornful; but his delight is in the law of the LORD, and in His law he meditates day and night. He shall be like a tree planted by rivers of water, that brings forth its fruit in its season, whose leaf also shall not wither; and whatever he does shall prosper (Ps. 1:1-3).

This is how the Hebraic concept works, how Torah works, how the Word of God works, and how Jesus taught. What may make the Law of the Seed difficult to understand is that our thinking is so linear; especially in business, our thinking gets stuck in a linear mode instead of a circular pattern of thought that allows creativity to enter. Circular thought allows for a "suddenly" and brings you to a place where God can use you for what He has seeded into you. You can then see cycles and trends, and you can see how to make shifts. You can see what's motivating you to make you happy, and you can be more creative so that you can prosper. If you meditate on (soak up) the life-giving Word, you will prosper (produce fruit).

If you look at a living tree, you will notice characteristics we share with it:

• This tree has leaves and branches.

• Isaiah 11:1 states, "There shall come forth a Rod from the stem of Jesse, and a Branch shall grow out of his roots." The tree has a rod out of the stem; it's one of Jesus' names (see Zech. 3:8; 6:12; Rom. 15:12). In other words, coming out of the stem is a rod that allows you to have authority. You can meditate on one word that provided the foundation of your vision and eventually have authority in an entire industry. This is because Jesus is the rod coming out of that stem from which the seed of that word created vision.

- The tree has vines, and you have to go through the pruning process of vines.

- The tree has vinedressers—people in your life who help the pruning process. If you don't have them in your life, you start growing out and producing weak shoots, because you don't have the actual nutrients to prosper. It doesn't mean you won't produce fruit; you just won't have the nutrients to prosper in a new way.

- Built into every seed (and into the tree) is the concept of firstfruits. Firstfruits is the principle of the seed bursting into resurrection. So when you are operating in firstfruits, you have the ability to burst forth into resurrection-type thinking. This allows you to look at something that has fallen dead and see how to re-create it. If you allow the power of firstfruits to be unlocked in you, you'll have access to incredible opportunity.

- When you are grafted into the natural tree, you have the right to prosper. But in the midst of it, it will always seem as if the ground isn't working—through culture, industry misuse, or some other reason. But you can go deeper into the soil of God's Word to increase and grow!

The Law of Recovery

Let me say yet again that we want you to prosper! We want you to recover what is lost and advance. The cares of this world are blinding. The debt structure of so many is overwhelming and preventing them from building and seeing clearly into the future.

We are given the liberty to borrow, but we must remember that whatever we borrow, we must take care of until the owner receives his or her return. Linda Heidler recently wrote me about a passage of

Scripture in 2 Kings 6. This story is better known as "The Floating Axe Head," or "Recover What Seems to Be Lost that You Have Borrowed." Linda writes:

> I saw something in the passage about the axe head being borrowed. The man who borrowed it was a good man. However, once he borrowed something, he was obligated to give it back. In the man's serving, he lost that which he was using. Not only is this a hard thing, but what he was using had been loaned to him. Because he lost it, he owed a debt that he could not repay. This is a key passage about getting out of debt. The young prophet had to seek wisdom from the seasoned prophet to recover his loss.
>
> Second Chronicles 20:20 encourages us to heed the word of the prophet and we will succeed. If we seek prophetic counsel and follow it, we will see God intervene to get us out of debt! This is what happened to Robert and me when we were so far in debt, and you told us to sell our house and pay off our debt. That was in 1997. It took almost a year, from February until November 1997, to get the house in good enough shape to sell. During that time, the property values in our neighborhood increased dramatically and the interest rates for home loans dropped dramatically. We sold our house, paid off our debts, and came out with enough to build our present house, which is almost twice the size and three times the value of our old house.
>
> Debt can be blinding. When we borrow, we must remember that we are obligated to pay it back. Many people feel trapped in the midst of their debt and come into a place of just wanting someone to remove the burden or pay off what they have borrowed. But to do this violates a principle of asking for, receiving, and following prophetic direction. Each one of us has something we can use. There is a resource that we have to pay off our debt. We can't allow fear to prevent us from letting go of what we have. We can't fear being left without any resources.
>
> Robert and I had considered selling our house to pay our debt before we went to you, but we were afraid of being left

with nothing. We had to trust God that if we followed the counsel you gave us, He would not leave us in need but would provide for us. We never imagined that He would provide so much and so far above even what we could have imagined. What happened with the axe head was a miracle, but when I think of what happened with us, it is no less a miracle. It takes faith to heed the word of the prophet for getting out of debt, but we will prosper if we do.[1]

Ask the Lord to remove any debt that has blinded you. Thank Him that He redeemed you from debt so that He can show you how to be delivered today from any debt that surrounds you. Even if you have lost what you borrowed, you can recover it! You can see your way past your debt.

The Law of Use

Use is an interesting principle. Use employs something for a specific purpose. Use takes something that is available for consumption and makes that item or resource active. In medieval English property law, there was a Law of Use that gave the right for one person to take the profits of land that belonged to another. It usually involved three people, although only two could be involved. One man (A) would convey land to another (B) on the condition that the latter would use it, not for his own benefit, but for the benefit of a third man (C), who could be A himself. C (or A), thus, had the profits, that is, the use of the land and could treat the land as he pleased.

This legal institution, which arose as early as the eleventh century, came to be employed not only as a legitimate method of providing for property management and for conveyancing but also as a method of defrauding creditors, depriving feudal landlords of their dues, and permitting religious institutions to derive the benefit of land that they could not own directly.

Here are some principles from the Word that utilize the Law of Use:

- *Give to someone more legitimate than you* (see Gen. 14). Abraham knew he had gained resources and spoils from war. However, instead of keeping what he had won, he presented all the spoils as an offering to Melchizedech, the high priest. He gave to someone more legitimate than himself. When he used these resources as firstfruits, God made a covenant with him shortly thereafter (see Gen. 15).

- *Outline your future* (see Gen. 22; 25:23; 27:29; 28:3-4,13-15). If we outline our future, we know what resources are available to us. We can then use those resources to advance.

- *Watch for angelic assistance* (see Gen. 28:12; Exod. 23:20-24; Luke 2:8-14). Angels are sent as messengers and helpers on our path. When we listen and use the revelation and protection they bring, we triumph.

- *Remember your commitments to serve* (see Gen. 28:18-19). Once we make a vow, we need to use the power in that vow to serve until the promise that the vow is connected to manifests.

- *Remember the memorial events in your life* (see Gen. 28:20-22; Hag. 1-2). When we use a portion of our resources to give as a memorial offering, God shakes loose the best that is ahead for us.

- *Be willing to operate in the principle of firstfruits giving, even in your need* (see 1 Kings 17:8-16). The widow first gave to the prophet what she had. He knew how to use this offering to multiply and sustain them for several days.

- *Evaluate your resources and enter into a new level of creativity* (see 2 Kings 4). The prophet asked another widow what she had in her house to use. This was after asking her what she wanted him to do for her. He took what she had, gave her a strategy, and she paid off all of her debt.

- *Give to an anointing greater than yours* (see 2 Kings 4; 8). The woman of Shunem was rich. However, she used a portion of her home and belongings for the prophet. This broke barrenness and death from her and caused the law of restoration to work on her behalf later.

- *Let love be your motivator* (see John 3:16). God the Father used His best to give so that humankind would be redeemed.

- *Everything you steward should multiply* (see Luke 19). We must never let fear keep us from using what God has given to us to multiply. How we use our resources is proportionate to our judgment and increase. Do not fear increase!

The Law of Multiplication

Newton's law of universal gravitation states that "every point mass in the universe attracts every other point mass with a force that is directly proportional to the product of their masses and inversely proportional to the square of the distance between them."[2] What happens if we violate this law of gravity? One object will hit another with great velocity!

There are spiritual laws of multiplication and prosperity just like physical laws, and these laws work the same way. When we violate one of the laws, instead of increasing we decrease; and instead of multiplying, we stay the same, divide or dwindle. Here are some of the Laws of Multiplication:

1. *The Law of Use—debt can be overcome through exploits* (see 2 Kings 4). Recognizing authority assures security. Notice in this story how each woman recognized the authority of the prophet and his ability to gain revelation that would cause them to increase. (We will discuss this law further in the next section.)

2. *The Law of Firstfruits—the best produces the rest* (see 1 Kings 17; Gen. 14; Acts 4). We have fully discussed this principle in this book. (For further understanding, see *A Time to Advance.*[3])

3. *The Law of Discipleship—learn to be a disciple of love* (see Matt. 14:13-21). When John the Baptist was beheaded, Jesus

pulled aside to seek the Father over how to shift His disciples to a new level of authority. The beheading of John
represented the end of a forerunner season and the maturing of the next wineskin. The first lesson the Lord
taught His disciples was a lesson on multiplication. They
wanted Him to feed the 5,000 people who were following
Him. Instead, He said, "You feed them!" He then activated
the Law of Use in His teaching and had them bring Him
the fish and loaves of a little boy. He broke the food into
pieces, multiplied what was there and fed all the people.
He taught His disciples that His love for the people could
multiply the resources available.

4. *The Law of Persistence—keep on and you will receive* (see Luke
   11:9-13; 18:1-8). The persistent widow did not relent in pe-
   titioning the judge until she received favor to get what she
   needed. Ask and keep on asking, seek and keep on seeking,
   and knock until the door opens.

5. *The Law of Waste—pour out in devotion* (see John 12:1-8). Mary
   poured out her savings and retirement. This seemed a
   waste, but it secured the future for humankind. Sometimes, when you pour out what you have, the Lord multiplies grace back to you.

6. *The Law of Giving—give out of love* (see John 3:16). God gave so
   that we could multiply in grace. Jesus taught giving. The
   apostles taught giving. Giving breaks the curse of robbing
   from God and opens the heavens.

7. *The Law of Worship—worship in faith to go higher* (see Gen. 22:1-
   19). In *The Worship Warrior*, John Dickson and I explain how
   faith and worship work together.[4] I believe this is our most
   important law. Learn to ascend in worship. Abraham ascended Mount Moriah for his faith to be tested. He worshiped, and this caused a revelation of God to come strongly
   into the atmosphere. The provision was there. After Abraham worshiped, he could see his provision for the future.

Gaining a Mindset of Multiplication and Use

If you are reading this book, I believe you picked it up because the hand of God is on you. God has brought you through some hard times, but He wants you to know He is with you and has a plan for your life. The best is yet ahead! To help you understand God's plan for your prosperity, I want you to understand 2 Kings 4. This chapter contains the stories of two women. Their situations were different, but through the prophet Elisha, God asked both of them the same question: "What can I do for you?"

This is a question that God is still asking. God had a plan to bring each of these women into His blessing and to meet the deepest desires of their hearts, and He has the same goal for you. Second Kings 4 begins with the story of a widow. Here's a condensed version:

> The wife of a man from the company of the prophets cried out to Elisha, "Your servant, my husband is dead and you know that he revered the Lord. But now his creditors are coming to take my two boys as his slaves." And Elisha replied, "What can I do for you? What do you have in your house?" "I have nothing there at all," she said, "except a little oil." Elisha said, "Go and ask all of your neighbors for all their empty jars, and don't collect just a few. Then go inside, close the door and, with the help of your sons, pour oil into all the jars." So the widow left him and did as Elisha had told her. When all the jars were full, she said to her son, "Bring me another jar," but he replied, "There's no jar left." Then the oil stopped flowing. She went to Elisha and he said to her, "Go and sell the oil and pay your debts. Then you and your sons can live on what is left."

What Elisha did for this woman was to show her a Kingdom principle: the principle of multiplication. In Mark 6:32-44, we find a similar story in which Jesus had compassion on a large crowd. He had been teaching them many things, and when it grew late in the day He told His disciples to give them something to eat. Here is a condensed version:

> When Jesus told the disciples to give the crowd something to eat, they said, "That would take more than half a year's wages.

Are You telling us to spend that much on bread and give it to them to eat?" "How many loaves do you have?" Jesus asked. "Go and see." When they found out, they said, "Five loaves and two fish." Jesus told them to have the people sit in large groups on the grass. Taking the five loaves and two fish, Jesus looked up to heaven, gave thanks, broke the loaves and then gave them to His disciples to distribute to the people. He also divided the two fish among all the people there. Everyone had enough to eat, and the disciples were even able to pick up 12 baskets of leftovers. About 5,000 men had been fed.

When God asks, "What can I do for you?" He's saying He wants to bless you. In Romans 8:32, Paul tells us, "If God loved you enough to send His Own Son to die for you, there's no good thing that He will withhold" (author's paraphrase). The word "blessing" means to cause to increase. A curse brings decrease, while a blessing brings increase. If we are walking in God's blessing, we should always be increasing. To increase is to prosper.

As I previously noted, during the Dark Ages most of the Church bought into the philosophy of asceticism, which said that God is happier when we are poor. Those who wanted to please God were told to take a vow of poverty. But that philosophy is not in the Bible. Almost all of the people we read about in God's Word were prosperous. Abraham was one of the wealthiest men in the land. Isaac, Jacob and Joseph prospered as well. David, Daniel and Paul were great men of God, and they were successful.

God wants you to be successful as well. He wants you to prosper and succeed in everything He has called you to do. That is His will, and that is His promise. You are not to worship money or let it control your life—the love of money will always get you in trouble. But God is not against money! He doesn't want His children to walk in poverty and His Church to be hindered by lack.

Failure is not more spiritual than success. Every day of your life, you're either walking in a blessing or walking under a curse. You can choose which you want to experience, but God wants you to know that His choice for you is blessing. Many don't know that God has promised increase and prosperity. Because of the Church's poverty mentality, many have been taught against prosperity.

I once heard a story about a group of deacons who were laying hands on the new pastor they had just hired. The head deacon prayed, "Lord, we thank You for this new pastor. We ask that You keep him holy, and we promise that we will keep him poor!" That's seriously how a lot of the Church thinks. There are those who teach that prosperity is a vice and that poverty is a virtue. If you've been exposed to that kind of false teaching, I have good news for you: the Bible is full of passages that teach prosperity! (See the passages we listed in chapter 4). So if you don't like teaching on prosperity, you will find it hard to read the Bible!

Some people don't know how to prosper. They try to practice what I call "Christian magic." If they need a new car, they claim it and confess it and visualize it and see the picture of a new car in their minds. They chant over and over, "New car, new car, new car." Then they look out their windows, waiting for new cars to appear in their driveways.

That is not how God works, and it is not how increase comes. God's plan for increase is called multiplication. In Hebrew the word for "increase" means to multiply.

The Meaning of "Multiply"

How would you describe what it means to multiply? Webster defines "multiply" this way: "To spread, to propagate, to increase by multiples, to increase greatly in number, to become progressively greater in amount."[5] Biblically, the concept means to take a small amount of available resources and see them increase and reproduce to fill every void and meet every need.

Picture a farmer with a small sack of seeds. He could take those seeds and grind them up and bake a couple loaves of bread and eat for a week and then die. Or he could sow those seeds in the ground; and when harvest comes, that which had been a very small amount will have become a significant resource for his future. Multiplication means that God has already supplied what you need—but He's given it in seed form! His plan is for you to take what you have and multiply it to meet your need. God's very first command to Adam and Eve was to be fruitful and multiply! That is still His desire.

When Elisha asked the widow, "What can I do for you?" he wasn't offering to have a wagon full of gold coins driven up and the coins dropped at her doorstep. He was offering something much more valuable. He was offering to show her a principle of the Kingdom.

God says He wants you to multiply as well (see Prov. 3:9-10). He wants to multiply your numbers, your offspring, your resources and the days of your life. He wants to multiply His miracles and multiply your seed for sowing. He wants to multiply grace and peace in your life.

The Steps in Multiplication

The steps of you need to take for multiplication to take place in your life can be seen in 2 Kings 4:

1. *Multiplication is to see your need.* The prophet's widow cried out to Elisha, "Your servant my husband is dead, and you know that he revered the Lord. But now his creditors are coming to take my two boys as his slaves." This woman saw her need very clearly. She was in desperate need. Her husband had died, she had lost everything except her two sons, and now she was about to lose them.

2. *See what you have.* Elisha's first question was, "What can I do for you?" His next question was, "What do you have?" The woman said, "All I have is a container with a small amount of oil." She knew what she had, but she didn't believe that it would be useful in solving her problem. Elisha, however, wanted to focus this woman's attention on what she presently had. That's what Jesus did when He told the disciples to feed the multitude. The disciples said, "We can't afford to buy food for all these people." Jesus said, "How many loaves do you have? What do you have now? Go and see." What you have is your resource to begin that multiplication process.

3. *Submit what you have to God.* The widow had to be willing to submit that little container of oil to the Lord's plan. That's

basically what Jesus asked the disciples to do when they showed up with the five loaves and the two fish. He said, "Bring them to Me. Put your resources in My hands." This doesn't mean that you put all your resources in the offering! Rather, this means you commit your resources to God and then receive God's strategy. Submission means that you commit to hearing God's plan and to walking it out by faith.

The Multiplication Process

In Matthew 14, we see that Jesus had a plan to multiply the loaves and the fish for the multitude. First, He had the people sit down in groups. He took the food and blessed it. He broke the loaves and gave the bread to the disciples to distribute to the people.

Have you ever wondered exactly when the multiplication took place? When He lifted it up to God and blessed it, did it suddenly start to multiply? Was it when He handed it to the disciples? I can't prove this, but I don't think the multiplication began until the disciples began handing it out. There were five loaves and 12 disciples, so each disciple got less than half a loaf. They started breaking off pieces and giving them to the people. They looked up, and there were thousands of people waiting to be fed. But they didn't focus on the thousands. They just had to say to themselves, *Jesus said to hand this out, so I'm obeying.* They moved by faith to follow Jesus' instructions, and as they did, it multiplied.

That's the same thing the widow did. Elisha said, "Ask your neighbors for empty jars. Don't just get a few. Then go inside, shut the door behind you and pour your oil into the containers." She obeyed and did what the prophet said, and as she poured the oil, it multiplied to fill each container. As long as there was a container to fill, the oil continued to flow. When she ran out of containers, the oil stopped flowing. A small amount of oil multiplied to meet her present need and become a resource for her future.

So the process of multiplication looks something like this:

1. You recognize your need: You don't have enough.
2. You see what you do have. You don't have enough now, but it can multiply. You ask yourself, *What do I have?*

3. You submit what you have to God and put it in His hands. You say, "Lord, here are my resources. Show me what to do with it."
4. You receive God's strategy (God always has a plan).
5. You walk by faith and receive breakthrough.

That's a picture of how God wants all of us to live. God wants you to have a mindset to multiply. In every situation, God wants to show you how to multiply what you have. When you look at your resources, don't just see your lack. Look to see what your present resources can become.

The multiplication of the widow's oil was a miracle, but a miracle is just one way God can cause you to multiply. Genesis 26 tells how Isaac was living in enemy territory in the midst of a famine. Things looked bad; the economy was in shambles. But the Bible says that Isaac planted in that time of famine and received a hundredfold return (see Gen. 26:12). Do you know why? He knew how to multiply! If you know how to multiply, you don't have to worry about what the economy is doing.

The King and the Chessboard

Anytime you operate in the principle of multiplication, the results will seem miraculous. One of Robert's favorite stories of multiplication is the story of the King and the Chessboard. A great and powerful king decided to honor a hero who had saved the nation in a time of great crisis. The king called the hero into his throne room and said, "You have done this country a great service, and I want to greatly reward you. Name your reward. Whatever it is, I will give it."

The hero thought for a moment and then said, "Take a chess board and put one small gold coin on the first square. Then put two coins on the second square, four coins on the third, etc. Each time double what was on the square before, until all the squares on the board are filled. With that reward, I'll be satisfied."

The king was offended that the hero had asked for such a small reward. But he finally agreed to the terms. They brought out a chessboard and put one small gold coin on the first square, two coins on the second square, and four coins on the third square. The king was embarrassed. He interrupted the process and said, "Please name a different reward. We want to give you more than this."

But the hero was insistent, so before all the court and all the officials, the king agreed and said, "We will do what you've asked." But as they continued to place coins on the chessboard, something happened that the king had not expected. As each square doubled the gold on the one before, the gold multiplied. By the time they got to the last row of the chessboard, the hero owned all of the wealth of the kingdom!

After sharing this illustration a few weeks ago, we did some checking on what the actual amount of this hero's reward would have been. If the king had used pennies instead of gold coins, the hero would have received a total of $184,467,440,737,095,516.15. (That's far above the value of all the gold ever mined in the history of the world!)

But the king would have run into a logistical problem long before the chessboard was full! As each stack of pennies doubled the height of the previous stack, the stacks would quickly reach impossible heights. For example, by the time you got to square 22, the stack of pennies would be over a mile high. The next square would double that! The pile of pennies on the twenty-ninth square would reach beyond the International Space Station. The pile on the thirty-ninth square would reach to the Moon, and the final square would hold a stack of pennies reaching one-third of the way to the nearest star! That's the power of multiplication!

The Ways to Multiply

The point is this: What you have now may seem small and even insignificant. What you have now may seem as if it won't do anything to meet your needs. But if you learn to multiply, what you have now will more than meet every need. God wants to change your mindset. He wants you to know that He's already given you what you need. You just need to learn to multiply it. How do you do that? The Bible tells a number of ways to multiply.

Multiplication Through Giving
The first way to multiply is through giving. In Luke 6:38, Jesus says, "Give, and it will be given to you. A good measure, pressed down,

shaken together and running over, will be poured into your lap" (*NIV*). In 2 Corinthians 9:6, Paul says, "Whoever sows generously will also reap generously" (*NIV*).

When I first met Robert Heidler, he did not understand the importance of these passages. He likes to share, "I didn't understand this principle until I met Chuck. But that is how he lives. Over the years, I have seen what Chuck does when he is faced with financial lack. He gets out his checkbook and starts writing checks! He begins giving money to people. He says, 'Lord, who should I give to? Who's in need?' He will give until his bank account is empty. But he knows that the next day, money will start to come in, and it always does."

Through the years I have learned that I cannot out-give God. Giving causes you to multiply!

Multiplication Through Investment

A second way we multiply is by investing. Investing is a way to multiply what God has put into our hands. In Jesus' parable of the talents, the master said, "You could have at least deposited it and earned interest" (see Matt. 25:27; Luke 19:23). You can multiply by putting money in a savings account that earns interest. You can make careful investments in stocks or in real estate. You can use extra money to start a business on the side. Just be sure to invest what you have where it will multiply.

Whenever I go into a 7-Eleven store, there always seems to be a line of people buying lottery tickets. If you had $5,000 and invested it in lottery tickets, in 25 years you would have no money. That's not a good investment! (Somebody once said that the lottery is a tax on people who are bad at math.)

If you took $5,000 and just hid it under your mattress, in 25 years you would have $5,000. (You haven't lost, but you haven't multiplied either!)

But if you had $5,000 and invested it where you could get 7 percent interest, in 25 years your $5,000 would have grown to become $30,000! Jesus said that earning interest is the least you should do.

Multiplication Through Wisdom

We can also multiply by gaining wisdom. Wisdom multiplies your time, and time is one of the most valuable commodities you can have.

When you have wisdom, you can accomplish more in less time, so your time is multiplied. If most people can do a job in 10 hours and you have the wisdom to figure out how to get it done in 5 hours, you have gained 5 hours. That is multiplication.

How do you get wisdom? The Bible is full of wisdom. If you need to gain wisdom, then start reading the book of Proverbs. The Bible promises wisdom to those who will read and study it. Read a chapter a day. Every day as you read, ask God to teach you His wisdom. Write down what He shows you.

Multiplication by Increasing Skills
Yet another way to multiply is by developing your skills. This is one of the most profitable ways to multiply. You increase your skills through training and instruction. At Glory of Zion International, located in the Global Spheres Center we have the Kingdom Force Institute. This is a great place to be trained. We also have conferences, books and training classes where people can hone their skills in ministry.

In the marketplace, you can take classes at community centers, job centers, and schools. You can take courses at a junior college. Your business may even hold training sessions. You might want to consider learning a new language. Here in Texas, knowing Spanish will greatly increase the number of jobs available to you. If you are hindered by a lack of computer skills, you can take computer classes at various places to increase those skills. The result of multiplying your skill is promotion. The Bible says that your gift will make a place for you.

So if you have a job and it's not paying what you need, multiply your abilities! If you take some training courses, you may get a promotion. I've known people who learned a new set of skills, got a new job, and doubled their income! That's a good return on your time and money. But you need to gain that mindset to multiply. Don't be satisfied with the skills you have now. Ask yourself, *How can I increase my abilities? How can I gain new skills?*

Multiplication Through Creativity
Finally, we multiply by drawing close to God and increasing creativity. God is the source of all creativity. He created everything. If you draw

close to God, He will impart creativity to you. You will learn to take what you have and use it to bring multiplication.

One of the ministries of the Holy Spirit is to give us divine creativity. Isaiah 11:2 tells us that God is the "Spirit of wisdom." In Hebrew, that word "wisdom" literally means "creative skill." So as you draw close to the Holy Spirit, you get creative ideas from God. You get ideas that you never had before. If you are a musician, you will get new songs. If you are an artist, you will paint new pictures. In your business, you will get creative solutions that no one else could have received. Somebody once said that one new idea can make you rich. A mindset to multiply says, "How can I walk in creativity to multiply the resources God has given me?"

A wonderful illustration of multiplication through creativity can be seen in Proverbs 31. Solomon writes:

> She looks for wool and flax and works with her hands in delight. She considers a field and buys it; from her earnings she plants a vineyard. She senses that her gain is good. She makes linen garments and sells them, and supplies belts to the tradesmen. . . . And she smiles at the future. (Prov. 31:13, 16,18,24-25, *NASB*).

Note the result of the multiplication of her creativity: "She smiles at the future."

We often read this passage but don't stop to realize what was taking place. This woman started out with very little. It says she had enough money to buy some raw materials—some wool and some flax. She could have taken that money and hidden it under her mattress, but she said to herself, *I have to figure out a way to multiply what I have.*

So she took her money and bought wool and flax. She worked with her hands in delight as she made belts and garments and sold them. I picture her going to the marketplace and walking up and down the stalls to see what people were buying. She probably looked at the garments that others had made and wondered how she could improve on them. She probably got to know people who had great skills and asked a lot of questions. "I really like the way you've finished this belt. Could you show me how you did that?" The result was that she produced something of quality that people wanted to buy, which led to earnings. Her income increased. She had more money than when she started.

She could have hidden that money under the mattress, but instead she said, "I want this to multiply more." Perhaps she saw a For Sale sign on a field she walked by every day. She thought, *That would be a great place for a vineyard.* So she took her earnings, bought the field and planted a vineyard. I think this also involved increasing her skills. She needed to learn how to grow grapes and make wine. She did what she had to do and the vineyard succeeded. The result was prosperity. We're told that "she smiles at the future," which means that when she thinks about the future, she is not filled with anxiety. She doesn't say, "Oh, Lord, what am I going to do?" Because she has learned to multiply, she can look at the future and say, "The best is yet ahead!"

God has a way for you to multiply and prosper just as this woman did. So in every area of life, look at what you have. God is saying, "What can I do for you?" Ask God, "How can I multiply what I have so that every need is abundantly met?" God wants you to know that you *can* multiply!

The Transformation of a Ring-tail Tooter

Let me tell you a brief story I think will explain why I am so sure that anyone can prosper. I have written much about my family. For those of you have not read what I've written in previous books, I'll just say here that my family had a tremendously traumatic past. Each member, especially my siblings, all had problems. My brother, Keith, was a "ringtail tooter," as they say in East Texas. I always say that he helped the enemy write his book. He was angry, manipulative and divisive, while being creative, funny and wonderful—all at the same time. I won't tell his story here, because that is for another book, but I will say this: He is the perfect example of fragmentation and recovery.

When the Lord met Keith and powerfully saved him, the change was so noticeable that you had to take a double look to believe you were seeing the same person. However, he was still fragmented. I remember him saying to me, "It will take seven years for me to go back and gather what I have scattered through Texas alone!" He had been promiscuous and hateful. He knew he would have to go back to many whom he had wounded; and he would have to repent, ask forgiveness and make amends. When he acted wisely in doing so, he was mended.

Today, Keith is an executive manager in a thriving title company. He not only prospers but also helps others prosper. God gave him a phrase that he uses today: "Discipline defines the gift!" I know very few people who were as undisciplined and fragmented as Keith and have become as disciplined and whole as he is now.

The Woman at the Well

The woman at the well in John 4 is a great example of someone being liberated from her past and having her shattered soul restored. In the book *Worship as It Is in Heaven,* I wrote:

> *We must worship in Spirit and truth to experience the reality of life in our time and space.* In the midst of our Lord's trials, He had a need to visit Samaria. Samaria was a nation that was hated by the Jewish people.
>
> I love the woman at the well (see John 4). She had a desperate need for change. Her questions and Jesus' answers changed the course of life for all nations. He asked for a drink of water and offered her water that would quench her thirst for eternity. If she gave Him the water she had access to, He would exchange that with what He had and she would never thirst again. The whole context of this exchange was within the differences of nationalistic worship between Jew and Samaritan. The interchange of communication in John 4:19-26 [AMP] around worship is revealing for all generations:
>
> > The woman said to Him . . . "Our forefathers worshiped on this mountain, but you [Jews] say that Jerusalem is the place where it is necessary and proper to worship."
> > Jesus said to her, "Woman, believe Me, a time is coming when you will worship the Father neither [merely] in this mountain nor [merely] in Jerusalem.

> You [Samaritans] do not know what you are worshiping [you worship what you do not comprehend]. We do know what we are worshiping [we worship what we have knowledge of and understand], for [after all] salvation comes from [among] the Jews. A time will come, however, indeed it is already here, when the true (genuine) worshipers will worship the Father in spirit and in truth (reality); for the Father is seeking just such people as these as His worshipers. God is a Spirit (a spiritual Being) and those who worship Him must worship Him in spirit and in truth (reality)."
>
> "The woman said to Him, I know that Messiah is coming, He Who is called the Christ (the Anointed One); and when He arrives, He will tell us everything we need to know and make it clear to us."
>
> Jesus said to her, "I Who now speak with you am He."

The understanding of this type of worship changed her forever. She did not let her past failures keep her from intimately worshiping and turning outward toward those around her. This woman tore down her prejudices, overcame her past, experienced a new reality of the Lord and left her mundane daily exercise of getting water to run and evangelize her entire city.

The disciples could not understand why the Lord would go to Samaria and visit with the woman at the well. They did not yet understand the type of worship that would produce reality in the earth. However, because of His love and boldness to break a religious standard, an entire city was saved. Thank God that Jesus talked to this person with a past, who was a Samaritan, and a woman. He was not afraid of His reputation being marred. He pressed through the mores of society to explain worship for a Kingdom that was forming.[6]

Jesus defied religion and sectarianism. The woman became part of this kingdom. She dropped her water pot, which represented her daily routine life, and ran back to visit with all of those with whom she had scattered herself. She had five husbands and was presently living with someone who was not her husband, but she was not ashamed of her past. When the opportunity presented itself for her to become whole, she did not hesitate. She embraced the moment, went and gathered the pieces of her past, and then entered her future. Her famous statement, "Come, see a Man who has told me everything that I ever did!" echoes down through the generations (John 4:29, *AMP*). She then led the entire city to the Lord and into the reality that she had found. Her fragmentation and scattering were re-gathered.

The Wisdom of the Ant

What is our plan of advancement? How do we move forward in the harvest? We must have a stewardship mentality before the Lord will release wealth. Proverbs 21:5 says, "The plans of the diligent lead to profit as surely as haste leads to poverty" (*NIV*). We must persevere against all odds and all enemy strategies. These are necessary characteristics of God's people that are needed to establish the Kingdom on earth.

Proverbs 17:16 says, "Of what use is money in the hand of a fool, since he has no desire to get wisdom?" (*NIV*). Therefore, if you ask for money, ask for wisdom also. Several years ago while I was on an airline flight, I shut my eyes and had a vision. I saw an ant. The Lord then quickened this passage to me:

> Go to the ant, you sluggard! Consider her ways and be wise, which, having no captain, overseer or ruler, provides her supplies in the summer, and gathers her food in the harvest. How long will you slumber, O sluggard? When will you rise from your sleep? A little sleep, a little slumber, a little folding of the hands to sleep—so shall your poverty come on you like a prowler, and your need like an armed man (Prov. 6:6-11).

The ant is used here as an example of the wisdom of setting aside in the summer for the wants of the winter. Not all ants store up seeds for winter use, but among the ants of Palestine, there are several species that do. Their well-marked paths are often seen about Palestinian threshing floors and in other places where seeds may be obtained. Such paths sometimes extend for a great distance from the ant nest. In every country in the world, the ant is synonymous with industry. Here are some important facts concerning the ant for us to consider:

1. The ants of many countries lay up vast stores of grain in their nests.

2. To facilitate their storage efforts, ants place their nests as near as possible to the places where grain is threshed and stored.

3. The grain the ants have stored provides food for them during the winter season.

From the example of the ant, we see that it takes diligence and perseverance to have the necessary supply to accomplish God's purposes. World economies are changing, so we need to be willing to change as well.

Many nations get wrapped up in their economies, or management of money. We must understand the business of heaven and apply heaven's principles to earth's economies. We must develop a mind to prosper.

This book concludes with several appendices, including "A Prayer Focus for the 50 Days from Passover to Pentecost" as well as "A 50-Day Prayer Focus for Harvest Praying." Both of these prayer focuses will lead you into a Pentecost understanding of being blessed and embracing increase. I encourage you to use these prayer focuses to break your old mindset and establish yourself in God's perfect timing.

May you experience your own personal Pentecost after reading this book. May your storehouses, wine vats, and barns be filled for the future. May you always remember: Anyone can prosper! This concept and principle were knit within you when God created you. You can overcome poverty. If you connect and align your gift properly, you can profit. This is a time of harvest. Enter into God's kingdom best for your life!

Chuck D. Pierce and Robert Heidler

Notes

1. Personal communication, February 5, 2010.
2. "Newton's Law of Universal Gravitation," formulated in Newton's Work *Philosophiæ Naturalis Principia Mathematica* ("the Principia"), first published July 5, 1687.
3. Chuck Pierce with Robert and Linda Heidler, *A Time to Advance: Understanding the Significance of the Hebrew Tribes and Months* (Denton, TX: Glory of Zion International, Inc., 2011).
4. John Dickson and Chuck Pierce, *The Worship Warrior* (Ventura, CA: Regal Books, 2002).
5. Merriam Webster's Dictionary, s.v. "multiply." http://www.merriam-webster.com/dictionary/multiply.
6. John Dickson and Chuck D. Pierce, *Worship as It Is in Heaven: Worship that Engages Every Believer and Establishes God's Kingdom on Earth* (Ventura, CA: Regal Books, 2010), pp. 221-222.

APPENDIX 1

A PASSOVER SEDER

ROBERT HEIDLER

The traditional Passover Seder involves a leisurely meal with many elements. While there is value in preserving this tradition, we will use a shorter version to more closely follow the biblical instruction that this be a meal "eaten in haste." It is likely that Jesus and the apostles followed an order similar to this when they met in the upper room to celebrate Passover. When observed in a "home group" setting, the group leader should read the sections designated for the father, and assign others to fill the roles of the "mother of the house" and the child. Hints for preparation are found at the end of this outline.

Lighting the Passover Candles

The mother of the house lights two candles, and prays: "Blessed are You, O Lord our God, King of the Universe, who has brought us safely through another year and blessed us with Passover, as a celebration of Your goodness. We thank You tonight for Jesus, our Savior and Messiah, Who is the Light of the World!" (Exod. 12:14).

Introduction

The father (or group leader) reads: "Now this day will be a memorial to you, and you shall celebrate it as a feast to the Lord; throughout your generations you are to celebrate it as a permanent ordinance. It is a Passover to the Lord who passed over the houses of the sons of Israel when He struck the Egyptians" (Exod. 12:14,27).

All participants: At one time we Gentiles were separate from Christ, excluded from citizenship in Israel, and foreigners to the covenants of the promise. But now in Messiah Jesus we who once were far away have been brought near through the blood of Christ.

The father reads: Consequently, we are no longer foreigners and aliens. . . . Through the work of Jesus we Gentiles are heirs together with Israel, members together of one body, and sharers together in the promise (see Eph. 2:12-13,19; 3:6).

All participants: "When the hour came, Jesus and His apostles reclined at the table. And He said to them, 'I have eagerly desired to eat this Passover with you before I suffer'" (Luke 22:14-15).

The Unleavened Bread Is Blessed, Broken and Buried

At this point in a traditional Passover celebration, the father performs a symbolic act called "Hiding the *Afikomen*." Before the celebration, three sheets of matzo are placed in a cloth bag called a "unity." (You can also use the three pockets of a folded napkin.)

At this point in the Seder the father removes the middle of the three sheets. By Jewish tradition, the sheet of Matzo has been pierced, striped and bruised. He holds it up and breaks it, then wraps half of it in a linen napkin and hides it away till later in the celebration. The middle piece of matzo is called the *afikomen*. *Afikomen* is not a Hebrew word. It's Greek, a form of the word *afikominos*. It means "He who is coming!" No Jew knows where this ritual came from, or what it means; it is just "tradition." As believers in Jesus, however, the meaning is obvious. As we do this, we celebrate the death of Jesus. This ancient ritual is still followed by Jews all over the world.

The father holds up the afikomen and reads: The three pieces of unleavened bread in one napkin are called a Unity. It symbolizes the unity of God: Father, Son, and Holy Spirit. This piece, the middle of the three, represents Jesus, the second person of the Trinity, our Passover Lamb!

The father breaks the middle piece of matzo. One half of the matzo is wrapped in a napkin and hidden under a pillow, picturing Jesus' burial.

The Invitation

The father reads: Let all who are hungry come and eat . . . "For Jesus, our Passover Lamb, has been sacrificed. Let us therefore celebrate the feast" (1 Cor. 5:7-8).

A child asks: Why is this night different from all other nights? What does this celebration mean?

The father reads: "It will come about when your children say, 'What does this celebration mean?' that you shall say, 'It is a Passover to the Lord who passed over the houses of the sons of Israel when He smote the Egyptians, but spared our homes'" (Exod. 12:24-27).

All participants: All Israel suffered as slaves in Egypt, but the Lord delivered them out of the hand of the enemy by His mighty hand and outstretched arm.

The father reads: In the same way, all of us were held in slavery and bondage to sin. Through Jesus, our Passover lamb, God delivered us. He set us free to live for Him.

All participants: So Passover is a celebration of God's love for all mankind. It celebrates Israel's release from slavery in Egypt and the redemption of all mankind from slavery to sin.

The father reads: "Now the Lord said to Moses and Aaron, Speak to all the congregation of Israel, saying, 'On the tenth of this month they are to take a lamb for each household. Your lamb shall be an unblemished male a year old. You shall keep it until the fourteenth day, then kill it at twilight. Moreover, they shall take some of the blood and put it on the two doorposts and on the lintel of the houses where they eat it. And they shall eat the flesh that same night, roasted with fire. They shall eat it with unleavened bread and bitter herbs.

'You shall eat it in haste—it is the Lord's Passover. For I will go through the land of Egypt on that night and will strike down all the first-born in the land of Egypt, both man and beast; and I will execute judgments against all the gods of Egypt—I am the Lord. And the blood shall be a sign for you on the houses where you live. When I see the blood I will pass over you and no plague will come upon you to destroy you when I strike the land of Egypt.

'Now it came about at midnight that the Lord struck all the first-born in the land of Egypt. Pharaoh arose in the night, he and all his servants and all the Egyptians; and there was a great cry in Egypt, for there was no home where there was not someone dead. Then he called for Moses and Aaron' at night and said, "Rise up, get out from among my people, both you and the sons of Israel; and go, worship the Lord, as you have said"'"(Exod. 12:1-13; 28-31).

All participants: Blessed is He who kept His promise to Israel. The Lord brought an end to bondage, and fulfilled His promise to Abraham: "Know for certain that your descendants will be strangers in a country not their own, and they will be enslaved and mistreated four hundred years. But I will punish the nation they serve as slaves, and afterward they will come out with great possessions" (Gen. 15:13-14).

The father reads: Rabbi Gamaliel, who taught the apostle Paul, said, "He who does not speak forth these three essentials of the Passover Seder has not discharged his duty: namely, the Passover Sacrifice, unleavened bread, and bitter herbs."

The Bitter Herbs

The father lifts up the bitter herbs and reads: These are the bitter herbs that we will eat.

The participants say: They picture the bitterness and sorrow of Israel, when they were held captive in Egypt and were oppressed by their cruel masters (see Exod. 1:14).

Pass the bitter herbs while the father reads: These bitter herbs symbolize the bitterness of slavery and Israel's miserable existence in Egypt. To us as Christians, the eating of bitter herbs also reminds us of our lives before we knew Jesus. They are symbolic of the bitter cup our Lord tasted on our behalf. The horseradish brings tears to our eyes as we taste it and remember.

The Passover Sacrifice

The father holds up the lamb and reads: This lamb pictures the lamb slain in Egypt, to set Israel free from bondage.

The participants say: "The Lord passed over the houses of our fathers in Egypt. As it is said, 'It is the Lord's Passover, for He passed over the homes of the Children of Israel, when He killed the Egyptians; He passed over our homes and did not destroy us'" (Exod. 12:27).

Pass the lamb around while the father reads: The Children of Israel were told how to protect themselves from the last plague. Each family was to take a lamb and kill it and drain the blood into a basin, and then take a bunch of hyssop and dip it in the blood and strike the upper lintel and two side doorposts of the house where they eat it. In doing this, they made the sign of the cross at each door.

All participants pray: Lord, we thank You that You gave Israel a place of protection under the blood of the Passover lamb. We now take this meal with thankful hearts, remembering Your faithfulness and love for Your people. We pray that all men and women everywhere would discover the place of blessing and protection You have provided under the blood of Jesus, who is the perfect Passover Lamb.

Eat the Passover meal. Following the meal, the Seder continues.

The Unleavened Bread

The father reads: In Passover, we not only remember the lamb slain in Egypt, but we also celebrate the true Lamb of God, the Messiah, who was sacrificed to bear the sin of the world. The Prophet Isaiah wrote:

> Surely He took up our infirmities and carried our weaknesses . . . He was pierced for our transgressions, He was crushed for our iniquities; the punishment that brought us peace was upon Him, and by His wounds we are healed. We all, like sheep, have gone astray, each of us has turned to His own way; and the LORD has laid on Him the iniquity of us all.
>
> He was oppressed and afflicted, yet He did not open His mouth . . . He was cut off from the land of the living; for the transgression of My people He was stricken. It was the Lord's will to crush Him and cause Him to suffer, and though the Lord makes His life a guilt offering, He will see His offspring and prolong His days . . . He poured out His life unto death, and was numbered with the transgressors. For He bore the sin of many, and made intercession for the transgressors (Isa. 53:1-12).

The participants say: "The next day John saw Jesus coming to him, and said, 'Behold, the Lamb of God who takes away the sin of the world'" (John 1:29).

In a traditional celebration, the children are now told to search for the *afikomen*. The one who finds it gets a reward. The father now takes the *afikomen*, unwraps it, and holds it up.

The father reads: This is the broken piece of matzo that was hidden early in our Seder. The unleavened bread is a picture of the body of Jesus. It is made of pure flour and water without yeast. When the dough is prepared, it is pierced and striped with a pointed tool. The prophecy of Isaiah 53:5 declares: "He was pierced for our transgressions, He was bruised for our iniquities: the chastisement of our peace was upon Him; and with His stripes we are healed."

When this sheet of matzo was broken at the start of the service, it symbolized Jesus' death. When it was wrapped in linen, it spoke prophetically of the wrapping of His body in linen after the crucifixion. When the broken and wrapped bread was hidden under the pillow, it symbolized His burial in the tomb of Joseph of Arimathea (see Matt. 27:57-60). Now after the meal is over, the pillow is removed, picturing the stone that was removed by the angel (see Matt. 28:1-2). The matzo is unwrapped and held up for all to see. This symbolizes the resurrection of Jesus.

The participants say: "On the first day of the week, at early dawn, they came to the tomb . . . they found the stone rolled away . . . Two men suddenly stood near them in dazzling clothing; and said to them, 'Why do you seek the living One among the dead? He is not here, HE HAS RISEN!'" (Luke 24:1-6).

The father breaks the *afikomen* into small pieces, and they are passed to each participant.

The father says: This is the place in the Passover celebration that was recorded in the Gospel of Luke, "Having taken some bread, when He had given thanks, He broke it, and gave it to them, saying, 'This is My body which is given for you; do this in remembrance of Me'" (Luke 22:19).

The father prays a blessing: Blessed are You, O Lord our God, King of the Universe, Who brings forth bread from the earth, and Who gave us Jesus, the bread of life.

All eat from the broken matzo.

The Cup of Redemption

The father reads: At this point in a Passover celebration, a cup of wine is poured. It is the third cup of wine poured in the traditional Passover meal, and it is the most significant.

The father lifts the cup and says: This cup is called the Cup of Redemption. At this point in the Passover, Jesus lifted the cup and said, "This cup is the new covenant in my blood; do this, whenever you drink it, in remembrance of me" (1 Cor. 11:25). This was the original context of the Lord's Supper.

The father prays: Blessed are You, O Lord our God, King of the universe, who brings forth the fruit of the vine, and who gave the blood of Your Son, Jesus, for our redemption.

All drink the Cup of Redemption.

At this point, a section of the book of Psalms, called the *Hallel*, is sung to praise God for His provision of redemption. This is the song Jesus and His disciples would have sung in Mark 14:26 to close their Passover meal.

The Hallel

Father: Not to us, O LORD, not to us,
Participants: But to Your name be the glory,
Father: Why do the nations say,
Participants: "Where is their God?"
Father: Our God is in heaven;
Participants: He does whatever He pleases.
Father: But their idols are silver and gold,
Participants: Made by the hands of men.
Father: They have mouths, but cannot speak,
Participants: Eyes, but they cannot see;
Father: They have ears, but cannot hear,
Participants: Noses, but they cannot smell;
Father: They have hands, but cannot feel,
Participants: Feet, but they cannot walk;
Father: Those who make them will be like them . . .
Participants: And so will all who trust in them.
Father: O house of Israel, trust in the LORD;

Participants: He is their help and shield.
Father: The LORD remembers us and will bless us:
Participants: He will bless those who fear the LORD,
Father: May the LORD make you increase,
Participants: Both you and your children.
Father: May you be blessed by the LORD,
Participants: The Maker of heaven and earth.
Father: Give thanks to the LORD, for He is good;
Participants: His love endures forever.
Father: The LORD is my strength and my song;
Participants: He has become my salvation.
Father: The stone the builders rejected
Participants: Has become the capstone;
Father: The LORD has done this,
Participants: And it is marvelous in our eyes.
Father: This is the day the LORD has made;
Participants: Let us rejoice and be glad in it.
Father: Blessed is He who comes in the name of the LORD.
Participants: From the house of the LORD we bless you.
Father: The LORD is God,
Participants: He has made His light shine upon us!

The Breath of Everything
Shall Bless His Name

The father says: To You alone do we give thanks, O Lord! Though our mouths were full of song like the sea, and our tongue of rejoicing like the multitude of its waves, and our lips full of praise like the breadth of the horizon, and our eyes were shining like the sun and the moon, and our hands were spread like the eagles of the sky, and our feet light as the hinds', we could never thank You enough, O Lord our God, for the good You have done for us.

The father says (triumphantly): "We have been redeemed by the blood of the Lamb!"

All say: "Out of the hand of the enemy!"

The father says: "Our redemption is complete!"

All say: "Bondage has been broken!"

The father says: "We have been released from captivity!"

All say: "We are set free to enter the promise!"

All participants pray: Holy One of Israel, we thank You for Your gift of salvation. We pray Your blessing on Your church, and on Your people Israel. We pray for the peace of Jerusalem. We pray that all of Israel be saved and come to know Messiah Jesus.

The father reads: "And they returned to Jerusalem with great joy and were continually in the temple, praising God" (Luke 24:52-53).

All the participants joyfully shout: "Next year in Jerusalem!"

[This traditional Jewish ending to the Passover celebration is optional!]

Preparation Hints

Elements for the Passover meal: Matzo (unleavened bread), horseradish (bitter herbs), wine (or grape juice), lamb (and other dishes for a complete meal). Also needed: a copy of this Seder for each person; 2 candles and matches, 2 white napkins.

Before the celebration, put 3 unbroken matzos in the folds of one napkin. You will use the other napkin to wrap the *afikomen*. You can use a small pillow as a place to hide the *afikomen*. Have a child—or the youngest adult—ready to ask the question that starts the celebration (page 1). The rest of the celebration provides the answer to these questions . . . passing on the remembrance of redemption from one generation to the next.[1]

Note

1. This Seder is reprinted from the book, *Messianic Church Arising* by Dr. Robert Heidler, © 2006, Glory of Zion International Ministries, and reprinted here by permission. Permission is granted for readers to make a copy of this Seder for each person attending your Passover celebration.

APPENDIX 2

DATES OF THE FEASTS
2013–2025

ROBERT HEIDLER

The appointed times begin at sundown on these dates.

	Passover	Pentecost	Trumpets	Atonement	Tabernacles
2013	March 25	May 14	September 4	September 13	September 18
2014	April 14	June 3	September 24	October 3	October 8
2015	April 3	May 23	September 13	September 22	September 27
2016	April 22	June 11	October 2	October 11	October 16
2017	April 10	May 30	September 20	September 29	October 4
2018	March 30	May 19	September 9	September 18	September 23
2019	April 19	June 8	September 29	October 8	October 13
2020	April 8	May 28	September 18	September 27	October 2
2021	March 27	May 16	September 6	September 15	September 20
2022	April 15	June 4	September 25	October 4	October 9
2023	April 5	May 25	September 15	September 24	September 29
2024	April 22	June 11	October 2	October 11	October 16
2025	April 12	June 1	September 22	October 1	October 6

APPENDIX 3

A PRAYER FOCUS FOR THE 50 DAYS FROM PASSOVER TO PENTECOST

CHUCK D. PIERCE

The purpose of this prayer focus is to have you cross over from the old season to stake your claim to the future. During the 50 days of focused prayer, you will be confronted with the necessity of unlocking and realigning your emotions so that the function of your "expectation" is restored and receptive to the Holy Spirit. This will cause your vision to be redefined and established. "Without a vision [prophetic revelation and utterance] a people perish" (Prov. 29:18, *NASB*).

The 50 days of this focus are designed to take you from Passover to Pentecost. However, you can also use this focus any time you want to stake your claim for the future!

One key aspect of understanding the shift from the Church season to Kingdom expression is the need to unlock the supply lines for your future. This will entail warring to break the conformity of your thinking processes and developing a harvest mentality. This focus will also include information about the dynamic of warring with structures that would stop the transference of wealth so that you understand what is going on. I decree that after doing this prayer focus your "end will be greater than your beginning."

The prayer focus is in five 10-day segments:

1. 10 Days of Crossing Over to Press into Your Promise
2. 10 Days of Decreeing Your Land or Boundaries Will Rejoice
3. 10 Days of Developing an Expectation for the Future
4. 10 Days of Restoring, Redefining and Establishing Vision
5. 10 Days of Warring for Increase and the Transference of Wealth

This Prayer Focus and the Timing of the Feasts

The Word of God revolves around the feasts that God appointed in the Old Testament. They were holy assemblies for holy rehearsals.

The remembrance of these physical events causes us to understand the spiritual significance of what came and what is to come! The feasts forecasted Jesus' sacrifice for us. Also, they foretold the full redemption of God's people and the alignment of all nations, which are His inheritance. When we participate in the waving of the first-fruits at Passover and then receive the anointing to gather and increase at Pentecost (Feast of Weeks), our faith is displayed and our confidence arises for our provision to be released.

Today, futility marks the legalistic participation in the feasts. We cannot legalistically keep the feasts, but we can honor the Father by remembering Him and receiving from Him at these appointed times (see Gal. 3:10). No longer do we have to seek an ultimate sacrifice—Jesus was given on the Cross. This broke Satan's headship over us personally, as well as humankind corporately. However, we must enter into the fullness of this plan. By participating and remembering the feast times *now*, they cease to be shadows of things to come. They actually cause us to see the future path to our promises.

May you eat the Word below and journey closer to His plan of fullness for your life.

10 Days of Crossing
Over to Press into Your Promise

Day 1: *Read Genesis 11–13; Luke 14:25-33.* All biblical understanding revolves around covenant. Notice in these passages that Abram came out of one societal structure and began his journey of faith. He then left his halfway mark and family ties to receive God's promise. Notice also how he received prophecy from the Lord along the way. Retrace your journey. Make sure you have not stopped halfway to your "there." This is a year to be positioned properly.

Day 2: *Read Genesis 14–17; John 2:23-24.* Abram became Abraham. The more we come into agreement with the Lord's plan and follow Him, the more we reflect His identity for us. Notice in Genesis 14:13 that Abram is referred to as the Hebrew, "the one who crosses over." Because we are grafted into the Abrahamic covenant, we are a people who are constantly crossing over. When Abram went to war and gave to Melchizedek, God made covenant with Him. He moved from promise and prophecy into covenant alignment. Be sure you keep going! Confess the sin of anytime you have resisted moving forward.

Day 3: *Read Exodus 2:23-25; 3.* Cry out for your future and watch the Lord acknowledge your cry. He will then start your deliverance process, which includes plundering the enemy's camp. Ask Him to deliver you from any oppression or hard labor that the enemy has unjustly put upon you.

Day 4: *Read Exodus 6; 12–14.* Find your place in the army. The Lord brought the Israelites out by armies. Decree that anything that has blocked your way will be removed. Do a faith exercise: extend your hand and decree that your way will open up.

Day 5: *Read Exodus 15–16; Matthew 14:13-21; Revelation 15.* Rejoice and sing the song of the Lord. Thank the Lord for your deliverance. Meditate on the song of Moses. The suffering covenant people sang this at their time of deliverance; we as Christians will sing it again. Thank God for all the provision that you are receiving. Even if it is "wilderness" provision, thank Him! Let Him take what you have and break it open and multiply it.

Day 6: *Read Exodus 20; 23; Matthew 17:5; 28:20.* These are key chapters in understanding justice. Ask the Lord to give you revelation of feast times. This will cause you to understand God's timing for your life as well as unlock supply. Ask God to make you aware of angelic visitation and leading. Confess as times of sin when you resisted being led properly. Ask Him about a firstfruit offering for the Feast of Pentecost. Much promise will be unlocked to you in these chapters.

Day 7: *Read Joshua 3–5.* These are chapters on preparation and how to follow (the Ark and the priests) into your future. Let me suggest a day of fasting. Focus on your place of crossing over for this season. Also, ask the Lord about those with whom you have relationship that are helping you move forward. Let the Lord revive your life by re-circumcising your heart. So many of us hang on to last season's provision. Declare that new provision will begin. The manna ceased and they had to learn to use the provision in the Promised Land.

This allowed them to reinstate the Feast of Passover to get them back on track. They were unable to do Passover for 40 years since all they had was manna and quail. God changes our provision many times to get us back in sync with His full plan. Get ready to face that thing that has always seemed invincible to you.

Day 8: *Read Matthew 14:22-36; John 6; Exodus 33.* Be willing to cross over into the place the Lord is calling you. You might want to pull aside into a quiet place to really seek the Father. Declare that you will not move forward without sensing His presence.

Day 9: *Read Acts 12; Esther 9. Memorize Philippians 2:27.* Ask the Lord to do a new thing in your prayer life. The beheading of James was during Passover. Ask the Lord to hide you from the religious world. Many times our past failures propel us into a whole new fervency of prayer. Pray and ask God for angelic help to come down so that you can move into the next season. Make a declaration that every decree that is set against you will be exposed and overturned and that you will advance.

Day 10: *Read Ephesians 1–4.* Recognize your condition as well as your position. Thank God for the change that the Holy Spirit has brought you. Thank Him for His love that has gotten you through so many situations. Thank Him that you are maturing into the fullness of His plan. Look at the government of the Church. Jesus ascended to heaven to take His throne next to the Father. He gives us access to Him. Ask the Lord to be sure your gift is aligned corporately.

10 Days of Decreeing Your Land or Boundaries Will Rejoice

While any sin can be an opening for demonic activity, there are certain sins that can defile (bring a foul, dirty uncleanness) in the land. These sins leave the land cursed and particularly susceptible to demonic footholds. When you stake your land, decree that the following structures break and let go. (Land can also be defined as your spiritual inheritance.)

Day 1: *Read Isaiah 54; Psalm 16.* Begin by doing the following: "Sing, O barren, You who have not borne! Break forth into singing, and cry aloud, You who have not labored with child! For more are the children of the desolate than the children of the married woman," says the LORD. "Enlarge the place of your tent, and let them stretch out the curtains of your dwellings; do not spare; lengthen your cords, and strengthen your stakes." Declare that this is a time of enlargement for your life.

Day 2: *Read Philippians 1–4.* Decree that all anxiety, fear, doubt, anger, frustration, guilt, jealousy and envy from past iniquity in your life will be removed.

Day 3: *Read Ezra 9; Psalm 81.* Decree revival! Get ready to embrace many changes. Declare that a window of revival is opening over your life and family. Declare that this revival will touch all generations.

Day 4: *Read Ezekiel 16; 36–37; 1 Corinthians 10.* Ask the Lord to break the power of idolatry in your bloodline. God hates idolatry. Just as the worship of God brings blessing upon the land, the worship of false gods brings curses.

Day 5: *Read Genesis; Acts 7.* Ask the Lord to remove illegal bloodshed from your land or inheritance. Remember the account of Cain and Abel. From this story we see that bloodshed affects the very land on which the violence occurred. As the blood of violence penetrates the ground, the Prince of the Power of the Air will gain legal right into the land. Curses attach to illegal violence and bloodshed.

Day 6: *Read 1 Corinthians 3–7.* Cut ties with any immorality that has been a part of your bloodline or the land where you are the steward. This issue is one that must be taken seriously. Immorality has become a vague term and a nonissue for those in power. Our society has come to believe that anyone can do whatever is right in his or her own sight. But Satan knows that every immoral act opens up a greater legal right for him to infiltrate land and homes. With the advent of the Internet, there is even greater access to things like pornography and adult chat rooms. None of these things is benign. What is done in secret can bring serious consequences through defilement—not only of those involved, but also of the land on which the sin occurred.

Day 7: *Read 2 Samuel 21.* Declare an end to covenant breaking. During the reign of King David, a great famine came on the land. When David inquired of the Lord concerning this famine, God said to him, "It is because of Saul and his bloodthirsty house, because he killed the Gibeonites" (see v. 1). The Gibeonites were a group of people who had entered into covenant with Israel in the days of Joshua. This covenant guaranteed their safety. Yet Saul broke covenant with the Gibeonites by murdering many of them and planning for the massacre of the rest. As a result, famine came on the land as God removed His blessing, and Satan was allowed access. The famine did not strike immediately but came when the new king came to power. Many of our homes in the United States have been built on land that was taken after treaties with Native Americans were broken. Those broken treaties from years ago can defile and give the enemy a foothold in the land where we live today!

Day 8: *Read Joel 1–3.* Declare that the land will begin to rejoice. Ask the Lord to stir the power of restoration in you.

Day 9: *Read Matthew 5–7.* Learn what the Lord taught His disciples to pray. Declare that heaven and earth will connect and that a new level of communion will occur in your life.

Day 10: *Read Ezekiel 34; Zechariah 8; 1 Corinthians 8; Hebrews 3–4.* Declare that your land will begin to produce in a new way so that your storehouses will become full. (Some of you might want to stake your land here and decree increase.) Declare that your land will also enter into rest (see Exod. 23:10-11; Lev. 25:2-7; Deut. 15:1-10; 31:10-13).

10 Days of Developing an Expectation for the Future

May this be a time of visitation where the presence and power of God invade your space and order your steps! May you be restored and healed—body, soul and spirit! Expect God to move!

Day 1: *Read Psalm 139; Ephesians 2.* May the Lord show you who you are in Him. You are an original, fearfully and wonderfully made! Thank Him for forming you in your mother's womb. Spend the day praising! This is very important in the process of breaking cycles.

Day 2: *Memorize and speak forth 1 Thessalonians 5:16-24.* Decree that your whole spirit, soul and body will be sanctified! *Also read Joshua 3.*

Day 3: *Sing or praise with Psalm 23.* Agree with God for the restoration of your soul. Soul is linked with "breathing" and refers to the entire inner nature and personality of a person. *Read Deuteronomy 26:16-19.* Declare that you will be set on high in a new place with a seal called Special. Decree life and life abundantly. *Read and underline Matthew 6:25; Luke 12:22; John 10:10.* Thank God for the prophets in your life (see Acts 3:23). If you have quenched the prophetic anointing in your life, confess it as sin. *Memorize Proverbs 29:18.* Ask the Lord to open up new vision and revelation over your life. *Memorize Jeremiah 30:17.*

Day 4: *Ask the Lord to make your heart pure!* Declare that the seat of your feelings, desires, affections and aversions will come under the alignment of the Holy Spirit. *Read the Beatitudes (Matthew 5:1-12).* Ask the Lord to send help or aid to your soul so that you can attain your highest end. Declare that your end will be greater than your beginning. *Read Haggai 2.* Ask the Lord for your soul to begin to prosper in a new way. *Read 3 John 2; Hebrews 13:17; James 1:21; 5:20; 1 Peter 1:9.* Now ask the Lord to make you "see." The pure in heart see Him (see Matt. 5:8).

Day 5: *Memorize Proverbs 18:14.* Ask the Lord to remove any vexation of the spirit of the world and its influence on your spirit. Thank God that you are a spiritual being and that you will live eternally with Him. If you do not have this assurance, stop and ask the Lord to remove any doubt from you. Receive a cleansing through His blood. *Read Hebrews 9.* Ask the Lord to cleanse your conscience and restore it to full working authority. Ask the Lord to renew your communion with Him. Take communion with Him. Your spirit is that part of you related to worship and divine communion. *Read and underline John 12:27; 1 Corinthians 16:18; 2 Corinthians 7:13; Matthew 11:29; 2 Corinthians 7:1; 1 Peter 2:11; James 5:20; 1 Corinthians 5:5; 1 Peter 1:9; Matthew 10:28; Acts 2:31; Romans 8:10; Ephesians 4:4; James 2:26.*

Day 6: *Read Romans 6.* Make a list of any place that sin "has dominion" over you. Decree that by the power of the Holy Spirit, you are freed and cleansed. Watch for sins of omission, such as gossiping, criticizing, judging, and so forth. At times, these are hidden from us and produce unbelief in us.

Day 7: The body is the lowest part of a person's triune being; it's where the soul and spirit reside. Honor the Holy Spirit who has chosen to dwell within you. *Read 1 Corinthians 6:19-20; 2 Peter 1:13-14.* Thank Him that your body is His. *Reread Romans 6:13,19.* Yield your members one by one unto God as instruments of righteousness rather than unto iniquity. If you have a part of your body that is not working properly, ask the Lord to heal and cleanse that portion. Include any organs that you know have been affected by sin. *Read Romans 7.* Declare that the "pull" of the old is eradicated.

Day 8: *Fast as the Lord leads you.* I suggest you fast from solid food and only drink liquids (water, herb tea, broth) on this day. *Read Romans 8.* Thank the Lord that you have been adopted by Him and that His blood is flowing through you to restore you!

Day 9: Declare all hope deferred is broken from you, loosed and removed from influencing your life. Declare the power of scattering is broken as you *read Ezekiel 36–37.* Thank the Lord for a new heart and spirit. Declare a new door of hope is opening. *Read Hosea 2; 6; 10.* Confess that the sin of unbelief is broken from your bloodline.

Day 10: *Read Psalms 32; 62.* Declare your emotions healed and your spirit free. Worship throughout the day. Use praise music. If you drive somewhere, then sing with the music. Healing Scriptures are important to recite. *Memorize Hebrews 11:6.* Ask the Lord for your next measure of faith. *Read and meditate on Isaiah 60.* Arise! Shine! Decree that all depression and oppression must leave. Expect God to move on your behalf. Expect miracles and healings to begin to happen in you and through you!

10 Days of Restoring, Redefining and Establishing Vision

Day 1: *Read Amos 9.* David's Tabernacle is being restored in the earth in this generation. Declare that the Tabernacle of David will be restored in your life, family, church, city, state and nation. You have a good future! Expect God to move on your behalf! Stake your claim!

Day 2: *Read Acts 15.* The Church agreed with the prophetic word from Amos 9 and declared that its identity would not reflect the legalism from the past. Ask the Lord to cut through all of the conflict that is keeping you from seeing the future.

Day 3: *Read Acts 8–9.* Notice how Saul's identity changed to Paul. Ask God to drop any scales from your eyes that are keeping you from seeing His plan for your future.

Day 4: *Read John 1; Matthew 16; Acts 10–11.* Notice the transformation of Peter. His identity was prophesied in John 1. He tapped into revelation in Matthew 16 and then began to come into his true identity in Acts. Follow this pattern in your own life. Also notice the difference between the church in Antioch and the church in Jerusalem. The identity of the church in Antioch was truly apostolic. Ask God to cause the Church today to begin to come into its new identity.

Day 5: *Read Revelation 1–3.* Notice the Revelator. Ask the Spirit of God to catch you up into a new place of revelation. Notice what the Spirit of God said to the churches. Ask the Lord to speak to you and let you hear what the Spirit is saying to the Church today.

Day 6: *Read Revelation 4–5.* Ask the Lord to bring you up into a new place of worship. Ask the Lord to reveal to you what is happening in the heavens.

Day 7: *Read Revelation 12; 18–19.* Ask the Lord to show you how to war in the earth. Ask Him to show you how to protect that which is being brought forth in this hour on your behalf. Declare Babylonian structures that have held you captive will begin to fall.

Day 8: *Read Revelation 20–22.* Ask the Lord to give you a vision of the River of Life. Ask the Lord to show you the armies of heaven. Declare all things are being made new and that you have a glorious new identity. Exalt the Lord for being Alpha and Omega in your life.

Day 9: *Read Isaiah 61–62.* You are anointed! Do not keep silent. Ask the Lord how to confess your faith. Go through your new gate. Decree that you are not a city forsaken but that you will be "sought out" (Isa. 62:12). The redeemed of the Lord say so. Shout "So!"

Day 10: *Read 1 Samuel 16–17; 30; 2 Samuel 1–2; 3:1,5-6.* I know this day has a lot of reading, but it will take you through the three anointings of David. David was anointed to be king, but his identity still had to form. Some of you have been in a hard place in regard to forming your identity. Do not be discouraged—there is a new anointing ahead. When you're finished reading these chapters (I suggest you read two in the morning, two at noon, and two at night), thank God for your next anointing. Anoint yourself before you go to sleep, and decree that your identity has shifted.

10 Days of Warring for Increase and the Transference of Wealth

Day 1: *Read Genesis 1–2, especially noting verses 1:26 and 2:15. Also read Ezekiel 28:13-19. Then read Genesis 3.* This will give you a good idea of God's plan of dominion and abundance for humankind. This will also reveal to you Satan's character and strategy. In the beginning, he was the keeper of wealth and resources. He covered these with sound. Upon his exaltation and fall, he has attempted to keep humanity in deception so that God's Kingdom plan in the earth will not advance. Agree with God that you will begin to see His strategy of abundance for you.

Day 2: *Read Genesis 12–15; 22.* All wealth is related to covenant. Notice the promise, the war, the giving aspect to Melchizedek, the ratification of covenant, and the testing of covenant. In the midst of this process, Jehovah Jireh revealed Himself. Stand up and honor Him as Jehovah Jireh.

Day 3: *Read Genesis 30; Daniel 11.* These are two wonderful chapters about God's ability through humankind to multiply resources. First, Jacob developed a new plan to breed goats and lambs. There are many new plans out there that God is willing to release to us. Daniel 11 promises that God will have a strong people who "carry out great exploits" (Dan. 11:32). Ask the Lord to give you an anointing to develop a new plan of multiplication.

Day 4: *Read Genesis 37; 39–41; 45.* The life of Joseph is worthy of special study this year. Joseph listened through his dreams for God's future plan. In the midst of his trials, his gifts remained active. He developed an administrative plan for multiplication—the Storehouse Principle. He guided Pharaoh and preserved the posterity of God's covenant plan for the future. Ask the Lord to develop the Storehouse Principle in your life.

Day 5: *Read Exodus 3; 23.* Ask the Lord to lead you into a new place of worship and favor. Declare that you will plunder Egypt. Declare that this is a year for you to gain the supply for your children's future. Ask the Lord to send angelic help to lead you in His next promise.

Day 6: *Read Deuteronomy 8; 28, especially noting verse 28:8.* The Lord gives you power and strength to gain wealth so that you can advance His covenant plan for your life. Ask Him for power and strength to gain wealth. Many times we are afraid to ask for this. Ask the Lord to "command the blessing on you in your storehouses" (Deut. 28:8). If you do not have a storehouse, ask the Lord to give you a plan to develop one.

Day 7: *Read 1 Chronicles 22, especially noting verse 14.* This is a year to build for our future. Ask the Lord to break from you the limits you have placed on Him to multiply in your life. Ask Him to take you "beyond measure" (1 Chron. 22:3). Most of us limit God to maintaining what we need. Ask the Lord to remove a maintenance mentality from you and move you into a beyond-measure mentality. Ask the Lord to send people to help you.

Day 8: *Read Proverbs 3; 2 Kings 4; 8:1-6.* Mistrust stops you from prospering. Trust the Lord and ask Him to redirect your path. That means to straighten out and make right the way ahead. Review your giving. Make sure you are aligned properly in giving. Honor the Lord with your firstfruits and tithes so that your barns will be filled and your vats will overflow. Prepare a special Pentecost gift. Send it to those who are helping you to advance spiritually. Look at the two women in 2 Kings 4 and 8. They began to prosper and their supply did not stop. Even in the midst of drought, the testimony of giving overcomes.

Day 9: *Read Malachi 3–4, especially noting verse 3:10.* Ask the Lord to open windows of heaven over you. Ask Him to rebuke the devourer. This is the only promise that we find biblically of us putting God to a test. Tell the Lord you want to be blessed so much that there will not be room enough for you to receive it. Ask the Lord to renew your giving process and bring revival upon it.

Day 10: *Read Matthew 14:13-21; Luke 12:22-48; John 5; 20; Acts 4.* Pentecost is a time of multiplication and prosperity. Read these Scriptures carefully. You will find much insight on how to prosper. God is preparing us to fill our baskets. Ask the Lord to gather all your fragments, reorganize what you have, and use you to supply for others in the future.

APPENDIX 4

A 50-DAY PRAYER FOCUS
FOR HARVEST PRAYING

CHUCK D. PIERCE

The purpose of this prayer focus is to help shift your mind and thinking processes toward harvest. Remember, the time between Passover and Pentecost is a time to watch new doors form. "Form" means develop or mold the shape or outline of something or to give meaning, character or nature to something.

Another way of looking at "form" is to think of something in the process of becoming what it will be in days ahead. This includes the conditioning of your mind and body in regard to the mental performance ahead. A forming season includes conceiving, training and disciplining. This denotes the arrangement of the part of a thing that gives its distinctive appearance.

A key Scripture about Pentecost is 1 Corinthians 16:8. Paul purposed to stay at Ephesus until Pentecost, because an effectual door was opened to him for his ministry. Like Paul, many enemies may be behind this forming door, but the Lord says, "Do not focus on your enemies during this season, but watch the door form and be ready to enter into this new opportunity. I will give you grace over your enemies."

Understanding Pentecost

In the New Testament there are three references to Pentecost: (1) 1 Corinthians 16:8, (2) Acts 2:1, and (3) Acts 20:16.

The most common reference is Acts 2:1 (we discussed 1 Corinthians 16:8 earlier). On this day, after the resurrection and ascension of Christ, the disciples were gathered in a house in Jerusalem and were visited with signs from heaven. The Holy Spirit descended upon them, and new life, power and blessing were evident. The 120 grew to 3,000 in one day. Ask for your 120 to turn to 3,000!

The early Christian believers, who were gathered in Jerusalem for observance of this feast, experienced the outpouring of God's Holy Spirit in a miraculous way. Peter explained that this was a fulfillment of the prophecy of Joel. The tongues symbolized the antithesis to Babel's confusion of tongues and represented the gathering of peoples under one mind and will to advance the kingdom of God. Jerusalem, the mount of the Lord, is the center of God's spiritual kingdom of peace and righteousness. Babel, the center of Satan's kingdom and of human rebellion, ignored God as the true bond of union. The city of Babel represented confusion. The Spirit of God given to Pentecost believers represented that God had come and His people would be keeping "the unity of the Spirit in the bond of peace" (Eph. 4:4).

The Pentecost Feast was known as the Feast of Weeks (see Exod. 34:22; Lev. 23:15-21; Num. 28:26-31; Deut. 16:9-12; 2 Chron. 8:13). This feast was observed in late May or early June, 50 days after the offering of the barley sheaf at the Feast of Unleavened Bread during Passover. Passover is a time to remember our deliverance. Pentecost is a time to thank God for our blessings and abundance and to rejoice over the harvest. Characteristics of this time include joy, happiness and celebration. During this feast, you enter into a time of offering concerning the firstfruit dedication (see Lev. 23:9-14; 2 Sam. 21:9-10; Ruth 2:23).

Pentecost was also known as the Feast of Harvest (see Exod. 23:16). The first sheaf offered at Passover and the two leavened loaves at Pentecost marked the beginning and ending of the grain harvest and sanctified the whole harvest season. The lesson for Israel was that the Lord had given them the best for the year ahead (see Ps. 147:14). The purpose of this feast was to commemorate the completion of the grain harvest. Its distinguishing features were the offering of two leavened loaves made from the new corn of the completed harvest, and seven lambs, one bull and two rams waved before the Lord as a thank offering (see Lev. 23:17-18).

Pentecost also was the time of the giving of the law on Sinai (see Exod. 12:2,19). At Pentecost the Lord wrote the law on our hearts and initiated the Church Age. This became the first feast in which Christians participated and celebrated. This should be a time of celebration each year. I believe the understanding of this feast is very important. The spiritual aspect of it is necessary if we are to multiply.

Time for Harvest!

Most of us do not understand harvest time. Because of our complex life, we are far removed from the actual production of our food supplies and the source of our provision. The harvest was a most important season (see Gen. 8:22; 45:6). Events were reckoned from harvests (see Gen. 30:14; Josh. 3:15; Judg. 15:1; Ruth 1:22; 2:23; 1 Sam. 6:13; 2 Sam. 21:9; 23:13).

The Pentecost Feast represents:

- A season of gathering (see Zech. 8)
- A season of judgment (see Jer. 51:33; Joel 3:13; Rev. 14:15)
- A season of grace (see Jer. 8:20)
- A time for the good news to be heard (see Matt. 9:37-38; John 4:35)
- An end of a season or age and the beginning of a new season of provision (see Matt. 13:39)

We must understand that harvest has a process:

1. The seed was broadcast and plowed under in late winter.
2. A prayer for rain—the early and the latter rain—was expressed (see Zech. 10).
3. The grain was grasped and cut with the sickle (see Deut. 16:9 and Mark 4:29).
4. The grain was gathered into sheaves (see Deut. 24:5).
5. The grain was taken to the threshing floor.
6. Tools were used for threshing. You have tools for harvest.
7. The grain was winnowed (tossed in the air). Let the wind blow away your chaff.
8. The remaining grain was shaken into a sieve (see Amos 9:9). Some of you are in this process.

9. The grain was brought into the storehouse. Find your storehouse.

Once in the storehouse, the harvest must be protected because harvest has major enemies:

- Drought—Ask the Lord to identify and break your dryness.
- Locust invasion—Ask the Lord to remove any devouring in your harvest.
- Plant diseases (mold, mildew)—Ask the Lord to remove any mold in your life.
- Hot, scorching winds—Ask the Lord to turn any adverse winds.
- War—The enemy wanted to live off the land. Declare that any enemy that has eaten your harvest will run out of your land.

Firstfruits: A Key to Blessing!

The Feast of Firstfruits was so called because it marked the beginning of the time at which people were to bring offerings of firstfruits (see Num. 28:26). It was a feast of joy and thanksgiving for the completion of the harvest season. These offerings were then presented as a wave offering for the people.

The first of ripe fruit, grapes and grain, the first production of oil and wine, and the first shearing of fleece were required as an offering (see Exod. 22:29; Lev. 2:12-16; Num. 18:12; Deut. 18:4; 2 Chron. 31:5; Neh. 10:35,37,39; Prov. 3:9; Jer. 2:3; Rom. 11:16). At this time, the Lord was credited as the source of rain and fertility (see Jer. 5:24). In the New Testament, the Holy Spirit came upon the disciples at Pentecost, at the festive time when Jews from different countries were in Jerusalem to celebrate this annual feast (see Acts 2:1-4); the interval between Pentecost and Tabernacles was the time for offering firstfruits. Ask the Lord for your firstfruits offering.

This is a time for harvest praying. I hope the following 50-day prayer focus will help you to understand and enter into this harvest season.

The 50-Day Prayer Focus

Day 1: *Read Hosea 6, especially noting verse 11* ("Also, O Judah, a harvest is appointed for you, when I return the captives of My people"). Ask the Lord to revive and raise you up. Ask Him to reveal your harvest to you.

Day 2: *Read Exodus 23, especially noting verse 16* ("And the Feast of Harvest, the firstfruits of your labors which you have sown in the field; and the Feast of Ingathering at the end of the year, when you have gathered in the fruit of your labors from the field"). Thank God for His leading. Be willing to follow Him. Thank Him that He has given you firstfruits.

Day 3: *Read Genesis 2 and 8:22* ("While the earth remains, seedtime and harvest, cold and heat, winter and summer, and day and night shall not cease"). Ask the Lord to reveal your harvest season to you.

Day 4: *Read John 16:7,13.* The old Jewish festival obtained a new significance for the Christian Church by the promised outpouring of the Holy Spirit. Ask the Holy Spirit to fill you new and fresh.

Day 5: *Read John 17.* Take Communion. Ask the Lord to reveal any horizontal relationships that are not right.

Day 6: *Read Job 5, especially noting verse 5* ("Because the hungry eat up his harvest, taking it even from the thorns, and a snare snatches their substance"). Ask the Lord to show you how the enemy has had access to your harvest.

Day 7: *Read 1 Samuel 12, especially noting verse 17* ("Is today not the wheat harvest? I will call to the LORD, and He will send thunder and rain, that you may perceive and see that your wickedness is great, which you have done in the sight of the LORD, in asking a king for yourselves"). Ask the Lord if there are any judgments on your harvest.

Day 8: *Read Proverbs 6:8.* The harvest mentality of ants is mentioned as a lesson for the sluggard. Break any apathy that is stopping you from moving forward.

Day 9: *Read Proverbs 20:4:* "The lazy man will not plow because of winter; he will beg during harvest and have nothing." Ask the Lord to reveal any area of laziness in your life that has stopped you from plowing.

Day 10: *Read Proverbs 10:5:* "He who gathers in summer is a wise son; he who sleeps in harvest is a son who causes shame." Break a spirit of slumber. Ask the Lord if you have gathered when you should have gathered.

Day 11: *Read Jeremiah 8:20:* "The harvest is past, the summer is ended, and we are not saved!" Ask the Lord to forgive you for any missed opportunities.

Day 12: *Read Joel 1.* Add fasting to your praying.

Day 13: *Read Joel 2.* Add fasting to your praying. Make a list of anything that needs to be restored.

Day 14: *Read Joel 3.* Add fasting to your praying. Ask the Lord for a new joy to enter your heart and the land you are praying for.

Day 15: *Read Psalm 16.* Thank God that He has an inheritance for you.

Day 16: *Read Matthew 7–8.* Let faith arise in your heart, a greater dimension of faith.

Day 17: *Read Matthew 9.* Ask the Lord for laborers. Let Him show you where you are to labor in His kingdom.

Day 18: *Read Matthew 10, especially noting verse 8* ("Freely you have received, freely give"). Prepare an offering.

Day 19: *Read Psalm 125.* Thank the Lord that this is a time for new joy.

Day 20: *Read Psalm 126.* Sing a song of deliverance. Declare that all captivity is broken.

Day 21: *Read Proverbs 25:13:* "Like the cold of snow in time of harvest is a faithful messenger to those who send him, for he refreshes the soul of his masters." Ask the Lord to surprise you with a message.

Day 22: *Read Isaiah 9.* Thank God for His government. Praise Him for the abundant harvest when government is in place. Pray for the government of the church that you are connected with.

Day 23: *Read Jeremiah 50:16:* "Cut off the sower from Babylon, and him who handles the sickle at harvest time. For fear of the oppressing sword everyone shall turn to his own people, and everyone shall flee to his own land." Pray for our troops overseas. Declare that every enemy of the harvest is revealed.

Day 24: *Read Jeremiah 51:33.* "For thus says the LORD of hosts, the God of Israel: 'The daughter of Babylon is like a threshing floor when it is time to thresh her; yet a little while and the time of her harvest will come.'" Call forth a harvest in Iraq.

Day 25: *Read Luke 10, especially noting verse 2* ("Then He said to them, 'The harvest truly is great, but the laborers are few; therefore pray the Lord of the harvest to send out laborers into His harvest'"). Ask the Lord to give you a revelation of the Lord of the Harvest.

Day 26: *Read Ruth 1.* Ask the Lord to reveal covenant to you.

Day 27: *Read Ruth 2, especially verses 21-23* ("Ruth the Moabitess said, 'He also said to me, "You shall stay close by my young men until they have finished all my harvest."' . . . So she stayed close by the young women of Boaz, to glean until the end of barley harvest and wheat harvest; and she dwelt with her mother-in-law' "). Ask the Lord to show you where you have been gleaning.

Day 28: *Read Ruth 3.* Notice how Ruth made her shift. Ask the Lord to give you a strategy to make a shift form gleaning to harvest.

Day 29: *Read Ruth 4.* Thank God that He has a full redemptive plan for your life.

Day 30: *Read Amos 9.* Ask the Lord to reveal to you the Tabernacle of David.

Day 31: *Read 2 Samuel 5.* Ask the Lord for the breaker anointing and strategies for breakthrough.

Day 32: *Read Acts 15.* Ask the Lord to settle any disputes that are keeping you from moving into full restoration.

Day 33: *Read Joshua 3, especially noting verse 15* ("And as those who bore the ark came to the Jordan, and the feet of the priests who bore the ark dipped in the edge of the water [for the Jordan overflows all its banks during the whole time of harvest]"). Do not be afraid to take that step of faith from wilderness to harvest.

Day 34: *Read 1 Samuel 8, especially noting verse 12* ("He will appoint captains over his thousands and captains over his fifties, will set some to plow his ground and reap his harvest, and some to make his weapons of war and equipment for his chariots"). Ask the Lord to show you your assignment and role in the harvest.

Day 35: *Read Levitcus 23, especially noting verse 22* ("When you reap the harvest of your land, you shall not wholly reap the corners of your field when you reap, nor shall you gather any gleaning from your harvest. You shall leave them for the poor and for the stranger: I am the LORD your God"). Prepare a gift for someone less fortunate than you.

Day 36: *Read Judges 14, especially noting verse 14* ("Out of the eater came something to eat, and out of the strong came something sweet"). Study the life of Samson. Ask the Lord to reveal any root of bitterness that needs to turn sweet.

Day 37: *Read Judges 15, especially noting verse 1* ("After a while, in the time of wheat harvest, it happened that Samson visited his wife with a young goat. And he said, 'Let me go in to my wife, into her room.' But her father would not permit him to go in"). See Samson's patterns that prevented victory in his life. Ask the Lord to break any similar patterns in your life.

Day 38: *Read Judges 16.* Ask the Lord for strength to break through. Ask Him to recoup your losses.

Day 39: *Read Exodus 34:21-22:* "Six days you shall work, but on the seventh day you shall rest; in plowing time and in harvest you shall rest. And you shall observe the Feast of Weeks, of the firstfruits of wheat harvest, and the Feast of Ingathering at the year's end." Find your Sabbath.

Day 40: *Read Mark 4, especially noting verse 29* ("But when the grain ripens, immediately he puts in the sickle, because the harvest has come"). Ask the Lord to show you when to put in your sickle for harvest.

Day 41: *Read Matthew 13:1-23.* Understand the process of harvest.

Day 42: *Read Matthew 13:24-58.* Understand the process of wheat and tares. Ask the Lord to reveal and release your treasures.

Day 43: *Read Matthew 14.* Ask the Lord to teach you to multiply and take you past the halfway point.

Day 44: *Read Psalms 1–2.* Thank the Lord for your personal harvest. Thank Him for the harvest He has in the nations.

Day 45: *Read John 4:1-34.* Ask the Lord to show you the "woman at the well."

Day 46: *Read John 4:39-54.* Declare that someone you know will get to know Jesus as his or her personal Savior.

Day 47: *Read Revelation 14:15:* "And another angel came out of the temple, crying with a loud voice to Him who sat on the cloud, 'Thrust in Your sickle and reap, for the time has come for You to reap, for the harvest of the earth is ripe.'"

Day 48: *Read Acts 2.* Thank God for filling you with His Spirit. Receive the wind of the Holy Spirit. Thank Him for the gift of tongues in the Church.

Day 49: *Read Acts 19.* Declare an awakening in your "Ephesus."

Day 50: *Read 1 Corinthians 16.* Ask God to show you your new door.

ALSO FROM CHUCK PIERCE

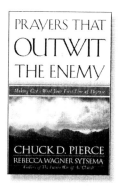
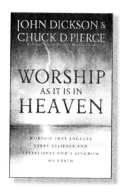